D1707503

ORIGINALISM AND THE GOOD CONSTITUTION

ORIGINALISM

—— AND THE ——

GOOD CONSTITUTION

JOHN O. McGINNIS

MICHAEL B. RAPPAPORT

HARVARD UNIVERSITY PRESS

Cambridge, Massachusetts

London, England

2013

Library of Congress Cataloging-in-Publication Data
McGinnis, John O., 1957–
Originalism and the good constitution / John O. McGinnis and Michael B. Rappaport.
p.   cm.
Includes bibliographical references and index.
ISBN 978-0-674-72507-2
1. Constitutional law—United States. 2. Constitutional law—Philosophy. 3. Origin
(Philosophy) 4. Judicial review—United States. I. Rappaport, Michael B., 1960–   II. Title.
KF4552.M34   2013
342.73'0011—dc23   2013007994

For Mother and Daddy
J.O.M.

For Erela, Jonathan, and Brandon
M.R.

CONTENTS

ORIGINALISM AND THE GOOD CONSTITUTION

1

ORIGINALISM: ITS DISCONTENTS
AND THE SUPERMAJORITARIAN SOLUTION

Originalism—the view that the Constitution should be interpreted according to its original meaning—has been an important principle of constitutional interpretation since the early republic. James Madison, the father of the Constitution, wrote: "I entirely concur in the propriety of resorting to the sense in which the Constitution was accepted and ratified by the nation. In that sense alone it is the legitimate Constitution. And if that be not the guide in expounding it, there can be no security for a consistent and stable . . . exercise of its powers."[1] Today this theory has prominent adherents on the Supreme Court in Justice Clarence Thomas and, at least in "faint-hearted" form, Justice Antonin Scalia. *Heller v. District of Columbia* recently featured both majority and dissenting opinions that were wholly originalist in style. Legal academics across the political spectrum espouse some version of originalism.[2]

Nevertheless, originalism continues to be plagued by challenges, the most salient being how it is to be justified. But originalism is also confronted by many other fundamental questions. What is the precise nature of an originalist method of interpretation? Isn't it wrong for the living to be governed by the dead hand of the past? How can an originalist jurisprudence address the hundreds of judicial decisions inconsistent with original meaning that are now deemed the law of the land?

A more general sense of disquiet underlies these specific questions. Law in general, and constitutional law in particular, should be measured by its contribution to our current welfare. Originalism seems to be focused on the distant past rather than the present and, on its face, does not concern itself with desirable results. Thus, it seems vulnerable to the central claim of living constitutionalism—that interpretation of the Constitution should be guided by a modern vision of a good society that likely differs substantially from that of the long-dead Founders.

In this book, we present a new normative defense of constitutional originalism that connects this interpretive method directly to the concept of a good constitution. We argue that originalism advances the welfare of the present-day citizens of the United States because it promotes constitutional interpretations that are likely to have better consequences today than those of nonoriginalist theories. The benefits of ordinary legislation for society and the proper theory of its interpretation are routinely connected to the virtues of lawmaking by a democratic legislature. We likewise connect the benefits of a desirable constitution and the proper theory of constitutional interpretation to the virtues of the constitution-making process.

A constitution that is enacted under a strict supermajority process is likely to be desirable because such a process has features appropriate for determining the content of constitutional provisions, just as majority rule is often appropriate for determining the content of ordinary legislation. Just as we interpret ordinary legislation according to the meaning given by the enacting legislature (whether we assess that meaning through text, intent, or purpose), so too should we interpret the Constitution according to its original meaning to preserve the benefits of the widespread agreement that gave it birth.

Although this justification of originalism is new, it has been hiding in plain view. One of the dominant ideas of the US Constitution is its use of supermajority rules to create good government. There are various specific supermajority rules in the Constitution, from the requirement that a treaty be ratified by two-thirds of the Senate to the requirement that a member of the House be expelled only through a two-thirds vote of his or her colleagues.[3] Even ordinary legislation, which may seem to be majoritarian, is in reality enacted by a procedure—passage by bicameral houses and presentment to the president—that is essentially an implicit and mild supermajority rule. We identify whether a provision is in the Constitution by asking whether it passed through a specific supermajority process—either through the original enactment under Article VII or through the amendment process of Article V. It is not too much to call the US Constitution "a supermajoritarian constitution."

Supermajoritarianism was not merely a theme of the Constitution but also a distinctively American contribution to the science of constitutionalism. Supermajoritarianism had not been an express feature of the English tradition nor had it often been recommended by past political philosophers. Just as the Americans had developed written constitutions by adapting English ideas to the new realities of the American experience, so did they develop supermajority rules. While the British had used a monarchy and hereditary aristocracy to place limits on democracy, the Americans, as republicans, eschewed these devices and substituted supermajority rules as one means of balancing the different interests in a nation. Given the centrality of supermajority rules to the US Constitution, it is not surprising that one kind of supermajority rule—the stringent kind that applies to constitution making itself—provides the key to understanding what makes the Constitution enduringly desirable and justifies interpreting it according to its original meaning.

This introductory chapter first outlines originalism's greatest unresolved problems. We then briefly explain how our theory resolves these difficulties. The purpose here is not to provide a detailed defense of our theory, which is what the rest of the book does, but to sketch how that theory, in an interconnected way, tempers originalism's discontents. It does so by showing that stringent supermajority rules are likely (and more likely than other methods, such as judicial fabrications) to generate good constitutional provisions. Thus, the beneficence of the Constitution is connected to the supermajoritarian process from which it arose. Originalism is the appropriate method of constitutional interpretation because it captures the meaning that passed through the supermajoritarian process. Consequently, the results generated by originalism are likely to be beneficial.

The Problems of Originalism

Existing Justifications for Originalism

Originalism has been defended in many ways. Some advocates focus on the good consequences that flow from originalism, while others emphasize the importance of following certain normative principles. But in our view, none of the existing justifications is adequate. Perhaps the least persuasive defense is that we should be originalists because the constitutional enactors were originalists. But this argument is circular because it purports to defend the authority of the original Constitution by appealing to the views of the original constitution makers.

Another nonconsequentialist argument for originalism is that it follows from the concept of law. If we are to be faithful to law, we must follow the law's original meaning. But this argument too is problematic. First, opponents of originalism are not generally arguing that the Supreme Court should not act lawfully. Rather, they may be employing a different approach to legal adjudication, one that includes prior cases and current normative principles as important guides to legal decision making. While one may disagree with this approach, it is hard to argue that the concept of law necessarily entails this one particular view of how the meaning of law is to be cashed out in constitutional decision making. Many legal systems, including the common law, seem to function through decision making that does not absolutely privilege a prior text. Finally, this defense would seem to suggest that we should follow the original meaning in constitutional decision making regardless of the quality of the Constitution. But it seems doubtful that originalism would have much appeal if the Constitution reflected the policies of a brutal dictator. Rather, the appeal of originalism seems to be implicitly linked to the high quality of the US Constitution.

Others argue that we should follow originalism because it comports with democracy, but this argument fails.[4] It is true that originalism requires judges to uphold the actions of an elected legislature or executive when the Constitution authorizes such action. But originalism also requires judges to strike down the actions of such entities when their actions conflict with the Constitution's original meaning. Originalism thus sometimes conflicts with the results of the contemporary democratic process. It might be argued that decisions overturning current legislation are democratic because they follow the democratic decision of the enactors of the Constitution. But simple invocations of democracy do not tell us why we should prioritize that previous democratic decision over the more recent one.

Other justifications of originalism are based on consequences or substantive policy. Some originalists, including Justice Antonin Scalia, have argued that originalism offers clearer rules to constrain judges than do other interpretive approaches.[5] This argument has been challenged as an empirical matter. But even assuming that it contains some truth, as we believe it does, it is nevertheless not enough to sustain a consequentialist case for originalism. The benefits of judicial constraint are limited if judicial decisions, even though they are not discretionary, are still generally harmful. Conversely, if constraint is the overriding objective, nonoriginalist doctrine may sometimes provide more constrained rules than the original meaning.[6]

Randy Barnett has argued that the Constitution's original meaning is likely to lead to just results and therefore we should follow that meaning.[7] We agree that the goodness of the Constitution is a potentially strong argument for originalism. But Barnett's argument assumes a thick theory of the good constitution. A thick theory, such as libertarianism or socialism, is not appropriate as the basis for a constitution in a pluralistic society in which the people hold differing views about the good (or justice). A constitution based on a thick theory will be open to attack by those who do not hold that particular view of the good. Instead, a constitution in a pluralistic society should rest to some extent on a compromise among people's views of the good in that society.

A thick theory of this kind may also be too strong to justify originalism because changed circumstances are likely in the future to lead the original meaning to consequences not in line with the substantive theory of the good constitution. One would then be forced to depart from the Constitution or to treat it as nonbinding. By contrast, our supermajoritarian theory imposes a weaker constraint. There may be many different constitutions that represent reasonable compromises among contending views and that are good enough to be treated as good constitutions. Thus, many changes in circumstances would still leave the Constitution a good one, especially given the ability of the amendment process to supply additional compromises.

Keith Whittington has sought to justify originalism based on a theory of popular sovereignty. For Whittington, the Constitution is understood as a creation of the whole people acting as a sovereign. Originalism, then, is justified as a means of both preserving the people's prior enactment and protecting their ability to pass new constitutional provisions in the future. Such acts of popular sovereignty constrain ordinary politics, creating "the security of a stable political system in which the fundamental decisions have already been made."[8]

We agree with Whittington that the normative case for originalism depends on a constitutive act of the whole people of the nation that creates a framework for ordinary politics. We also agree that originalism depends on the capacity of the people to change the Constitution through the amendment process. But we do not believe that popular sovereignty is the best way of justifying either the Constitution or originalism. If the enactment of constitutions by the people collectively led systematically to undesirable constitutions, then popular sovereignty would not be attractive from a normative perspective. This conclusion suggests that popular sovereignty is not the primary value we care about in considering a constitution or its interpretation.

It might be argued in response that popular sovereignty does in fact generally lead to good results. After all, the people are choosing a constitution for themselves. Just as individuals usually make good choices for themselves, the argument would run, so do the people collectively. But there is a significant difference between individual choice and collective choice. It is clear when an individual acts, but it is not at all clear within popular sovereignty theory when the people act. As Whittington himself admits, the idea that the people are choosing when they enact a constitution is a metaphor.[9] Depending on which rules govern their choice, very different entrenchments could result. Some theories of popular sovereignty hold that the people can act when a simple majority makes a choice.[10] But a mere majority can easily take actions that harm the minority. To avoid all risk of such harm, something close to unanimity is required for the people to act.[11] But that requirement would block almost all constitutions from being enacted.

In our view, the best way to define the actions of the people concerning constitutions is as actions taken under strict supermajority rules. In this way, a mere majority cannot speak in the name of the people, but at the same time a very small minority cannot block a constitution. In Chapter 3, we show how this kind of supermajority rule in fact likely leads to desirable results. Thus, while Whittington is correct that the case for originalism depends on a constitution's being generated by popular choice, our theory is essential to determine the appropriate rules by which the people exercise that choice.

The approach that comes closest to our own is expressed by Akhil Amar in his article "The Document and the Doctrine."[12] Amar attempts to justify primarily following the meaning of the document, rather than judicial precedent, based on the goodness of the document and the advantages of following it. He views the goodness of the document as deriving in large part from how it was enacted, coming from the people in a system that promotes deliberation, long-term decision making, and the benefits of multiple minds. Moreover, he argues that it has improved substantially over time through the amendment process. The goodness of the document is not based on a simple approach, but on one that appears to take account of the multiple needs of a complex society unfolding over time.

But Amar's argument is not as clear and systematic as would be desirable. He points out advantages of the process of enactment, but does not provide a theoretical or comprehensive discussion of what a desirable process looks like. For example, "The Document and the Doctrine" does not even make clear whether Amar believes a supermajoritarian or majoritarian constitutional enactment process is superior. We are also unclear about how he believes the document should be read—whether it should be interpreted solely as an originalist textualist would interpret it, as he suggests at some points, or whether it may also be interpreted with an eye to reach desirable results in particular cases, as he seems to suggest at other times. Although we agree with many of the insights in Amar's article, we believe that they need clearer and more methodical development before one can determine whether they state a persuasive case for originalism.

Our argument justifying originalism expands on the most desirable features of its most persuasive predecessors. Like Justice Scalia, we defend originalism on the basis of consequences, but we enlarge the scope of consequences to include the beneficence of rules rather than merely their clarity. Like Keith Whittington, we stress that originalism reflects fidelity to the authoritative decision of the people, but we show how supermajority rules are necessary to capture an authoritative decision of a whole people, including minority views. Like Akhil Amar, we emphasize that the advantages of the enactment process are essential to defending the virtues of originalism, but we provide a systematic account of what those virtues are. Thus, while our argument is new, it has a family resemblance to a variety of previous arguments. It gains strength from the recognition that it builds on familiar foundations rather than erecting an edifice with completely unknown materials.

The Content of Originalism

Since its reemergence in the latter part of the twentieth century, originalism has also been plagued by debates about its content. At first, original intent was the touchstone. The original meaning of a constitutional provision was said to depend on the intent of the enactors. But over time, the original intent view came to be criticized. One of the most influential criticisms was that it was difficult, if not conceptually impossible, to discover a single intent of a document with multiple authors.[13]

Because of such criticisms, original intent has given way to original public meaning as the predominant methodology of originalism. Theories of original public meaning, in contrast to original intent, interpret the Constitution based on how the words of the document would have been understood by a competent speaker of the language when the Constitution was enacted.[14] Original public meaning thus avoids the problem of ascertaining the intent of multiple authors. But this theory was in turn criticized, in part because the Constitution's original public meaning was thought often to be vague or ambiguous.

More recently, a new form of originalism, which we call constructionist originalism, has arisen in response to this critique of original public meaning. Constructionist originalists argue that interpreters are bound by the Constitution's original meaning only when it is clear.[15] When a provision is ambiguous or vague, interpreters may resort to nonoriginalist materials to determine the Constitution's meaning. But constructionist originalism raises its own difficulties because it significantly reduces the scope of originalism. Indeed, some theorists have questioned whether constructionist originalism's embrace of nonoriginalist methods to resolve ambiguity and vagueness does not largely collapse originalism into living constitutionalism.[16] Constructionist originalism also leaves unanswered the question of what replaces originalism when originalism does not apply?

Contemporary originalism thus has substantial methodological controversies at its heart. One problem is to decide which methodological approach is correct. But a second challenge is to relate the content of that methodological approach to the justification of originalism.

The Dead Hand

Another persistent complaint about originalism is that it forces the current polity to be governed by the past. Everyone who enacted the original Constitution is long dead, which raises the question whether present-day Americans should be ruled by those long buried.[17] This complaint surfaced during the Progressive era, but recent opponents have revived it.[18]

The dead hand complaint highlights some of the weaknesses of originalism's traditional justifications. The dead hand argument undermines the democracy justification because it exposes the countermajoritarian nature of using the provisions of an old Constitution to invalidate the decisions of contemporary democracy. It also illustrates a weakness of the clear rules justification for originalism. No matter how clear, the rules are a message from a distant past that may not seem adapted to the present.

Finally, the dead hand critique raises serious questions for defenses of originalism that rely on its desirability. Such defenses must explain why a Constitution that was desirable in 1789 remains desirable in the present day. In fact, some constitutional theorists have recently suggested that originalism might make sense as an interpretive methodology in the years immediately following the enactment of a Constitution but that it loses its power as the constitutional settlement becomes more distant.[19] Given these renewed arguments about the limited relevance of originalism to the present, answers to the dead hand argument are more imperative than ever.

The Exclusion of African Americans and Women

Much of the current Constitution was enacted when African Americans and women did not have the franchise and could not participate in the constitution-making process. Not surprisingly, a constitution so fabricated did not include provisions that reflected their interests—most notably, of course, a prohibition on slavery. It can be argued that a constitution so created is fundamentally defective, and so its original meaning should not be honored.

This criticism of originalism is relatively new, reflecting the sensitivity to excluded groups that has emerged in recent decades. It has, however, been pressed by prominent thinkers. At the bicentennial of the Constitution, for instance, Justice Thurgood Marshall argued that the original Constitution should not even be celebrated because of the exclusion of blacks and the unjust provisions that flowed from it.[20]

This focus on the original document's exclusions makes more pointed and general the difficulty for originalism created by the famous holding in *Brown v. Board of Education* that invalidated school segregation.[21] Opponents of originalism have argued that *Brown*, a decision both morally compelling and foundational to contemporary jurisprudence, cannot be reconciled with originalism.[22] They argue that the right response is to retain *Brown* and dismiss originalism as a bankrupt judicial philosophy. Originalists have responded to this attack in a variety of ways, including with arguments that attempt to show that *Brown* is indeed consistent with originalism.[23]

Strikingly, however, originalists have not substantially addressed the more pervasive critique—that the original meaning of a document built on exclusion cannot be a guide to constitutional interpretation in a society where that exclusion is almost universally condemned as unjust and is indeed rightly seen as the original sin of the United States. In this sense, originalism can be portrayed as incompatible both with the long struggle for redemption from this original sin that has marked US history and with, more generally, the ever greater integration of the groups specifically excluded from participation in creating the original Constitution.

The Problem of Nonoriginalist Precedent

Precedent also poses a problem for originalism because much of Supreme Court jurisprudence is nonoriginalist. Originalists have had two ways of treating such precedent. The first is to dismiss nonoriginalist precedent as inconsistent with the Constitution. While precedent might be consulted for any evidence it provides about the original meaning, precedent itself would not have any independent weight in contemporary constitutional decision making. Under this view, the Constitution must be interpreted according to its original meaning because nothing in the document permits precedent to trump the original meaning.

The problem with this view is that, while it appears to retain the purity of originalism, it renders it a wholly impractical jurisprudence. Some core contemporary practices of government are founded on nonoriginalist decisions. To overrule these decisions would plunge the nation into chaos. Moreover, no Supreme Court has ever suggested that precedents should not be given any weight in its decision making. To do so now would be to repudiate two centuries of Supreme Court jurisprudence.

Alternatively, some originalists advocate following nonoriginalist precedent in certain circumstances. Antonin Scalia, for instance, has sometimes followed constitutional precedent that he appears to believe is nonoriginalist.[24] The difficulty with this approach is that, without further explanation, it appears unprincipled and ad hoc. How exactly is precedent to be reconciled with originalism? Without a resolution, the deployment of precedent within an originalist theory lacks justification. Further, if some precedent can be reconciled with originalism, what are the rules that integrate originalism and precedent, and how do they flow from originalism?

A Sketch of the Supermajoritarian Answers

Our supermajoritarian theory responds to these discontents with originalism. The theory provides a normative defense of originalism from a consequentialist perspective. Thus, we argue that interpreting the Constitution according to a meaning established in the past will promote human welfare in the present. But our theory does not rely on a controversial view about those good consequences. Rather, we merely assume that good consequences are produced by a constitution that incorporates the core principles of the liberal tradition and has the support of the people.

Although our argument for originalism has its complexities, its essence can be captured in three relatively simply premises that lead to a conclusion favoring originalism. First, desirable constitutional provisions (or as we also call them, entrenched laws) should take priority over ordinary legislation because such entrenchments establish a structure of government that preserves democratic decision making, individual rights, and other beneficial goals. Second, appropriate supermajority rules are a sound method of producing legitimate and desirable entrenchments and no superior method is available. Third, the Constitution and its amendments have been passed in the main under appropriate supermajority rules, and thus the norms entrenched in the Constitution tend to be desirable. From these premises, it follows that the desirability of the Constitution requires that judges interpret the document based on its original meaning because the drafters and ratifiers used that meaning in deciding whether to adopt the Constitution.

In short, it is the supermajoritarian genesis of the Constitution that explains both why the document is desirable and why that desirability requires that it be given its original meaning. While there is one significant way in which those supermajority rules were not appropriate—the exclusion of African Americans and women from voting for and serving as constitutional drafters and ratifiers—this defect, which we address at length in Chapter 6, has rightly been removed.

Note the structure of this defense of originalism. It defends the quality of constitutional provisions largely by reference to the likely consequences flowing from the process that created them. It avoids the Scylla of completely formal defenses of originalism and the Charybdis of completely contestable assertions of what constitutes goodness. It is also consistent with perhaps the most common defense of originalism: that it generally ties judges to rules.[25] These rules consist of the interpretative rules of originalism itself as well as the substantive rules in the Constitution.[26] But to the virtue of rule following, it adds the even more important virtue of following beneficial rules.

Justifying Originalism as the
Means for Preserving a Good Constitution

Our central argument for originalism is that it preserves the benefits of a desirable Constitution. Thus, like some other originalists, we premise our defense of the Constitution on its desirability. But unlike other defenses, we do not define desirability based simply on our own political philosophy. Instead, crucial to our defense of originalism (as we elaborate in the next three chapters), is our argument that the best way to create a good constitution is through relatively stringent supermajority rules and that the supermajoritarian procedures for enacting the US Constitution are largely the appropriate ones.

A key issue for our defense is the proposition that supermajority rules are the most desirable way of creating good constitutional provisions and, in particular, that they are better than majority rule. While majority rule is thought to generally produce ordinary legislation that is desirable,[27] permitting a majority to entrench norms would be problematic. Entrenchments need to be bipartisan and to reflect consensus to create allegiance and stability, but majority rule does not generate such consensus and bipartisanship. Entrenchments, which are designed to endure, also need to reflect the long view and to protect minority rights. But majority rule neither creates the deliberation needed for the long view, nor is conducive to protecting minority rights.

By contrast, the passage of entrenchments under appropriately stringent supermajority rule would compensate for majority rule's defects in the entrenchment context and produce good entrenchments. Supermajority rules, for instance, directly address the need for consensus by permitting only norms with the support of a substantial consensus to be entrenched. Supermajority rules also dampen partisanship by making it less likely that entrenchments could be passed with the support of only one party. Wide support for a constitution helps to create the legitimacy and allegiance for the nation's fundamental law that is especially important in a pluralist country like the United States.[28]

Supermajority rule also encourages a nation to make good long-term decisions about entrenchment by creating a veil of ignorance and improving deliberation. A strict supermajority rule (for both enactment and repeal of entrenchments) improves the quality of entrenchments by helping to create a limited veil of ignorance.[29] Because proposals so entrenched under supermajority rules cannot be easily repealed in the future, citizens and legislators cannot be certain how the provisions will affect them and their children. Hence they are more likely to consult the interests of all future citizens—the public interest—to determine whether to support a provision. Citizens are also more likely to support minority rights because they cannot be certain whether they or their families will be in the majority or minority in the future.

Having set forth the desirable process for constitution making, we then show that the enactment of the US Constitution largely tracked that process. The Constitution and its amendments were mostly products of the kind of stringent supermajority rules that generate beneficial entrenchments.[30] Constitutional amendments must be approved by two-thirds of each house of Congress and ratified by three-quarters of state legislatures.[31] The original Constitution was also a product of a double, if not triple, supermajoritarian process. Article VII expressly required nine of the thirteen states to ratify the Constitution before it took effect.[32] Equally important, but less obvious, is that a supermajority of states also had to support the calling of the Philadelphia Convention and that the Constitution was endorsed by a very substantial proportion of the convention's delegates.[33]

A last step to our argument is that beneficial judicial review requires a form of originalism. It was the meaning that the enactors believed the Constitution had—the original meaning—which defined the consensus that made the Constitution desirable. It was not the meaning favored by Richard Posner or Ronald Dworkin. Following a meaning that was not endorsed by the enactors would sever the Constitution from the process responsible for its beneficence.[34]

Our description of the desirability of a constitution enacted by a supermajority not only helps to justify originalism, but also offers a critique of other interpretive theories, such as living constitutionalism, that give the Supreme Court substantial authority to generate constitutional norms. A comparison of constitutional lawmaking with case-by-case Supreme Court norm creation reveals what is wrong with such Supreme Court–centered theories. First, only a very small number of justices generate norms through their decisions, but desirable constitutional lawmaking requires the broader participation of many. Second, the Supreme Court is drawn from a very narrow class of society: elite lawyers who then work in Washington.[35] In contrast, supermajoritarian constitutional lawmaking enables participation by diverse citizens with a wide variety of attachments and interests. Constitutional lawmaking is supermajoritarian, while the Supreme Court rules by majority vote. Perhaps worst of all, Supreme Court updating of the Constitution preempts the amendment process and redirects political energy from the rich deliberative process of constitution making that the supermajoritarian amendment procedure affords. In short, these several reasons suggest that the doctrines fabricated by Supreme Court justices are likely to lead to worse consequences than doctrines that flow from the Constitution's original meaning.[36]

The Type of Originalism: Original Methods Originalism

Our justification for originalism also dictates its methodology. The constitutional enactors voted to ratify the document based on their understanding of the text and how they believed it would be interpreted by subsequent generations. Thus, modern courts should interpret the Constitution using the same interpretive methods that the enactors would have used—a process we call original methods originalism. The normative reason for interpreting the Constitution as the enactors would have done is that the meanings they deemed applicable were part of the expected costs and benefits of the provisions and thus crucial to obtaining the consensus that made the Constitution good.

This conclusion is of major importance to originalism because it shows that the original interpretive rules are integral to the originalist approach. Discarding these rules severs the connection between the document that existing judges implement and the document passed by a consensus of past enactors. To embrace originalism without embracing the enactors' interpretive rules is like trying to decode a message using a different code than the authors of the message employed.

This argument suggests that originalist theories are mistaken insofar as they advocate an interpretive approach based on policy or philosophical considerations. Even if an interpretive theory could be shown to be the best philosophical account of meaning, that discovery would not show it should be employed. If that philosophical approach was not followed by the enactors, then employing it to interpret the Constitution will produce a different meaning than the one the enactors employed. Thus, the content of the original interpretive rules becomes crucial to defining originalism. In subsequent chapters, we argue that the enactors' interpretive rules generally fall within the family of originalism in that they appealed either to original public meaning or original intent, or both. These interpretive rules did not, however, permit the updating of the Constitution through arguments akin to living constitutionalism—the notion that the meaning of the Constitution should be adapted to contemporary conditions.

This analysis also bears on a contemporary debate among originalists—the question of whether construction is a legitimate part of originalism. Adherence to the theory of construction is a central part of what is sometimes called the new originalism. So-called new originalists (or, more accurately in our view, constructionist originalists) believe that original meaning controls the interpretation of provisions that are not ambiguous or vague, but that constitutional construction provides judges and other political actors with discretion to resolve ambiguity and vagueness based on values not derived from the Constitution. Under our view, construction based on extraconstitutional values would be legitimate only if the original interpretive rules endorsed construction. But we find no substantial support for constitutional construction, as opposed to constitutional interpretation, at the time of the Framing or even at the time of subsequent amendments. Rather, the evidence suggests that ambiguity and vagueness were resolved by the enactors and their generation by considering evidence of history, structure, purpose, and intent. Whether or not construction has a philosophical justification, the Framers' generation does not appear to have considered it.

Equal Generations and the Benefits of Inheriting a Constitution

Our supermajoritarian theory also provides an answer to the complaint that, under originalism, the dead hand of the past rules the present. First, we show that each generation largely has equal formal authority to entrench its political principles into the Constitution. The original Constitution came into being through stringent supermajority rules, and each generation can amend the Constitution through similar, although not exactly the same, rules. Thus, the Constitution is not ruled by a dead hand but instead by a generationally fair procedure that allows a consensus of any generation to enact provisions.

Our response to the dead hand argument is not merely formal but also consequentialist. One might argue that the first generation had a greater practical opportunity to insert their values into the Constitution, even if they were subject to largely the same formal rules. But even if this difference is real, the disadvantages of being a later generation are more than compensated for by the advantages. There are great benefits to inheriting a constitution that has the support of the people, has generally been followed, and has promoted stability and prosperity. If the living generation preferred the ability to insert their own values into a constitution more than inheriting the benefits of a good constitution, they could dispense with the existing constitution and replace it with a new one. That few people of any generation even consider the possibility suggests that the living consider themselves better off with their inheritance.

A Reformed, Inclusive Constitution

Our theory also responds to the complaint that the exclusion of African Americans and women from much of the constitution-making process undermines the case for originalism. While we ultimately reject this critique, we believe it is the most serious of all criticisms of originalism. Thus, it is all the more surprising that no previous defense of originalism has seriously grappled with it.

In fact, it is our explanation of the characteristics of a good constitution that underscores the potential power of this critique. The exclusion of African Americans and women goes to the heart of how supermajority rules produce a good constitution. The constitutional enactment process depends for its desirability on representation of the entire population. Supermajority rules have the virtue of creating consensus solutions, but if a class of voters is excluded from the process, their absence casts doubt on the existence of a consensus. The supermajoritarian process is supposed to help protect minorities, but it has difficulty doing so if those minorities cannot participate.

We develop a theory of supermajoritarian failure to address this issue. The mere existence of a flaw in the supermajoritarian process does not necessarily mean that originalism is not the best interpretive rule, any more than the mere existence of a market failure means that government regulation is superior to the market outcome. Interpretive theory has too long been under the grip of a nirvana fallacy.

One must instead examine the costs and benefits of following originalism with the other alternatives in light of the failure. There are three conceivable responses to supermajoritarian failure. First, one can dispense with the existing constitution and attempt to establish a new one. Second, one can simply apply the original meaning of the imperfect constitution, even though it has defects. Third, one can purport to apply the imperfect constitution, but then selectively depart from that constitution in an effort to correct it, such as when judges depart from the original meaning through interpretation.[37]

We compare these three alternatives. Dispensing with our existing constitution is a drastic alternative that is not justified for the United States because the US Constitution's existing defects are less costly than the burden of dispensing with the document and attempting to create one of greater desirability. Very few scholars or politicians have ever argued for such a solution. Correcting these failures through judicial interpretation is also generally problematic because such judicial correction requires substantial discretionary decisions that have the potential to unravel a constitution.

Through the amendment process, subsequent generations have now corrected the most obvious and worst consequences of the exclusion of African Americans and women. The original supermajoritarian failure has been followed by supermajoritarian corrections in the form of the Thirteenth, Fourteenth, Fifteenth, and Nineteenth Amendments. In light of these corrections, we argue that further judicial correction has more costs than benefits. Originalism remains the best theory of constitutional interpretation for our supermajoritarian constitution.

Precedent

Our theory also shows how originalism can be reconciled with precedent in a principled and beneficial way. The claim that originalism is incompatible with precedent is wrong because the Constitution itself contemplates precedent. First, the Constitution incorporates a minimal notion of precedent as an aspect of judicial power. Second, the Constitution treats precedent as a matter of federal common law that is revisable by congressional statute. Thus, the courts in the first instance and Congress ultimately have significant discretion over what precedent rules should be adopted.

The consequentialist nature of our theory of originalism then permits us to develop a normatively optimal approach to precedent under originalism. A balance must be struck between the benefits of following the original meaning of desirable provisions and the benefits of following precedent, such as predictability, judicial constraint, and protection of reliance interests. Examining these relative benefits and the circumstances when they are most valuable can be used to generate a precedent doctrine that consists primarily of rules rather than one that is dominated by judicial discretion.

Our normative theory of precedent thus is intermediate between that of those originalists who reject all precedent, and that of the current Supreme Court, which claims to invoke a strong presumption in favor of precedent. In contrast, we believe that, given the benefits of the Constitution's original meaning, there must be strong countervailing benefits to justify following nonoriginalist precedent. Nevertheless, we do identify circumstances where following precedent has such great benefits. First, precedent should be followed when it is necessary to avoid imposing enormous costs. For example, even if one believed that Social Security violated the Constitution's original meaning, one should still follow the precedents holding it constitutional to avoid the enormous costs and disruption that invalidating the program would cause. Second, precedent should be followed when it is entrenched—that is, when the precedent enjoys such strong support that it is comparable to that necessary to pass a constitutional amendment. Thus, our theory of precedent does not necessitate the elimination of nonoriginalist precedents around which our society is based. But it does permit the Constitution's original meaning to apply when precedents do not have deep roots in the legal soil. It thereby allows today's polity to reap the benefits of past consensus decisions and not remain permanently stuck with the ill-considered decisions of some particular set of justices.

The test of a compelling theory of originalism is whether it meets the salient objections that have accumulated to this venerable theory over many years of disputation. We believe our theory meets these objections better than others through its focus on the good consequences of following a good constitution produced by a good constitution-making procedure. We next turn to setting out the nature of the relationship of a good constitution-making procedure to a good constitution.

2

THE NATURE OF THE ARGUMENT

In this book, we argue that a constitution enacted pursuant to appropriate supermajority rules is likely to be a good one and that securing the benefits of such a constitution requires that it be interpreted using originalist methods. Our argument involves two basic claims. First, we maintain that a good or desirable constitution is one that promotes the welfare of the people and that such a constitution should be followed. Second, we hold that passing a constitution through a strict supermajoritarian process provides the best method for discovering and enacting a good constitution.

In this chapter, we attempt to clarify the nature of our argument. In particular, we explore several basic aspects of our argument: the source of the obligation to follow the original meaning of a supermajoritarian-enacted constitution, the characteristics of a good constitution, the nature of the welfare consequentialism that we employ as a premise of our argument, a normative classification scheme of constitutions, the normative consequences from the possible enactment of a less-than-good constitution, and how the good constitution relates to an individual's ideal constitution. In exploring these ideas, we are not attempting to summarize our argument, which we have done in the previous chapter. Instead, we define central concepts and focus on certain important aspects of the argument, which we know, from past experience, can easily be misunderstood.

The Obligation to Follow the Original Meaning of the Supermajoritarian-Enacted Constitution

We begin by clarifying our basic argument for following the original meaning of a supermajoritarian-enacted constitution. Our normative approach to constitutions and interpretation is welfare consequentialist. We believe that constitutions and interpretive methods should be assessed based on their consequences for the welfare of the people of the nation.

Under our welfare consequentialist view, an ideal constitution is one that produces the maximum net benefits for the nation. Because ideal constitutions are rare, the most desirable constitutions in the real world are good constitutions. We distinguish here between two different types: a *genuinely good constitution* and a *pretty good constitution*. A genuinely good constitution is one that is inferior to an ideal constitution but nonetheless does a good job of promoting the welfare of the nation. The genuinely good constitution may have various imperfect provisions, but few of them are seriously deficient. Overall, then, the genuinely good constitution operates to significantly further public welfare. When a nation has a genuinely good constitution, the strong normative case for following that constitution flows directly from the desirable consequences that following it would promote. While some people might seek to secure an ideal constitution by replacing the genuinely good constitution or departing from its provisions extraconstitutionally, such departures or attempts at replacement are unlikely to be worthwhile because the good constitution is relatively near the ideal, the costs of change are significant, and the production of an ideal constitution is extremely difficult.

While still a good constitution, a pretty good constitution is inferior to the genuinely good one. The genuinely good constitution has few serious defects, but the pretty good constitution has a greater number and may contain various other less significant imperfections. Overall, though, the pretty good constitution still does an adequate job of promoting welfare.

The normative case for following a pretty good constitution, however, differs somewhat from that of following a genuinely good constitution. Unlike the case of the genuinely good constitution, the normative case for following the pretty good constitution does not turn on the claim that enacting a new constitution is unlikely to produce a better constitution. In fact, we believe that a constitution enacted through an appropriate mechanism is likely to be better than the pretty good constitution.

Instead, the case for following the pretty good constitution is that, until a new constitution is enacted, following this constitution is better than the alternative of violating it. If the legislature or judges were to depart from this constitution extraconstitutionally, that departure would not, we argue, lead to better results because the legislative and judicial processes do not have the attributes to regularly produce better norms than those contained in a pretty good constitution. If one is living under a pretty good constitution, the appropriate response is to follow it until one can amend it or enact a new one.

So far, our argument has not referred to supermajority rules or the method for enacting the constitution. It is simply a consequentialist argument for following either type of good constitution. The supermajoritarian passage of a constitution becomes relevant when we begin to ask how a good constitution can be enacted. A nation needs a method for enacting a constitution. While some have argued that majoritarian enactment is beneficial, we maintain here that the best way of enacting a constitution is through strict supermajority rules. Supermajoritarian passage generates many benefits, including promoting consensus and encouraging desirable long-term provisions. We argue that a supermajoritarian process not only provides a better way of enacting a constitution than a majoritarian or minoritarian process, but is also likely to produce a genuinely desirable constitution.

Our argument that a supermajoritarian enactment process likely leads to a good constitution should be distinguished from a distinct argument with which it might be confused. This latter argument maintains that whatever passes through a strict supermajoritarian process is necessarily justified. Just as some people argue that whatever the majority passes is justified by its democratic pedigree, so one might argue that whatever secures a strict supermajority is justified as a constitution. But this is not our argument. We do not believe that a constitution is necessarily good because it was enacted by a supermajority. Rather, we believe that a supermajoritarian process is likely to produce a good constitution.

To put the point differently, passage of a constitution through a strict supermajoritarian process is neither a necessary nor a sufficient condition of a good constitution. It is not necessary because one could produce a good constitution through some other method. Nor is it sufficient because it is possible that a supermajoritarian process could generate a less than good constitution (a point we discuss in a moment). But passage through the supermajority rule is still a desirable method for enacting a constitution because it is both more likely than any other method to produce a good constitution and quite likely to produce such a constitution.

If supermajority rules are likely to produce a good constitution, then we argue that the original meaning of that constitution should be followed. It is the original meaning of the constitution that should be followed because only the original meaning would have been treated as the document's meaning during the supermajoritarian process. Therefore, it is only that meaning that is likely to have the desirable attributes generated by that process.

The Characteristics of a Good Constitution

Because we claim that a supermajoritarian process is likely to produce a good constitution, it is necessary to give some account of the characteristics of a good constitution. As a broad generalization, we believe that good constitutions are those that have been recommended by the Western liberal tradition.[1] We largely leave this description at the level of a broad generalization because the differences between societies suggest that no one constitution makes sense for every nation at all times. Nonetheless, we do feel confident making some general claims about desirable constitutions.

First, such constitutions establish certain types of governments. These governments are limited governments, are accountable to the people, are subject to mechanisms that shield minorities from exploitation by majorities, and include institutions that protect vital interests such as individual rights.[2] Thus, one would expect a good constitution to employ a variety of familiar institutions, such as representative democracy and checks and balances. One would also not be surprised to find other common institutions, like the separation of powers, federalism, and judicial review, although it is possible that alternative institutions could be employed to further the goals that these institutions promote. Good constitutions are also designed to produce long-term structures that enable future generations to inherit the benefits of stable constitutional institutions.[3] Thus, a good constitution tends to have an indefinite term and is difficult to change.

Second, a good constitution will also be one that is desired by the people of the nation. Most importantly, a good constitution will be the product of a consensus of the nation.[4] A constitution that was strongly opposed by a significant minority would cause great disaffection and alienation because that constitution would be so difficult to eliminate. Moreover, a good constitution will not just be not strongly opposed, but should, to a significant extent, be actively supported by the people. Such support will occur in part if the constitution reflects the preferences, values, and factual views of the people. While the active support of everyone may not be possible, the stronger the support, the better the constitution is for the nation.

We have divided the characteristics of a good constitution into two categories. The first involves characteristics that produce good results. The second focuses on the people's approval of the constitution based on their values and understanding of how its provisions will function. Some aspects of a constitution, such as accountable government and the protection of individual rights, are desirable because they produce good results. By contrast, some constitutional aspects, such as provisions that limit freedom of speech to protect religious or racial groups, probably do not produce good results but are desired by people either because the provisions conform to their values or because they mistakenly believe they produce good results. While people may support provisions in the first category, these provisions are desirable even if people do not directly value them because they generate good results. By contrast, provisions in the second category are beneficial only to the extent that people directly value them.

In our view, a good constitution attempts to incorporate both types of characteristics. While some might argue that the best constitution is one that contains only provisions that produce good results, that claim would be mistaken. If provisions are strongly disliked, that result is undesirable in itself and also has bad effects by reducing the support for the constitution. It would be best if the country desired only provisions that produced good results, but a good constitution must take the population as it comes and cannot wish away their values.

Although a good constitution incorporates both types of characteristics, we are not attempting here to define precisely the correct combination because that combination depends on the specifics of the provisions at issue and the population's values and understanding. But in our view, both types are important and should be represented in any good constitution.

Finally, we note that a supermajoritarian enactment process is likely to produce a constitution with both types of characteristics. Certain aspects of the supermajoritarian process are likely to produce provisions that have the support of the people. But others are likely to produce provisions that have desirable results, even if they do not enjoy visceral support from the people. For example, we argue that supermajority enactment rules produce a limited veil of ignorance and therefore force people to consider what institutions they want without knowing whether or not they will be in power. This effect may cause them to include checks on the government that they might have avoided if they knew they would control the government in the future.

The Nature of Our Welfare Consequentialist Premises

Our argument for originalism is one that assumes a welfare consequentialist approach. Welfare consequentialism is a modern version of utilitarianism, which holds that the morally correct act is the one that produces the greatest welfare for people. In the constitutional context, welfare consequentialism holds that the best constitution is the one that produces the greatest welfare for the people of the nation.[5] Our aim here is not to defend this view but simply to explain our position.

Although an approach that seeks to further the welfare of the people has obvious intuitive appeal, welfare consequentialism is a controversial foundation for moral and political theory. One major criticism is that an act consequentialist approach is unattractive because it would sometimes require people to take actions that violate important moral principles. In our view, this criticism is misplaced. While we do embrace an approach that assesses actions based on whether they produce the best results for human welfare, we believe that various aspects of the human condition— such as bias, limited knowledge, the value of coordination, and the need to internalize behavioral guides to action—produce a world where the best way for an individual to promote good consequences is to take actions that followed settled rules and practices. This view would not require people to violate accepted moral principles. This two-level consequentialist approach has been developed most extensively by R. M. Hare.[6]

This approach strongly supports the argument that we make here. First, it suggests that there are strong reasons to follow a procedure for enacting the constitution rather than simply making the decision on a case-by-case basis. We are all open to bias, limited knowledge, and other infirmities. Therefore, determining the best constitution for a society with diverse views is best accomplished by employing a broadly acceptable procedure. Second, this type of consequentialism supports a rule that judges should follow the Constitution's original meaning. Because the supermajoritarian procedure generates a good constitution, judges can make good decisions by following that good constitution. Although some might argue that judges could better promote good results by departing from the original meaning when they believe that a different decision would have better consequences, we reject this notion. As we argue below, the same infirmities, such as bias, limited knowledge, and the need for coordination, that require ordinary people to follow rules strongly argue here for judges also to follow the original meaning. Moreover, in the context of constitutional adjudication, the arguments appear to be even stronger because departures from the original meaning are made in public and are easily discovered.[7]

The Different Types of Constitutions

Our basic argument is that an appropriate supermajoritarian procedure is very likely to lead to a good constitution and that a good constitution should be followed by political actors, such as judges and legislatures. To develop this argument, however, it is useful to draw some finer distinctions between different types of constitutions, expanding on the conceptual discussion we have already begun earlier in this chapter. In particular, we identify the following categories of constitutions: the ideal, the genuinely good, the pretty good, and the fair. These types provide an analytical device to explain the quality of constitutions and the reasons for following or not following constitutions, depending on their quality.

We start at the top. An ideal constitution for a country, under our consequentialist approach, is a constitution that maximizes the net benefits for the nation. Because perfection cannot be expected from humans, this ideal constitution is likely to remain merely a goal and a standard by which other constitutions are measured.

Next is the genuinely good constitution. It is, of course, inferior to the ideal constitution. It is not even the best constitution that one could expect imperfect humans to devise (which might be termed the very good constitution). Instead, the genuinely good constitution is one that enjoys many of the characteristics of an ideal constitution, but also has various defects. Among existing constitutions, the ones that are considered the best are very likely to fall in this category.

The pretty good constitution is the next type of constitution. In contrast to the genuinely good constitution, which is in the core of the good constitution range, the pretty good constitution is closer toward the bottom. The pretty good constitution shares many of the characteristics of the genuinely good constitution, but has more defects, including a number that are significant. Among existing constitutions, the pretty good constitution is generally regarded as successful but imperfect. Still, such constitutions can govern nations that are relatively prosperous and free.

Together, the genuinely good and the pretty good constitutions are what we refer to in this book as the good constitution. Clearly, though, there is a substantial difference between them in quality.

The fair constitution, on the other hand, is inferior even to the pretty good one. Compared to the pretty good constitution, it has even more defects and may include a substantial number of serious flaws. Of real-world constitutions, we judge the constitutional arrangements existing prior to the US Constitution—the combination of the Articles of Confederation and the state constitutions—as generally falling into the category of a fair constitution.[8]

While we could continue identifying types of constitutions, the types we list here are sufficient for our purposes. Constitutions inferior to the fair constitution, which provide even fewer of the liberties and checks on government that are the foundation of a desirable constitution, lie largely outside our main purpose, which is to justify following the original meaning of one particular good constitution—that of the United States.

The Genuinely Good, the Pretty Good, and the Fair Constitution

Having defined various types of constitutions, we are now in a position to clarify the nature of our argument that an appropriate supermajoritarian process is likely to lead to a good constitution and that the original meaning of such a constitution should be followed by government officials, including the courts. In short, we believe it is extremely likely that an appropriate supermajoritarian process will result in a good constitution—either a genuinely good constitution or a pretty good one. We also believe that these good constitutions should be followed by the government.

In our view, the most likely outcome of following an appropriate supermajoritarian enactment procedure will be a genuinely good constitution. The various virtues of that supermajoritarian procedure (which are discussed in Chapter 3) make it likely that the procedure will result in a genuinely good constitution. But there can be no guarantee that the supermajoritarian procedure will produce this result. A supermajoritarian process is affected by a large number of variables, including the knowledge and values of the participants involved. In the real world, it is quite possible that a combination of circumstances might lead to a worse than expected constitution. Thus, a second possible outcome of the supermajoritarian procedure is that of a pretty good constitution. While we believe this result is relatively unlikely, it could occur, and therefore we feel compelled to include it as one of the two possible results. By contrast, we believe it is extremely unlikely for the supermajoritarian procedure to generate an even less desirable constitution, such as a fair constitution.

In the case of a genuinely good constitution, the constitution should be followed because it is quite desirable and there is no reliable way of generating a better one. If one were to apply the supermajoritarian enactment procedure again, it would lead at best to a genuinely good constitution. Thus, government officials should implement the genuinely good constitution because they will be enforcing desirable provisions and are unlikely to discover better provisions.

In the case of a pretty good constitution, the constitution is only moderately desirable. Thus, unlike the case of the genuinely good constitution, it is quite possible that the nation could secure a better than pretty good constitution by enacting a new one through the supermajoritarian procedure. So the reason for following the pretty good constitution is not that there is no reliable way of generating a better constitution. Instead, the reason is that judges and other government officials are unlikely over the long run to achieve better results by departing from the pretty good constitution than by following it faithfully.

The supermajoritarian process employs a diffuse and diverse public to produce a constitution that is supported by a consensus, that has high-quality provisions, and that has provisions that can be known ahead of time. Even if that process does not work perfectly, the constitution will at least be a pretty good one. By contrast, we argue that explicit or implicit judicial "correction" of the constitution through nonoriginalism creates partisan disagreement, lower-quality provisions, and greater uncertainty about the constitution's meaning. While it might seem that judicial correction would improve the constitution (at least from the perspective of the justices who seek to do the correcting), we argue that this proposition is not true in the long run because such nonoriginalism will prompt other groups, with differing views, to engage in their own nonoriginalist decision making. Thus, while it is possible that supermajority rules might sometimes generate only a pretty good constitution that could be improved upon, judicial correction will not be the way to improve it. Rather, the only reliable mechanism is to replace or amend the constitution with a supermajoritarian process.

We do not want to exaggerate the differences in the reasons for following a genuinely good and a pretty good constitution. Although the distinction is important analytically, it may be less important when assessing real-world constitutions. First, the goodness of a constitution exists on a spectrum, with the better versions of a pretty good constitution shading into the weaker versions of a genuinely good constitution. As a result, observers will often have a difficult time determining whether a particular constitution is genuinely good or pretty good. Second, constitutions that were unambiguously genuinely good or pretty good when enacted can change over time. A constitution that was genuinely good when first enacted may need to be changed over the years to reflect altered circumstances. Until amendments can be passed, that constitution may deteriorate and become only pretty good. Similarly, a constitution that is only pretty good when enacted may improve through amendment and become a genuinely good constitution. Thus, it will often not be clear how to classify a particular constitution, especially when the possibility of change over time is considered.

In most of this book, we do not make a distinction between genuinely good and pretty good constitutions, but simply refer to good constitutions. In the first place, the distinction is not relevant to our primary purpose in the book, which is to justify following the original meaning of the US Constitution. Even if a constitution is only pretty good, the courts and the political branches should still follow it because following the constitution is better than judicial or legislative departures from its original meaning. Next, as we have just mentioned, in the real world, it is often difficult to determine whether a constitution is genuinely good or pretty good. Therefore, it makes sense to focus on the wider category of good constitutions to the extent that there is a common answer to whether we should follow its original meaning.

We can further clarify the nature of our argument by discussing the default constitution—the type of constitution in place when the supermajoritarian enactment process is operated. This analysis is important because the constitution that would continue to operate after the failure to adopt the proposed one can be significant in determining what result the supermajoritarian process will produce. If the default constitution were very undesirable, then it is possible (although not necessarily likely) that the constitution produced by the supermajoritarian mechanism might not be all that desirable. People who had significant privileges under the prior regime might hold out to protect them. And other people might agree to the new constitution because it was better than living under the prior regime.

In this book, we assume that the default constitution is at least as desirable as the fair constitution. There are several reasons for this assumption. First, in the case of the US Constitution, the default constitutional regime of the Articles of Confederation and the state constitutions was, in our judgment, a fair constitutional regime. Second, we do not need to explore default constitutions that are worse than the fair constitution because that would needlessly complicate the argument without generating significant benefits. Most constitutions in the Western world are at least fair constitutions. Addressing other types of societies with worse constitutions is itself an interesting inquiry but not our concern here.

The Good Constitution and an Individual's Preferred Constitution

We now move to another important question that can be asked about our understanding of a good constitution: In what sense can the constitution produced by supermajority rules, or any single constitution, be described as a good constitution in a society consisting of people with diverse political views?

Although the supermajoritarian process is likely to produce a genuinely good constitution, the constitution that it generates will not appear that desirable to everyone. Individuals in a nation may hold a great range of views. They may be, to name just a few possibilities, conservatives, welfare liberals, libertarians, or socialists. In a sense, then, no single constitution will appear genuinely good to all of them. Here, we argue that a genuinely good constitution must take into account the views of the bulk of the people in the polity. Therefore, even from the perspective of someone with outlying views, such as a socialist or libertarian, the genuinely good constitution is likely to be a compromise between those views and those of the public at large. Still, people with outlying views may, because of their differences with the bulk of the population, conclude that the constitution produced by supermajority rules is not genuinely good.

Under a consequentialist approach, the different preferences or values of the people in a pluralistic society do not present a serious conceptual or practical problem. Although people have different preferences, the consequentialist approach simply recognizes those differences as a fact about the society. A society in which there are diverse preferences requires pluralistic institutions that allow for these different preferences to be realized. To the extent that preferences are incompatible, the consequentialist approach simply attempts to select those rules and institutions that maximize the satisfaction of preferences.

But the differences in preferences among individuals are only part of the differences among people that a good constitution must overcome. Under consequentialism, the different political views of conservatives, welfare liberals, socialists, and libertarians result primarily from differing factual views about which institutions promote the greatest welfare. These different factual views cannot be resolved in the same way that differing preferences can. Consequentialism deems the best constitution to be the one that *actually* maximizes net benefits, and therefore consequentialism requires the correct view of the facts, not simply a fair compromise between different factual views. As a result, it appears that a socialist will not view as genuinely good a constitution based on nonsocialist factual views.[9]

Although people with outlying views may therefore believe that the constitution produced by supermajority rules is not genuinely good, it is important to emphasize the several ways in which the good constitution will take into account the views (both factual and preferential) of the population at large. Once these ways are considered, it becomes clear that, even for a reasonable person who has outlying views, the genuinely good constitution will not exclusively reflect those views. The genuinely good constitution for a reasonable socialist living in the contemporary United States would not be largely socialist.[10]

The first reason why a genuinely good constitution for an outlier will take into account the views of the public is the importance of a constitution being supported by a consensus of the nation. Even if one wants a particular constitution, one should not favor that constitution if it would be strongly opposed by any significant group. Thus, the importance of a consensus may rule out many constitutional provisions favored by individuals, especially if they have unusual views.

Second, the importance of having a constitution that is strongly supported by the people will also place limits on obtaining a constitution preferred by a particular person. While it might be possible to have a consensus constitution that is not strongly opposed by any significant group, the diversity of people's views makes it extremely difficult to have a constitution that is strongly supported by all significant groups. People will therefore realize that a compromise is necessary. But to secure people's support, they must believe that it was a fair and reasonable compromise. This is not based on any Rawlsian notion of political legitimacy, but simply on the psychological requirements for supporting a constitution that has some provisions one does not approve of. One of the best ways of demonstrating that the constitution represents such a compromise is to enact it through a fair procedure, such as a supermajoritarian process. In that way, people know that their views had a fair chance of being taken into account. But this process means that the views of outliers will have limited influence on the constitution's content.

A third reason why a constitution should take the views of the public into account is the ordinary consequentialist goal of furthering the preferences of the people. A socialist who is a consequentialist will recognize that the preferences for different constitutions should be taken into account. It is true that the socialist will discount these preferences because the socialist believes that the people support nonsocialist provisions based on mistaken views of what their results will be. But while he or she might reasonably discount their preferences, he should not ignore them entirely because their preferences are still part of the good under consequentialism.

Finally, it is important for a constitution to reflect the interests of the people generally rather than of a small group or elite. A powerful method of ensuring that the constitution does this is to require that it be approved though a procedure, such as strict supermajority rules, that gives the public significant influence so that it can block any constitution that does not support its interests. If a process that gives the public significant input is extremely useful, then this process makes it unlikely that the constitution will reflect the views of outliers because the public will reject a constitution of that type.

Overall, then, it should be clear that a genuinely good constitution, even from the perspective of an outlier, will take into account the preferences and factual views of most of the people of a nation. Yet it also seems that the good constitution for the outlier should, to a significant extent, include his or her factual views. Thus, it appears that the good constitution for the outlier will involve a compromise between his or her views and those of the public. The outlier will be constrained by considerations such as the need for consensus and support for the constitution, but will believe that these needs should be balanced against the good provisions that his or her views supply.

Several important implications flow from this compromise. First, it seems likely that the outlier will not regard the constitution produced by supermajority rules to be a genuinely good one. The supermajoritarian constitution will not sufficiently reflect these outlying views. But, second, the supermajoritarian constitution will also unlikely be a fair constitution (or worse). Even if the outliers' views are far from those of the public, the importance of consensus and the other reasons to take into account public views make it likely that the supermajoritarian constitution, while not a genuinely good constitution, will still be, from the outlier's perspective, a pretty good constitution.

Finally, while the genuinely good constitution for the outlier will be superior to the supermajoritarian constitution, it is not clear how that good constitution could be produced. Although it is possible that the outlier could design it, the country is not going to accept such a constitution.

In sum, our view of the good constitution is not at base procedural, but substantive—the good constitution promotes the welfare of the nation. Yet our argument claims that the supermajoritarian process is the best means of producing a substantively desirable constitution. In this respect, the supermajority process of generating a constitution resembles another key legal institution: the criminal trial. A trial that follows desirable procedures is neither a necessary nor a sufficient condition for getting the right outcome, but we have devised no other better human institution for reaching that outcome.[11] Consequently, when a case has complied with the appropriate procedures, we treat the outcome as final. So should we treat the constitution produced by appropriate supermajority rules. Given that supermajority rules are the best procedural device for generating a constitution, constitutions generated in compliance with such rules have a strong claim to substantive correctness.

3

THE SUPERMAJORITARIAN
THEORY OF CONSTITUTIONALISM

In this chapter, we explain why strict supermajority rules are very likely to generate a good constitution—either a genuinely good or a pretty good constitution. Such supermajority rules create the consensus and nonpartisanship necessary for fostering allegiance to a constitution that desirably regulates politics and society. Supermajority rules also afford the deep deliberation that helps correct for difficulties that legislators have in framing constitutional provisions that are designed to endure. Finally, supermajority rules generate a veil of ignorance that helps promote rights for minorities.

In showing that supermajority rule provides an appropriate mechanism for constitution making, we use two different approaches to evaluate the function of democratic representatives.[1] The first views representatives as acting to further the preferences of their constituents.[2] Under this approach, a desirable enactment is one that maximizes the net benefits of the society as measured by the preferences of the citizens. Thus, the normative goal of a voting rule is to aggregate preferences in the way that best satisfies citizens' preferences. The question on which we initially focus is whether majority or supermajority rule is the better aggregator of citizen preferences when the vote is on an entrenchment—a provision that cannot be repealed by a simple majority vote.

The second approach views representatives as mainly assessing proposals to determine whether they further the public interest.[3] Under this accuracy approach, the normative goal of a voting rule is to aggregate the conflicting judgments of representatives to determine most accurately whether an enactment actually promotes the public interest. The question on which we initially focus is whether majority or supermajority rule is the better aggregator of judgments when the issue being voted upon is an entrenchment.

We conclude that supermajority rule is superior to majority rule for enacting constitutional entrenchments under both the preference and accuracy approaches. Having addressed the comparative question of whether majority or supermajority rule is superior, we then turn to whether supermajority rule is likely to result in a good constitution. Our conclusion is that the virtues of the supermajoritarian process under both the preference and accuracy approaches are sufficient to produce good entrenchments.

Although both approaches make markedly different assumptions about the behavior of representatives, they complement one another by each capturing important aspects of the behavior of representatives. A representative, for instance, tends to reflect the preferences of his or her constituents, as the preference view assumes. In an election, the representative runs on a platform that appeals to these preferences, and is unlikely to be reelected or otherwise advance in politics if his or her voting record does not largely correspond with the constituents' desires. On the other hand, legislators also assess the actual effects of proposed laws on the world. Representatives may evaluate a law based on the public interest for two kinds of reasons. First, they may genuinely be concerned about the public interest. Second, they may seek to pass laws that actually have desirable effects because their constituents are then likely to hold them in higher regard and support them in the future. Thus, an inquiry into the appropriate voting rule for constitutional entrenchments should take account of how that voting rule aggregates both the preferences of the people and judgments about the public interest.

In the next sections of this chapter, we provide separate analyses of constitution making from the preference and accuracy perspectives. First, we consider the defects of majority rule that make it difficult for legislators to translate the preferences of citizens into beneficial entrenchments. We then explain how supermajority rule addresses these defects. Second, we consider the defects of majority rule that prevent legislators from making accurate judgments concerning entrenchments. We then describe how supermajority rule both remedies and compensates for these defects. That supermajority rule for the enactment of constitutional provisions can be shown to be desirable under both the preference and accuracy approaches provides reinforcing evidence that supermajority rule is likely to be desirable for constitution making in the real world. Finally, we argue that, under both the preference and accuracy approaches, strict supermajority rule does not merely generate better entrenchments than majority rule, but also leads to good entrenchments.

In this chapter, we focus on the question of the desirable voting rule for enacting entrenchments. Chapter 5 then focuses on the role of the judiciary, arguing that supermajority rule is superior to the judicial enactment or modification of entrenchments. We should note that this chapter summarizes and relies on more extended discussions of these issues in our prior scholarship. For those interested in the fuller and more complex versions of the argument, we refer you to those articles.[4]

The Preference Perspective

In this section, we first discuss the preference perspective and explain how it operates with regard to laws generally. We then focus on entrenchments—constitutional provisions that cannot be repealed by majority vote. We argue that it does not make sense to use majority rule to enact provisions that cannot then be repealed by majority vote. Instead, we maintain that supermajority rule is superior to majority rule for entrenchments because supermajority rule better promotes constitutional provisions that are supported by a consensus, that are not based on partisan considerations, and that are protective of minority rights.

It is important to emphasize here that the comparison we are making is between two different voting rules for entrenchments, which are constitutional provisions that cannot be repealed by ordinary legislative enactment. Thus, the majority voting rule discussed here is not the intuitive one of majority enactment, majority repeal, but instead the unfamiliar one of majority enactment, supermajority repeal. The reason we do not focus on a majority enactment, majority repeal voting rule is that such a rule would not really allow for any entrenchments. A majority of the legislature could enact any rule it sought, but could also eliminate that rule at will. Thus, the real alternative to a supermajority entrenchment rule is the majority entrenchment rule that we discuss. Later in this chapter, we briefly discuss and reject the majority enactment, majority repeal rule on the grounds that it would fail to exploit the benefits that genuine entrenchments generate for a stable and desirable political order.

Majority and Supermajority Rule under a Preference Perspective

We start with a simple model, but one that captures some essential aspects of the legislative process. First, the simple model assumes that legislators act based on their preferences, which are identical to those of their constituents. We later relax this assumption to reflect the reality that representatives sometimes follow the interests of their party rather than their constituents. Nevertheless, we continue to assume that legislators are always connected in a significant way to the preferences of the citizens they represent.

Second, the model assumes that legislators and citizens have equal intensities of preferences. In other words, the benefit that each legislator (or citizen) derives from a bill he or she supports is equal to the harm that each legislator (or citizen) suffers from a bill he or she opposes. We will also relax this assumption later because minorities may have intense preferences of which a constitution should take account, even if they are opposed to the milder preferences of a substantial majority.

Third, for reasons of tractability, the simple model normatively assesses laws based on an efficiency standard, with good laws producing net benefits and bad ones generating net costs. Later we argue that our results would not change under a welfarist standard based on measures that take the poor's interests into account more than efficiency does.

Under this simple preference model, majority rule is efficient. A legislature operating under majority rule will pass any efficient laws that come to a vote on the floor. The reason is straightforward: By gaining a majority, a law signals that its presence satisfies more people than does its absence. Under majority rule, a legislature will also never pass inefficient laws.[5] Again the reason is straightforward: By failing to gain a majority, a law signifies that its absence satisfies at least as many people as does its presence.

Supermajority rule does not work as well in these circumstances. Under a sixty-vote supermajority rule, for instance, some efficient laws will fail to pass. More specifically, laws that can secure between fifty-one and fifty-nine votes would produce net benefits but would not pass under the supermajority rule. It is true that no inefficient laws will pass under supermajority rule because inefficient laws cannot gain a majority, let alone a supermajority. Nevertheless, supermajority rule prevents the enactment of laws that would create more net benefits than their absence. Thus, we believe that, at least under some circumstances, majority rule may be better for ordinary legislation.[6]

The simplest way to understand when supermajority rule is better than majority rule is to focus on a concept we call marginal legislation. Marginal legislation is defined as legislation that can pass under majority rule but cannot secure enough votes to pass under supermajority rule. Under majority rule, both marginal legislation and legislation that can secure a supermajority will pass. Under supermajority rule, however, only legislation that can secure a supermajority will pass. Thus, it is the marginal legislation—the legislation blocked by supermajority rule—that differentiates majority from supermajority rule.

When comparing majority to supermajority rule in this simple model, one need consider only the marginal legislation and decide whether it has net benefits. If the marginal legislation has net benefits, then this means supermajority rule blocks more good than bad legislation and is therefore undesirable. If the marginal legislation has negative net benefits, then this means supermajority rule blocks more bad than good legislation and is therefore desirable.

We can apply the concept of marginal legislation to constitutional enactments through the notion of marginal entrenchments—entrenchments that are blocked by supermajority rule. If such entrenchments produce negative net benefits, then supermajority rule for entrenchments is desirable. In making the case for such entrenchment rules, we examine the factors that tend to make marginal entrenchments harmful. Marginal entrenchments lack consensus and are likely partisan. They may also reflect the mild preferences of a majority at the expense of the intense preferences of a minority, thus creating the risk of undermining important minority interests.[7]

Of course, at some point of stringency, a supermajority rule may block more good than bad entrenchments. A unanimity rule in a democratic body of any size, for instance, would likely block almost all entrenchments and thus defeat the purpose of constitutionalism. Exactly how strict supermajority rule should be depends on both the natural requirements of entrenchment and the history of the particular polities. Certainly, the nature of entrenchments demands a supermajority rule that is strict enough to obtain broad consensus and prevent partisanship. Achieving these goals ordinarily requires a supermajority rule in the range of at least two-thirds or three-quarters. On the other hand, it must not be so strict that it prevents a polity from generating an initial constitution or adding or repealing entrenchments as the circumstances of the world change. A unanimity rule would obviously be problematic because it would permit each citizen to hold up the constitution for idiosyncratic preferences and no coalition could afford to exclude him or her.

The precise range of strictness that is viable also depends to a certain extent on the circumstances of a nation. For instance, a nation with two large groups of different sizes divided by ethnicity or religion might want to choose a rule that requires substantial buy-in from the minority group. Only then would the rule for entrenchment likely generate widespread allegiance to the constitution. In Chapter 4, we make the case that the supermajority rules for the US Constitution are within the appropriate range for the United States, and in particular are not too strict to prevent necessary constitutional amendments.

We are now in a position to explain more clearly how relatively stringent supermajority rule for constitutional enactments is likely to achieve a polity's preferences better than would majority rule. That is, we explain why it is superior to enact entrenchments (that cannot be repealed by a majority) through supermajority rule rather than through majority rule. In making this argument, we relax two assumptions of the simple model: that legislators always reflect the preferences of their constituents, and that citizens have equal intensities of preferences about the entrenchments that are passed. We relax these assumptions because they often do not hold in the real world and because relaxing them provides insight into the advantages of supermajority rule over majority rule.

Supermajority Rule and Consensus

One advantage of a supermajority entrenchment rule is that it requires consensus support to enact constitutional provisions. Consensus support for a constitution is valuable because it allows a nation to develop a widespread and stable allegiance to its framework of government. This kind of allegiance is particularly important at the birth of a nation or a regime when strong attachments have not had time to develop. But it remains very useful even as the regime ages because a felt allegiance provides incentives to follow one's duties and to sacrifice on behalf of the nation, tempering the problem of free-riding that besets any society. In contrast, a constitution with only narrow majority support might be divisive because it might be strongly opposed by a significant portion of people in the country and could not be changed. Alienated from their fundamental governing law, they would feel less of a stake in maintaining the political structure generated by the constitution.

Thus, one can assume that a well-informed public wants a consensus for entrenchments, even if it could tolerate substantially more divisiveness for ordinary legislation. But even when the public places a high value on passing a consensus constitution, its representatives would likely fail to enact one under majority rule because majorities face a prisoner's dilemma in expressing this sensible preference for consensus.

If a majority acted on its belief that it would be beneficial to entrench only those provisions that have the support of a consensus, such self-restraint could hurt that majority if future majorities did not exercise similar restraint. Thus, if the first majority refrained from entrenching provisions that it favored and others opposed, but then subsequent majorities did not follow such restraint, the original majority would enjoy neither the benefits of consensus nor the inclusion and retention of its preferred provisions into the constitution. As a result, a majority may be extremely reluctant to exercise the restraint necessary to obtain consensus, both in refusing to entrench provisions that lack widespread support and in making compromises that would result in entrenchments with widespread support. A strict supermajority rule, by contrast, largely permits the entrenchment of only those provisions that enjoy consensus support. It thereby defuses the prisoner's dilemma that may encourage a majority to ignore the sensible preference of their own members for consensus constitutional provisions.

Supermajority Rule and the Absence of Partisanship

A second desirable characteristic of a constitution is that it should not be based on partisan motivations. Partisan constitutional provisions are opposed by the opposition party not merely based on their merits, but also because they are seen as a standing affront to that party. As we discuss below, partisan entrenchments are likely to be divisive provisions that are based on short-term considerations and are weakly rooted in a broad understanding of the public interest. While a majority voting rule for entrenchments allows the majority party to enact partisan entrenchments, a supermajority rule greatly inhibits their passage, leading instead to bipartisan entrenchments.

A majority entrenchment voting rule promotes partisan entrenchments for two reasons. First, partisan political action is often beneficial to members of a party. If such partisanship strengthens the party, then it may be able to secure additional benefits for its members. As a result, both legislators and citizens of a particular political party may support partisan behavior. Second, legislators may favor partisan behavior even if citizens do not. If partisan behavior increases party cohesion in the legislature, then legislators from the party may be able to secure more benefits for special interests that can help reelect the legislators.

It might be posited that such partisanship need not be problematic under a preference model because at least under the first reason that partisan entrenchments would occur under majority rule, citizens may actually support the partisan action. If citizens favor their party's agenda as a means of securing their interests, then why ignore those preferences? But this preference for their party's interest is a strategic, rather than a primary, preference. A citizen's preference for a party is largely, if not entirely, instrumental. People use parties to obtain goods that satisfy their primary preferences for items like those about the level of spending for national defense or the appropriate trade-off between economic growth and equality. Furthering the party thus is a cost of obtaining the citizens' actual preferences. If politics could be structured so that citizens could obtain their preferences without having to sacrifice to further their party's interests as much—as we suggest supermajority entrenchment rules allow—citizens would be better off.

While we will argue that inhibiting partisanship through supermajority rules would have significant advantages, one might argue that it would also have significant costs because political parties serve an important information function. Citizens are rationally ignorant of politics, and political parties provide simple signals to guide their voting.[8] We thus recognize that these information benefits of political parties must be balanced against the costs that partisanship causes. The better balance is to allow significant partisanship for ordinary politics, while inhibiting partisanship at the constitutional level. Under this arrangement, the partisanship in ordinary politics would permit people to use the information provided by political parties, while bipartisanship at the constitutional level would allow the constitutional enactment process to avoid the significant costs of partisanship in that sphere.

The harm that partisanship imposes on the constitutional enactment process is not only substantial but also worse than the harm that it imposes on ordinary politics. In the first place, partisan action often generates an us-versus-them attitude. This attitude can create a cycle of increasing bitterness and revenge, which is particularly dangerous to constitution making. Today we witness such escalating partisan feuds in the appointments process, where one party tries to obstruct the nominees of the other party's president, in part because the other party obstructed the nominees from its own party. Such cycles can be damaging in ordinary politics, but they do greater damage in the constitution-making area by leading to poor and contested decisions about the nation's fundamental law. Second, partisan concerns are especially problematic for a constitution because they often involve a political party's short-term interests. Provisions based on such concerns may rapidly become out-of-date and therefore are particularly inappropriate for a law designed to endure. Also, partisan constitutional measures are typically divisive because a large portion of the public consists of members of the opposite party. Like constitutional provisions lacking consensus support, partisan constitutional measures may undermine the allegiance that a constitution, which cannot easily be amended, must enjoy.

Under a majority entrenchment rule, legislators (with or without the support of citizens) are likely to indulge their partisan preferences because they can entrench their parties' interests without significant constraint.[9] Indeed, partisanship may become even more prominent for entrenchments than for ordinary legislation because the parties may be led into a race to entrench. The representatives of each party may fear that the other party will entrench its agenda unless the representatives entrench their own agenda first.[10] This race may cause legislators to support entrenchments that are not in accordance with the citizens' primary preferences. For instance, one party might decide to entrench low taxes and low debt to make it harder for the other party to entrench entitlements, even when, in the absence of the strategic considerations created by partisanship, citizens prefer the entrenchment of neither low taxes nor entitlements.[11]

Supermajority rule tempers partisan motivations in the entrenchment process, thus making it less likely that the fundamental structure of government becomes an object in a partisan tug of war. Under a relatively stringent supermajority rule, measures could not generally be enacted unless they received significant support from both parties. This requirement largely prevents partisan measures from being passed. It also obliges the parties to cooperate in order to entrench provisions. Thus, supermajority rule generates a different kind of politics for entrenchment than that for ordinary legislation, leading legislators to focus less on defeating the other side and more on creating a workable entrenchment. In this more cooperative environment, legislators are more likely to focus on the interests that citizens have in common rather than their parties' narrow interests.

Minority Rights and the Veil of Ignorance

Another desirable characteristic of a constitution is that it should protect the rights and interests of minorities. When the intensity of people's preferences varies, majority rule for the passage of legislation may lead to undesirable results. A majority may enact a measure that it mildly prefers but that is intensely opposed by a minority. For instance, a majority may find some religious practices distasteful and mildly prefer that they be banned. But the minority that engages in these practices may strongly prefer that they be allowed.[12]

A supermajority entrenchment rule helps temper the problem of intensity of preference under majority rule by establishing a limited veil of ignorance. A veil of ignorance provides citizens with greater incentives to protect minority rights by depriving citizens of concrete knowledge about whether they will be part of the intense minority or the mild majority. A supermajority entrenchment rule helps create a limited veil because its requirement of a supermajority, both to enact and to amend, makes it difficult to change constitutional provisions. Because constitutional provisions last for long periods, citizens cannot easily predict whether they and their families will, as political, economic, and social climates change, be in the majority or minority on various issues.[13] Therefore, citizens have an incentive to protect the vital rights and interests of minorities.[14]

Adrian Vermeule attempts to cast doubt on the strength of the veil-of-ignorance effect from constitutional provisions or other durable rules, but we continue to believe that this effect is important. First, Professor Vermeule suggests that a high discount rate may make actors discount the long-term effects of entrenched provisions.[15] Although a high discount rate certainly does limit the veil-of-ignorance effect, it does not eliminate it. Indeed, one factor significantly reduces the discount rate. Despite people's discount rate for themselves, many people care greatly about what happens to their children (and grandchildren), as when they save in order to leave their offspring an inheritance or when they decide where to live based on the schools available for their children. Thus, parents are likely to be concerned about the effect of entrenchments on their children. Because it is hard to be certain about the position and status of their children, they are more likely to choose provisions that advance the general welfare.

Second, Professor Vermeule suggests that the ability of actors to change entrenchments weakens the veil-of-ignorance effect,[16] as when the coalition that passed legislation repeals it as soon as that legislation no longer serves their interests. We agree that an easily amended constitution can undermine the veil of ignorance, but, as we show in detail below, the US Constitution imposes a double supermajority rule for amending the Constitution, and that rule itself can be changed only through a double supermajority rule. At least in the United States, the ability of political actors to change the formal rules of the game is sharply limited.[17]

Finally, Professor Vermeule suggests that specific, as opposed to general, provisions can gut the veil-of-ignorance effect because very specific provisions have little prospective constraining power.[18] But a supermajority rule for originating and amending a constitution tends to lead to provisions of general applicability. Supermajority rules for entrenchment permit the passage of only constitutional provisions that benefit large numbers of people. Such benefits can be provided through general provisions or through a set of specific special-interest provisions that are grouped together as a means of securing wide support.

A set of special-interest provisions, however, is unlikely to secure the necessary supermajority. The veil-of-ignorance effect applies not merely to general provisions, but also to specific provisions, making it difficult for people to predict the ultimate effects of these specific provisions on their interests or those of their families. As a result, they are likely to support the provisions only if they believe they will be beneficial to the public generally. Thus, general provisions that provide long-run net benefits to the public, such as freedom of speech or due process, are likely to secure supermajority support, but even collections of provisions that benefit only special interests are unlikely to do so. In ordinary politics governed by majority rule, one frequently observes the passage of so-called Christmas tree legislation where many special-interest provisions are intertwined to gain majority support. But one does not observe Christmas tree constitutional amendments in the supermajoritarian constitution-making process. In fact, the US Constitution, which is subject to strict supermajority enactment rules, is exemplified by many provisions of striking generality.

Narrow Preferences

We have argued that supermajority rule does a significantly better job of promoting consensus, bipartisanship, and minority rights than does majority rule. These three significant benefits of supermajority rule must be balanced, however, against one advantage of majority rule. Majority rule is probably superior at realizing one type of preference: a person's preference for an entrenchment based only on his or her view of the content of the entrenchment, independent of any concerns about consensus, bipartisanship, or minority rights. Under this type of preference, a person determines whether he or she prefers a particular entrenchment without considering whether it would be supported by a consensus, whether it would be bipartisan, or whether it would harm minority rights. This type of preference, which we call a person's narrow preferences, is a subset of the overall preferences that people are likely to have about entrenchments.[19]

Majority rule is likely to do a better job than supermajority rule of enacting entrenchments that satisfy people's narrow preferences. The reason is that the marginal entrenchments are likely to produce net benefits in terms of the people's narrow preferences.

This benefit of majority rule, however, is very likely to be smaller than the benefits produced by supermajority rule for two reasons. First, the marginal entrenchments are likely to be the least beneficial entrenchments that are passed, even from the perspective of narrow preferences. Because these marginal entrenchments are supported by a mere majority, they are likely to produce small net benefits. Second, because these marginal entrenchments are only supported by a mere majority, they are also likely to do poorly in terms of the other factors such as consensus and partisanship. Thus, the combination of their low net benefits, as judged in terms of narrow preferences, with their high costs in terms of the other factors suggests that they are unlikely to be desirable overall. We therefore confidently conclude that supermajority rule is likely to be superior based on this simple preference model.

Unequal Intensities of Preference and Vote Trading

We have (with the exception of the veil-of-ignorance argument) proceeded in our comparison of majority and supermajority rule on the assumption that citizens have equal intensities of preference. We now relax this assumption and explore the results for the choice between majority and supermajority rule. Under an equal intensities assumption, the benefits to each person who gains from an entrenchment equal the costs to each person who is harmed by it. By contrast, under an unequal intensities assumption, the benefits to each person who is bettered by an entrenchment may be greater than or less than the costs to each person who is harmed by it.

Unequal intensities of preference diminish the connection between votes for a provision and the preferences for it. In particular, a provision might be enacted, but have less preference support for it than its votes suggests because opponents may be intensely against it. Similarly, a provision can be blocked, but have significant preference support because its supporters intensely favor it.

The results, in a situation of unequal intensities, depend in part on whether vote trading is permitted. If vote trading is not allowed, then the disconnect between votes and preferences continues to exist and may lead to worse results. If vote trading is permitted—if persons who strongly favor one measure can trade their votes on another measure they care about less in return for votes on the one they care about more—then vote trading can reduce the disconnect between votes and preferences. Here, we focus on the situation where vote trading is permitted because we believe it is more likely to exist in the real world and leave to an endnote a discussion of the situation where vote trading is assumed not to exist. Note, however, that even assuming that unequal intensities are possible does not mean all or most laws have such unequal intensities. It is quite possible that the politics relating to some or most measures resembles the model of equal intensities. In that event, the analysis involved in equal intensities applies and supermajority rule is preferable.

In a model with unequal intensities and vote trading, supermajority rule should once again be superior to majority rule for enacting entrenchments because supermajority rule does better in terms of consensus, bipartisanship, and minority rights. First, supermajority rule does a better job of ensuring that entrenchments have consensus support. It is true that under majority rule, a minority that strongly opposes an entrenchment might be able to trade votes in order to block that entrenchment from passing. But it is quite possible that no such vote-trading exchange may be available. For example, the intense opponents may not be sufficiently numerous to buy off enough of the majority to block the measure. Or there may not be a measure—either an entrenchment or ordinary legislation—for which the supporters of the entrenchment are willing to trade their votes. The supporters may not need the extra votes to pass the other measure, or they may not care enough about the other measure to trade their votes, or they may not have a way to structure the deal so that it is enforceable enough for them to rely on it. By contrast, supermajority rule better protects consensus because it not only allows opponents of an entrenchment to trade votes and block it, it also starts with a voting rule that makes it easier for opponents to block an entrenchment either through vote trading or in other ways if no eligible vote trading is possible.

Second, supermajority rule also does a better job of ensuring bipartisanship than does majority rule. Once again, it is true that under majority rule, the minority party might be able to buy off enough voters to block partisan entrenchments. But, of course, it might not be able to do so for many of the same reasons that we mentioned in relation to consensus. One additional consideration is that it is likely that party loyalty is stronger in the case of partisan measures and makes it extremely difficult for party members to defect. By contrast, under a supermajority rule, the minority party usually does not have to rely on the precariousness of trading votes to block partisan entrenchments. Third, supermajority rule is also superior to majority rule at protecting minority rights because it generates a limited veil of ignorance.[20]

These three significant advantages of supermajority rule must be balanced, however, against one advantage of majority rule that we identified in the model with equal intensities of preference: Majority rule is more likely to realize people's narrow preferences—their preferences for provisions independent of any concerns about consensus, bipartisanship, or minority rights. But as with the equal intensities model, the net benefits in terms of narrow preferences from majority rule are likely to be small because the marginal entrenchments—the entrenchments with the least majority support—are the ones that have the smallest net benefits. These small net benefits are very unlikely to outweigh the significant benefits from consensus, bipartisanship, and minority rights.[21]

Supermajority rule also manages better than majority rule the principal downside of vote trading. Some scholars believe that vote trading is harmful because it adds to legislative instability.[22] The argument is that vote trading may make any majority coalition more unstable because vote trading increases the number of potential coalitions that can replace the majority coalition, making majority rule subject to cycling. Cycling is the process by which legislative majorities change among different and inconsistent policies.[23] Such instability and inconsistency obviously undermine sound public policy.[24] While cycling can be avoided through agenda control, such agenda control also reduces the extent to which the legislature represents voters' desires. Whatever the validity of these concerns about vote trading, supermajority rules are more likely to ameliorate than exacerbate this problem.[25] The political science literature suggests that supermajority rule reduces cycling because it decreases the number of possible winning coalitions and thereby limits the number of possibly inconsistent policies.[26] Thus, we conclude that supermajority rule is superior to majority rule in a preference model with unequal intensities.

Efficiency and Welfare

One last issue remains in our initial discussion of the preference approach. To make the preference model more tractable, we have used efficiency as the criterion for evaluating whether supermajority rule is superior to majority rule for entrenching provisions. Although our welfare consequentialist approach applies a different, more defensible criterion of welfare than efficiency, we do not believe that the results of comparing majority to supermajority rule under such a criterion is likely to diverge from those under efficiency. The reason is that the differences between these approaches do not seem to map onto any systematic differences between majority and supermajority entrenchment rules.

We can illustrate this point by considering what is perhaps the most important difference between the efficiency standard and a more defensible welfare standard. Under efficiency, preferences are measured based on ability to pay and therefore poor people's preferences count less. By contrast, under a welfare standard, the measure of a person's welfare is measured based on how it contributes to the actual happiness or preferences of the person independent of his or her ability to pay. Thus, the welfare standard is likely to require better treatment of poor people than the efficiency standard.

But majority and supermajority rule are unlikely to differ systematically from the perspective of poor people. One salient reason is that distributional coalitions can vary under either voting rule. The poor may be part of a supermajority coalition no less than a majority coalition. It is true that the wealthiest may be able to block provisions they do not like under supermajority rule, but that is true of the poorest as well. Given the symmetry of position between the relatively wealthy and relatively poor in distributional coalitions under the two voting rules, majority and supermajority rule are unlikely to have systematic distributional consequences.[27]

The Accuracy Perspective

We now turn to the accuracy perspective. Under this approach, we are not concerned with the preferences of the citizens. Instead, we explore which voting rule is most likely to pass good entrenchments as judged by an external standard. We show that democratic representatives are likely to make less accurate judgments about entrenchments than about ordinary legislation, thus making majority rule a relatively poor method for generating sound entrenchments. We then explain how supermajority rule remedies and compensates for these defects, improving the accuracy of judgments about entrenchments and thereby making sound constitutions.

The Accuracy Framework

On balance, we believe that the preference model more faithfully captures the behavior of legislators than the accuracy approach does. The reason is that the nature of democracy generally forces democratic representatives to favor the interests of their constituents over their own assessments of the public interest. Nevertheless, a model that understands democratic representatives as evaluating legislation in part based on the public interest does describe an essential part of the complicated picture of legislative voting. First, legislators usually claim to be voting in the public interest, and at times they incur such substantial costs and indeed opprobrium for their votes that a concern for the public interest should be counted as a partial motivation.[28] Moreover, legislators must attempt to accurately assess states of the world, including the consequences of legislation that they support, even to understand where their interests and those of their constituents lie. Constituents are unlikely to remember that they preferred a policy if that policy leads to bad results. Support for legislation that is harmful, or is seen as such during the legislators' tenure in office, can be politically damaging even if a majority of constituents supported it at the time. Given that legislators actually appear to vote, at least sometimes, based on their views of the public interest, we believe it is important to consider whether majority or supermajority rule is the superior voting rule under these circumstances.

To provide a framework for our accuracy analysis, we turn to a model of legislative voting associated with the Condorcet Jury Theorem.[29] That Theorem is often thought to show that majority rule is the best decision-making rule, causing some theorists to extrapolate that majority rule is the optimal voting rule in legislatures.[30] Although we too use the model underlying the Condorcet Jury Theorem to form the basis of our analysis, we believe there are important limitations of that model as applied to the legislative world. By modifying the model to make it represent the legislative world more realistically, we can show why supermajority rule leads to more accurate judgments about the public interest in the context of entrenchments.

The Condorcet Jury Theorem is the most famous approach to modeling the accuracy of group decision making.[31] In its simplest form, it assumes that the two alternatives from which voters choose have an equal a priori chance of being true.[32] It then holds that when individuals in a group make decisions independently of one another about the truth of propositions and each has a greater than 50 percent chance of being correct, the decision reached by majority rule is more likely to assess the truth of the proposition than that reached by other voting rules. Moreover, as the number of decision makers in the group increases, their collective judgment becomes more accurate.[33]

We must modify the model underlying the Condorcet Jury Theorem to make it more applicable to representative democracy. Unlike the decision makers envisioned by that Theorem, representatives do not traditionally evaluate the truth or falsity of a proposition. Rather, they evaluate legislation based on the good or bad effects it is likely to generate.[34] The analytic framework of the Theorem can be adapted to the situation where decision makers evaluate whether a measure is good rather than whether a proposition is true. Here, we assume that representatives consider whether to vote for legislation based on whether it promotes the welfare of the people. It is true that this notion of welfare must be given a specific definition so that representatives can judge whether legislation advanced it as a matter of fact. For example, the definition must make clear what the trade-off should be between considerations of efficiency and distribution. But as long as the content of the welfare of the people is specified, representatives can determine whether to vote for the legislation based solely on their judgment of the facts concerning the legislation.[35]

Although the Condorcet Jury Theorem is usually thought to favor majority rule, we believe that, in the context of constitutional entrenchment, the Condorcet approach to legislative decision making favors supermajority rule.[36] We reach this conclusion by adapting the approach to the context of a representative assembly that is determining whether to enact a constitutional provision. Once these adaptations are made, the model supports the superiority of supermajority rule, not of majority rule, in the entrenchment context.

First, under the Condorcet approach, majority rule in a body with a large number of decision makers is very likely to lead to the correct result. But that condition is not present in legislatures. Although legislatures normally have a relatively large number of members, they have far fewer independent decision makers because all representative bodies operate by faction. With a reduced number of independent decision makers, the truth-discovering effects of majority rule are far weaker than they are with a larger number of independent decision makers.

Second, the Condorcet approach to legislative decision making normally assumes that the independent decision makers have accuracy rates (that is, the probability of a representative reaching a correct decision) that are greater than 50 percent. With such accuracy rates, majority rule reaches the correct decision more often than any other voting rule (assuming the other conditions of the Condorcet Jury Theorem are satisfied). But under majority rule for entrenchments, various biases, such as partisanship and heuristic mistakes involved in thinking about the future, are likely to cause accuracy rates to fall below 50 percent. Under such circumstances, a core premise of that Theorem's endorsement of majority rule no longer holds.

Third, there are good reasons to believe that accuracy rates will improve under supermajority rule. By making it difficult to enact partisan entrenchments, supermajority rule should lead legislators away from partisan motivations and more toward public policy considerations. Supermajority rules also lead to a limited veil of ignorance and fewer measures to be considered, both of which should increase the accuracy of legislative judgments. In the language of social science, the accuracy rate for entrenchments is endogenous to the voting rule. Thus, supermajority rule and accurate judgments about entrenchment are inextricably linked.

Fourth, the assumption of the Condorcet Theorem that representative bodies vote on an equal number of good and bad entrenchment proposals under majority rule is also likely to be false. Most constitutional provisions voted on are likely to be bad ideas because it is difficult to come up with good ordinary legislation, let alone provisions that will produce long-term net benefits for an ever changing society. Because a larger number of bad proposals makes it more likely that supermajority rule is superior to majority rule, this aspect of entrenchment decision making provides additional support for the relative beneficence of supermajority rules.

Finally, supermajority rule acts as a form of insurance. Because accuracy rates for entrenchment are uncertain and low accuracy rates may yield bad results, supermajority rule helps to minimize the risk of the worst results. Because entrenchments can be very important and because citizens are risk-averse, supermajority rule may provide a particularly useful form of insurance in the entrenchment context.

The combination of these five different effects in the accuracy model renders supermajority rule superior to majority rule for entrenchment decisions. We now turn to discuss each effect in more detail. Elsewhere we have developed a model that describes these effects more formally and mathematically to which we refer the interested reader.[37] Here, we offer a more intuitive discussion.

Independence and the Number of Decision Makers

We begin our analysis by fitting the Condorcet approach to the legislative context. To make the Condorcet approach more realistic, one must reduce the number of decision makers in the legislature from the formal number of legislators to the number that vote independently. The Condorcet approach assumes that decision makers are independent, but most legislators, for a variety of reasons, do not vote independently from one another. First, legislators are influenced by the positions and votes of other members of their party. Like most people, legislators are influenced by people they respect and who have similar positions. Second, legislators with similar perspectives tend to acquire information from common sources. Thus, conservatives may read the *Wall Street Journal* and get information from certain interest groups, whereas liberals may read the *New York Times* and get information from other interest groups. Overall, we believe that the interdependence of legislators significantly reduces the number of independent decision makers in the legislature.

For our purposes, it is enough to observe generally that the number of independent decision makers is much reduced from the formal number of legislators. Reducing the number of decision makers to reflect more realistically the measure of independence in a legislature has direct implications for the choice between majority and supermajority rule. As the number of independent decision makers declines, the Condorcet approach indicates that the legislative decision under majority rule are less accurate.[38] Although majority rule remains superior to supermajority rule if the other conditions support the Condorcet Jury Theorem, the reduced number of independent decision makers significantly reduces that superiority. Given this reduced superiority, if other factors favor supermajority rule as a better voting rule for reaching accurate legislative judgments, as we argue later in the chapter, supermajority rule can more easily become the superior voting rule.

Low Accuracy Rates for Entrenchment under Majority Rule

Perhaps the most important reason that the Condorcet approach may favor supermajority rule for constitutional entrenchments is that the accuracy rates of individual representatives may be less than the 50 percent accuracy required for majority rule to be the preferred decision-making rule. There are at least three reasons why legislators are less likely under majority rule to make accurate judgments about entrenchments than about ordinary legislation. First, individuals have a heuristic problem in evaluating the future: They are too disposed to believe that existing patterns will continue indefinitely.[39] This heuristic appears to be one of the causes of speculative bubbles in the stock and housing markets.[40] People take the favorable trend in prices as a baseline and extrapolate to the future without justification.

This same behavioral tendency can encourage representatives to make bad entrenchments. For example, representatives may enact entrenchments that create favorable results under current conditions but will not do so in the future as circumstances change. More subtly, the heuristic can also discourage legislators from making good entrenchments by making those legislators too likely to believe that entrenchment of a norm is unnecessary because no current threats to the norm exist. For instance, in a period of financial stability, legislators might not anticipate the strong pressure for disruptive debt abrogation legislation that can emerge during harder times and might thereby mistakenly vote against constitutional provisions that restrain such legislation.[41]

Second, the public generally cannot appropriately assess the desirability of entrenched legislation until significant time has passed and the representatives have long since left office. Entrenched legislation is a framework for government that is designed to endure long into the future. Thus, the desirability of entrenched legislation does not turn merely on its immediate effect, but also on its long-term effects. By that time, legislators are likely to be out of office. If the public cannot determine the accuracy of legislators' decisions until they are out of office, legislators will be under less pressure to reach good decisions.

Third, under majority rule, partisanship is likely to distort legislators' judgments for many of the same reasons that it is likely to impede legislators from reflecting their constituents' true preferences. As we discussed earlier in the chapter, partisanship leads legislators to support or oppose an entrenchment based on the identity of its supporters rather than on its merits. One additional reason why partisanship occurs in the accuracy model is that both legislators and citizens develop nonrational antipathies.

For example, when legislators often vote on a party basis, an us-versus-them attitude can develop that leads legislators and citizens to oppose legislation based on the identity of its supporters rather than on their actual preferences. Partisan bias has an even greater effect on entrenchments than ordinary legislation because, as we discussed earlier in the chapter, each side has a partisan incentive to entrench its program before the other side can entrench its conflicting program. This tendency can obviously distort judgments about whether entrenching a provision advances social welfare.

A related danger is that aberrational elections can make the collective judgment of the legislature less reliable. A party may take office because of a scandal, like Watergate or some other unique event, and proceed to entrench legislation on matters that are unrelated to the reason for its election. An aberrational majority is likely to have a bias in favor of entrenching bad legislation. Because it recognizes that it may lose power in the future when the fallout from the scandal subsides, an aberrational majority is likely to focus on entrenching matters that an ordinary majority would not entrench. Partisanship thus presents a greater risk of distorting legislative judgments in the entrenchment context.

The Supermajority Rule's Capacity to Improve Entrenchment Accuracy Rates

Supermajority rules improve the accuracy of judgments about entrenchments either by directly addressing the problems under majority rule or by making judgments more accurate in other ways. With regard to partisanship, supermajority rule directly addresses the forces that particularly distort judgments under majority rule. A more inclusive voting rule makes it difficult, if not impossible, for one party to entrench without assistance from the other party. This need for cooperation gives legislators less incentive to promote party interests while also decreasing the parties' emotional aversion to one another. Consequently, legislators are likely to approach entrenchment with a greater spirit of bipartisanship, or at least partisan neutrality, rendering their judgments less distorted and more acute.

Supermajority rule does not directly address the other problems caused by majority rule for entrenchments—either the heuristic problem in predicting the future or the reduced pressure on legislators from voters to make accurate judgments about provisions whose principal effects will be felt long in the future. Instead, supermajority rule creates other forces that improve the accuracy of entrenchment decisions. First, as discussed in the section of this chapter on preferences, supermajority rule for entrenchment helps establish the conditions for a beneficial veil of ignorance. Because entrenched provisions cannot easily be repealed and therefore endure for long periods, citizens and representatives cannot readily know how these provisions will affect them and their families in the future.[42] Consequently, they are more likely to consider how these provisions will affect citizens generally—that is, how they will affect the public interest. This effect is likely to increase the accuracy rates of representatives.

The advantages of such a public interest perspective are pervasive. For example, if people did not know whether future presidents would be from their party or the opposing one, they would not be able to assign presidential powers based on their party's interest. Instead, they would have an incentive to allocate such powers based on whether the power makes sense for a president to possess—that is, based on their honest view of the public interest.

Second, a supermajority rule is likely to improve legislative judgments about entrenchments by restricting the legislature's entrenchment agenda. Because of the higher hurdle for supermajoritarian passage, fewer entrenchments are seriously considered and put up for a vote. But those that gain a place on the legislative agenda consequently receive more attention from legislators, the press, and the public.[43] This greater scrutiny should make for more accurate judgments because more deliberation generates additional sources of information as well as more reflection on the accuracy of these sources.

The High Proportion of Bad Entrenchment Proposals

Another factor supporting the desirability of a supermajority entrenchment rule is that a large percentage of the entrenchments voted on by representatives are likely to be bad ones. This claim is relevant to our general argument in two ways. First, one might worry that, although supermajority rule would raise accuracy rates for entrenchments, it would do so at a high cost of preventing too many good entrenchments from passing. But this tendency to block entrenchments becomes less problematic if most of the entrenchments on which democratic representatives vote are bad. As we have demonstrated more formally elsewhere,[44] the more bad entrenchments that are voted on, the greater the virtues of the supermajority rule.

Even if one disagrees with our contention that the accuracy rates for entrenchment under majority rule are often likely to be less than 50 percent and that supermajority rule raises them, one could still believe that supermajority rule would be superior if the ratio of bad to good entrenchments voted on was sufficiently high. Supermajority rule blocks the passage of more measures than does majority rule. Thus, if the set of measures that are voted on contains more bad than good measures, supermajority rule will have the beneficial effect of blocking many more of these bad proposals. If the percentage of bad entrenchments voted on is large and the accuracy rate for entrenchments under majority rule is not much higher than 50 percent—both plausible conditions for entrenchments under the assumptions in this paragraph—these blocking advantages of supermajority rule may outweigh the other advantage of majority rule, resulting in the superiority of supermajority rule. This result holds even if one assumes that supermajority rule does not raise the accuracy rate of representatives.

We argue that democratic representatives are likely to vote on substantially more bad than good entrenchments. Even for ordinary legislation, we suspect that most proposals voted on are bad. First, the set of legislative ideas from which measures that are voted on are selected is likely to contain mainly bad ideas. It takes serious intellectual effort to come up with a good idea and substantial dispassion to guard against one's own biases, or those of friends or constituents, in formulating an idea.[45] Moreover, the set of public policy ideas contains many contradictory proposals (such as one proposal requiring spending and another preventing it), and often two contradictory proposals can both be bad.

Although review of legislative proposals by committees might improve the mix of legislation voted on by the legislature, committee review is unlikely to prevent such proposals from still being mostly bad for several reasons. First, a committee has fewer members than the general legislature and this reduced number will make the Condorcet pooling effect, by which large numbers of decision makers raise the legislature's accuracy rate, less powerful (even assuming that the accuracy rates of individual members are above 50 percent). Second, committee members are often susceptible to special-interest influence on matters within their jurisdiction. Outside special interests are likely to have more influence over committees than the legislature at large because there are fewer people to influence, and therefore they can concentrate their spending on the committee members.

While these considerations suggest that the proportion of good bills that are voted on is not likely to be large, the proportion of good entrenchment proposals that are voted on is likely to be considerably smaller. Relatively few provisions have the high quality that is necessary to be entrenched against the vicissitudes of future change. Thus, the proposed entrenchments that are voted on are even less likely to constitute good entrenchments. As a result, a supermajority rule is more appropriate for entrenchments because a higher proportion of proposals that are voted on are bad ones.[46]

The Insurance Rationale for Supermajority Rules

A final consideration favoring stringent supermajority rule involves risk reduction, or insurance. So far, we have compared supermajority rule to majority rule based on which rule produces the greater net number of good measures. But one might also consider how much risk a voting rule imposes on the public. Risk-averse citizens might prefer a voting rule that led to a lower expected number of good laws if it imposed less risk.[47] In this way, a voting rule may operate like an efficient form of insurance.

Under an accuracy model, citizens may experience risk because the accuracy rates of legislators may not be known. If legislators had a single accuracy rate that was known, then one could predict the expected net number of good laws that they would generate under different voting rules. By contrast, if the legislators' accuracy rates might lie anywhere in a range, then there will be far more uncertainty about what the result of the voting rule will be. Moreover, if that range included accuracy rates that are both above and below 50 percent, the risk would even be more pronounced. If accuracy rates were above 50 percent, the entrenchments would be likely to be desirable, whereas if the accuracy rates were below 50 percent, the entrenchments would be more likely to be undesirable.[48]

Supermajority rule has the capacity, however, to reduce this risk. Because it blocks more measures than majority rule, it will reduce the number of bad measures that are enacted if accuracy rates turn out to be on the low end of their possible range. It thus prevents some of the worst results that entrenchment voting rules can generate. By preventing some of the worst outcomes, it also reduces the risks of employing these voting rules. While supermajority rule may also decrease the expected net number of good measures passed compared to majority rule, the benefits provided by its risk reduction might outweigh the costs of its reduction in the net number of good measures. Thus, supermajority rule may serve an insurance function.

Given that supermajority rule reduces risk, it is quite possible that citizens would prefer a supermajority rule to majority rule where the accuracy rate is uncertain. That supermajority rule eliminates the worst results produced by majority rule might be valuable as insurance.

The insurance rationale for supermajority rule has particular force in the entrenchment context because the risk experienced by citizens is likely to be higher here than in the context of ordinary legislation for two reasons. First, as discussed earlier in this chapter, problems such as the heuristics of predicting the future and partisanship contribute to lowering the accuracy rate for constitutional entrenchment. Citizens face a more substantial risk in the entrenchment context that the accuracy rate for entrenchment will be below 50 percent and thus a correspondingly greater need for insurance.

Second, these downside risks are exacerbated by the importance of entrenchment decisions. Entrenched constitutional provisions are difficult to eliminate. As a result, they are generally more important and have a greater effect than ordinary statutes. Thus, the passage of a bad entrenchment is worse than the passage of a bad statute, just as the passage of a good entrenchment is better than the passage of a good statute. The higher stakes increase the range of results and the risk.

To summarize our arguments in this section, the Condorcet approach ordinarily favors majority rule in legislatures, but it may do so only to a modest degree if one reasonably concludes that there are relatively few independent decision makers. In the context of constitution making, this preference for majority rule may then be outweighed by various considerations. First, several factors suggest that entrenchment accuracy rates under majority rule may be less than 50 percent, which would make majority rule undesirable. Supermajority rule can raise these accuracy rates. Supermajority rule may also counteract the problem that a high ratio of bad to good constitutional proposals is voted on by representative bodies during the constitution-making process. Finally, supermajority rule may also provide insurance to citizens by eliminating the worst-case outcomes that majority rule for entrenchments can produce. For these reasons, supermajority rule is likely to be the best method for generating entrenchments under an accuracy approach. Although we believe the preference model provides the more representative picture of legislative behavior, the conclusions arising from the accuracy model strengthen the overall case for supermajority rule over entrenchments.

Comparing Supermajority Rule
to Majority Rule without Entrenchment

In the previous section, we compared supermajority and majority enactment rules when both are combined with a rule of supermajority repeal. Here, we briefly compare that supermajority rule to a purer majoritarian rule of majority enactment, majority repeal. Because this purer majority rule allows all provisions to be repealed by a majority, it essentially eliminates entrenchments.

A supermajority entrenchment rule is clearly superior to this purer majority rule. This majority rule would essentially eliminate entrenchments and therefore prevent the constitution from providing the stable framework of government and the protections for minorities that entrenchments allow. Because a majority could repeal and add provisions to the constitution at will, the polity could not rely on any constitutional provisions to endure. The resulting instability would be the reverse of what a constitution is supposed to achieve.

Provisions such as the separation of powers, federalism, bicameralism, and bills of rights structure politics in order to generate good results. Without such provisions, a majority would have unlimited authority to exercise political power to do as it desired. This majority could walk over the opposing interests in the society. In addition, such majority power might lead to the political lurching and weaving that can undermine social peace and stability.

Supermajority Rules and Good Entrenchments

In the previous sections, we compared entrenchment under a supermajority voting rule to entrenchment under a majority voting rule, and we concluded that the former is superior. We also compared entrenchment under a supermajority rule to a purer majority voting rule of majority

58

enactment–majority repeal—again concluding that the supermajority rule is superior.

But our argument requires more than a comparison of a supermajority voting rule with other voting rules. We are claiming that a supermajority rule is not merely better than other voting rules, but that it is likely to result in good entrenchments—either genuinely good or at least pretty good entrenchments. Here, we argue that an appropriate supermajority rule will produce good entrenchments in both the preference and the accuracy models.

In analyzing this issue under the preference model, the first question is how to determine whether the supermajority rule results in good entrenchments. Our test for comparing supermajoritarian entrenchment with majoritarian entrenchment focused on marginal provisions because marginal provisions pass under majority rule but are blocked by supermajority rule. The test here, in contrast, focuses on the provisions that actually pass under the supermajority rule because we are evaluating the desirability of these provisions. If the entrenchments that pass under supermajority rule generate net benefits, then the supermajority rule will produce favorable entrenchments compared to the status quo.

But producing entrenchments that are better than the status quo is not necessarily sufficient to produce good entrenchments. In making our prediction that a supermajoritarian process will generate a good constitution, we assume (for the reasons specified in Chapter 2) that the constitution in existence when the supermajoritarian process is employed is a fair constitution. In those circumstances, if the supermajoritarian process merely results in slightly favorable entrenchments, the new constitution will be better than the status quo, but will probably not be a good constitution. And to produce a pretty good constitution, the supermajoritarian process must generate entrenchments that are beneficial enough to represent a substantial improvement. To produce a genuinely good constitution, the supermajoritarian process must generate entrenchments that are considerably better than minimally beneficial. Of course, even genuinely good entrenchments will not be perfect or even the best that humans can produce. But they will be quite attractive and among the best of the constitutions that actually exist in the world.

The supermajoritarian process is very likely to produce a good constitution for many of the same reasons why it is superior to the majoritarian enactment process. Under the preference model, the supermajoritarian process is likely to produce a constitution that is bipartisan, has consensus support, tends to protect minorities, and accords with the preferences of the people.

A supermajoritarian process is particularly good at generating a consensus constitution. If a proposed constitution has consensus support, it is likely to pass under the supermajority rule. If it does not have such support, it is exceedingly unlikely to do so. Thus, a supermajority is a very effective filter for generating a consensus constitution. Of course, not all of the provisions of such a constitution would have consensus support. Obtaining a consensus might require compromising on individual provisions, but overall the constitution would be unlikely to be strongly opposed by a significant percentage of the public. The supermajoritarian process is also likely to produce bipartisan provisions for many of the same reasons that it produces a consensus constitution. Under ordinary circumstances, only bipartisan constitutional provisions can secure supermajority support, and partisan provisions cannot secure such support.

The supermajoritarian process is also well designed to produce a constitution that protects minorities. The process does not virtually guarantee such a result, as it does with consensus or bipartisan provisions. But the limited veil of ignorance that supermajority rules produce does give the constitutional enactors an incentive to enact provisions that protect minorities. This operates to significantly improve on the operation of a simple majority enactment rule with respect to protecting minorities.

Finally, the supermajority process is also well designed to adopt a constitution that accords with the narrow preferences of the people with regard to the content of its provisions. Because a supermajoritarian process takes into account the views of the public (through their representatives in legislative bodies), it is likely to reflect the public's preferences about provisions.[49] Legislators who vote for unpopular provisions may lose their jobs. In the case of conventions, convention delegates win their positions based on the views of voters about whether a provision should be adopted.[50]

We now turn to our second model, the accuracy model. We believe that this model also predicts that entrenchments passed under appropriate supermajority rules will be good ones. As with the preference model, for supermajority rules to generate good entrenchments under the accuracy model, it is not enough for them to produce entrenchments that are merely better than the status quo. Rather, they must produce entrenchments that are beneficial enough to produce a pretty good or a genuinely good constitution.

But strict supermajority rules produce such good entrenchments under the accuracy approach. The main reason is that they significantly improve the accuracy rates of representatives through various methods, such as checking partisanship, limiting the bias created by aberrational elections, promoting a veil of ignorance, and restricting the agenda of possible amendments. Each of these effects is likely to be significant, and overall we can easily imagine them raising the accuracy rate substantially.

This higher accuracy rate has two main advantages in producing beneficial entrenchments. First, it allows representatives to pass a significant number of good entrenchments even though they must do so under a strict supermajority rule. The higher accuracy rate means that representatives are more likely to vote for good provisions, and this effect generally offsets the increased difficulty of passing provisions under a supermajority rule. Second, the higher accuracy rate operates, in conjunction with the strict supermajority rule, to prevent most bad entrenchments from being enacted. With the higher accuracy rate, representatives are more likely to vote against bad provisions and, in combination with the increased difficulty of enacting provisions under a supermajority rule, very few bad provisions are enacted.[51] Overall, then, the higher accuracy rate, combined with strict supermajority rules, should lead to a desirable constitution.

Supermajority rules should produce most of the same net benefits even though we argue that a high percentage of the entrenchments that are voted on are likely to be bad ones. Because representatives with high accuracy rates, operating under a strict supermajority rule, prevent a very high percentage of bad entrenchments from being enacted, desirable provisions should still be enacted.

Thus, we conclude that under both the preference and the accuracy models, appropriate supermajority rules result in a good constitution.

4

THE COMPLIANCE OF THE US CONSTITUTION
WITH DESIRABLE SUPERMAJORITY RULES

In the previous chapter, we showed why a strict supermajoritarian process is the best mechanism for generating a good constitution. In this chapter, we start the process of showing that the rules for enacting and amending the US Constitution largely follow this prescription. First, we show that these rules impose strict supermajoritarian requirements and that such requirements have produced some of the most beneficial constitutional provisions. Second, we argue that the supermajority requirements imposed by these rules are, in the main, not too stringent. Third, we show that there is a rough symmetry between the rules for originating the US Constitution and those for amending it—a symmetry that permits each generation to enact constitutional provisions under similar rules.

While this chapter largely focuses on showing that the Constitution's enactment rules are not too strict, Chapter 5 supplements the discussion by arguing that it is the nonoriginalism of the Supreme Court, rather than the strictness of the amendment rules, that has prevented the enactment of constitutional amendments. In Chapter 6, we address what was historically the most serious departure from the desirable supermajoritarian enactment rules—the exclusion of African Americans and women from the voting process. We argue that those exclusions, while extremely harmful historically, have now been largely corrected.

The Supermajority Rules for
Creating and Amending the Constitution

The rules for creating and amending the US Constitution are not merely supermajoritarian but also relatively stringent supermajority rules. Thus, they help create the consensus, absence of partisanship, veil of ignorance, and deliberation that we have identified as the key features of a good constitution-making process. Although there are some complications, which we address below, it is not too much to say that the dominant supermajoritarian character of the process for enacting and amending the US Constitution mainly conforms to the normatively appropriate process for enacting a good constitution.

The supermajoritarian nature of the Constitution's amendment provisions is evident from an examination of Article V.[1] The Constitution requires two-thirds of each house of Congress to propose a constitutional amendment or two-thirds of the state legislatures to apply for a constitutional convention. It then requires three-quarters of the state legislatures or three-quarters of the states acting through conventions to ratify an amendment.[2] Thus, amendments must surmount a double supermajority requirement.

The process for enacting the original Constitution was also supermajoritarian. Article VII of the Constitution required nine of the thirteen states to ratify the Constitution. But the process for drafting the Constitution also had consensus support in various other ways. The decision to draft a constitution had supermajority support in the Congress under the Articles when it endorsed the call for a constitutional convention. The final draft of the Constitution secured the support of twelve of the thirteen states in the Philadelphia Convention, as well as thirty-nine of the fifty-five delegates who attended. Thus, the enactment of the original Constitution secured supermajoritarian support during at least two, if not three, stages.

Akhil Amar has argued that the ratification process for the original Constitution was majoritarian because the state conventions ratified the Constitution by majority vote.[3] But properly characterizing the ratification vote requires a more discriminating analysis. From Amar's perspective, it may be correct to describe the ratification as majoritarian. His focus is on what was necessary at the state level to adopt the Constitution, and it is true that a majority of each state's convention was all that was necessary. But our focus is on what was necessary at the national level to adopt the Constitution. It is clear that, from the perspective of the new nation, a nine-thirteenths supermajority rule was employed. From the national perspective, the fact that each state used a majority rule is not crucial. In a complex democratic system, rules can contain majoritarian elements, and yet their overall effect can be supermajoritarian. For instance, senators are elected by a majority in each state, and yet no one would doubt that the requirement that a treaty receive a two-thirds vote for advice and consent is supermajoritarian. So it was with the ratification of the Constitution.

The supermajoritarian provisions were not only desirable in the abstract but were also responsible for key provisions of our Constitution that have been admired throughout the world, such as a bill of rights and constitutional federalism. For example, if the ratification of the Constitution had merely required a majority of the states, then it is likely that the Federalists would not have had to agree to provide a bill of rights.[4] Similarly, without the need for supermajoritarian support, the nationalists at the Philadelphia Convention may not have had to agree to provide significant autonomy to the states through constitutional federalism.[5]

More generally, the Constitution of 1789, despite serious flaws, has received praise not only from Americans but also from foreign observers. Famously, William Gladstone wrote: "[T]he American Constitution is, so far as I can see, the most wonderful work ever struck off at a given time by the brain and purpose of man."[6] The supermajoritarian origins of the Constitution explain that the "brain and purpose" that generated it was the collective consensus of the nation. The Constitution was not simply the creation of a few great Americans; it distilled the essence of Americans' philosophy of governance through a supermajoritarian process.

Thus, our theory of constitution making contains within it a new view of what made our founding great. It is the supermajoritarian constitution-making process that helps to account for the beneficence of the Constitution, not merely, or even primarily, the greatness of men such as Hamilton, Madison, and Franklin. Many of these men's proposals did not survive the supermajoritarian gauntlet; other proposals, of which they disapproved, became part of the compromise document. Although most Americans believe that the amended Constitution is an exemplary document, we believe that most explanations of its success rely too much on suppositions of happy accidents, claims of US exceptionalism, or hero worship. We see the greatness of the Constitution as largely the result of the supermajoritarian process that enacted it.

The Reasonable Stringency of the Constitution's Supermajority Enactment Rules

In this chapter, we focus on the most frequent criticism made about the Constitution's supermajority enactment rules: that these rules are too strict. With a few qualifications, we maintain that the supermajority rules for making our Constitution are of reasonable stringency. These supermajority rules, despite frequent claims to the contrary, are not too strict, although we would not want them any stricter. Here, we offer some substantial evidence for the reasonable stringency of the constitution-making rules in the US Constitution, focusing on the amendment rules that have continuing practical importance.

Our argument that the amendment process is reasonably stringent is necessarily an extended one. We begin here by showing that it has permitted a host of amendments that have changed the basic politics of the republic, even when those changes worked against vested majority interests, let alone strong minority interests. It is simply not the case that the amendment process creates such a strong minority veto that fundamental changes cannot take place. We also argue that an evaluation of the proposed amendments that passed Congress but were not ratified by the states—amendments that might have been enacted under a less stringent amendment process—does not suggest that the amendment process is too strict.

The full force of these arguments may not be fully appreciated until the next chapter, where we contrast living constitutionalism (or judicial updating of the Constitution) with originalism. We show that it is judicial updating's rebellion against originalism, rather than Article V's formal voting requirements, that undermines the amendment process and renders it less effective. The Supreme Court's updating of the Constitution crowds out the formal amendment process. Citizens also rationally invest less effort in passing amendments that a nonoriginalist Court may not enforce according to their terms.

We do acknowledge that in a few respects the rules may make amendment too difficult: They make it extremely difficult to eliminate each state's equal Senate representation, and the procedure for amending the Constitution through a national convention does not work very well. Perhaps the most far-reaching problem is that the stringency of the amendment process both provides judges with the temptation to interpret the Constitution in a nonoriginalist way and makes it difficult for the people to overrule these decisions. But these problems do not render the constitutional enactment rules undesirable overall.

The Appropriate Stringency of Supermajority Enactment Rules

Determining the appropriate stringency of the origination and amendment processes is necessarily a judgment call, but that judgment can be informed by both theory and practice. For origination, a supermajority rule should be stringent enough to generate good provisions that both enjoy consensus and have the other virtues, such as establishing a veil of ignorance, that we have identified. Yet it should not be so stringent that it prevents a beneficial constitution from coming into being. We have already said enough about Article VII to (a) suggest that it created a beneficial constitution for its time, as well as an amendment process that could correct its serious defects, and (b) show that supermajority rules were crucial to generating that result. The origination process also does not seem too stringent because we know ex post that it did not prevent a beneficial constitution from being created.

The appropriate stringency of an amendment process must balance two considerations. On the one hand, it must be stringent enough to prevent bad provisions from being added to the Constitution by mistake or in moments of passion.[7] Relatedly, it must be stringent enough to prevent good provisions of the Constitution from being easily repealed. If a majority or even a weak supermajority could amend the Constitution, the document would no longer represent the consensus support that offered a stable framework for governance. It would not even place limits on the majority.

On the other hand, the amendment process must be lenient enough to permit new provisions to be added or defective ones repealed, particularly when these are needed to address technological or social change.[8] A unanimity rule, for instance, would obviously be too strong because it would permit individuals with idiosyncratic preferences to block needed change. Even a requirement of unanimous approval by states would be problematic because it would permit parochial preferences to block change in the national interest. The founding generation recognized this reality: The rule requiring unanimous agreement by the states to change the Articles of Confederation was strongly criticized for its rigidity.[9]

In the next sections, we present evidence that the constitutional amendment process is not too strict. It is instead within the range of stringency that is desirable, even if it is at the most stringent edge of that range.

Proposed Amendments That Have Been Defeated

One way to determine whether the amendment process is too strict is to evaluate the amendments that it has blocked. Although current political debates turn on ideological disagreements that are hard to resolve, one might hope to evaluate amendments from decades ago more dispassionately. Of course, it is not possible to assess here all the amendments ever introduced. But presumably some of the most plausibly beneficial ones would be the amendments that came closest to passage by receiving the support of two-thirds of both houses of Congress but that foundered on the requirements for obtaining three-quarters of the states. We look briefly at this limited set of six proposed amendments and conclude that their failure was not damaging to the republic and that not a few would have had obviously bad consequences.[10]

The original congressional proposal for the Bill of Rights included a provision that regulated the number of representatives in the House rather than leaving that number to be set more at Congress's discretion.[11] While adopted by Congress, the amendment was never ratified. This outcome seems salutary. The amendment was poorly drafted.[12] And it would have put a ceiling in the long run on the membership of the House—a result in tension with the intent of its sponsors.[13]

In 1810, Congress sent to the states a proposed amendment barring anyone who had ever held a title of nobility or received an emolument from a foreign government from holding federal office.[14] This proposed amendment does not seem to be of significant consequence. At worst, it might have excluded some meritorious people from consideration for public office, and at best, it might have excluded some unmeritorious ones, who were unlikely to be elected. It does not seem worthy of being placed in the Constitution.

The next amendment passed by both houses in 1861 was far from trivial in that it constitutionally protected slavery and barred any future amendment from interfering with the institution.[15] The case for such an amendment was that its passage might have prevented the Civil War. Nevertheless, given the lateness of the hour, it is not clear that it would have done so. And it would have done so at enormous cost—the entrenchment of slavery as part of the Constitution of the United States. This entrenchment would have been far deeper than an ordinary amendment because it purported to prevent future amendments that would have prohibited slavery. Thus, a less stringent amendment process might have permitted the imbedding of an evil institution into the heart of a document designed in many other respects for the promotion of human freedom.

In 1924, Congress passed an amendment that would have permitted it to regulate child labor.[16] Assuming that the objectives of the Child Labor Amendment were sound, its failure to be ratified provides little evidence that the amendment process is too stringent. As we discuss in Chapter 5, the Roosevelt Administration likely had the clout to pass and ratify an amendment that would have given Congress substantial power over economic matters that would have encompassed the rather circumscribed authority in the proposed Child Labor Amendment. It chose instead, however, to persuade the Supreme Court to change its interpretation of the Constitution. The Roosevelt Administration did this first by pursuing a Court-packing plan that was not realized, and then by replacing enough justices so that the Court would finally eliminate any restriction on Congress's power over economic matters, including those related to labor. As a result, the Child Labor Amendment became superfluous.

In 1971, Congress passed a proposed Equal Rights Amendment (ERA).[17] As we discuss at length in Chapter 5, the failure of an amendment accomplishing the objectives of providing equal rights for women is largely the result of the nonoriginalist Warren and Burger Courts. These Courts both judicially updated the Constitution by providing substantial equality rights for women and practiced such a nonoriginalist jurisprudence generally that citizens lacked confidence that the Court would not use the ERA to pursue objectives its enactors never intended. Thus, the failure of the ERA underscores the dangers of nonoriginalism rather than inadequacy of the amendment process.

In 1977, both houses sent to the states an amendment that would have treated the District of Columbia as a state for purposes of representation, thus giving the District a representative and two senators.[18] The desirability of this amendment is itself controversial. Proponents suggest that it enfranchises citizens of the District who otherwise have no voting representative in Congress. Although the representation provided in the Senate would give District citizens influence far out of proportion to their numbers, this lack of proportionality is no worse than the disproportionate influence enjoyed by citizens of Vermont or Wyoming. Opponents suggest that problems in the current proportionality of representation are no excuse for exacerbating the problem, particularly when the citizens of the District enjoy other financial advantages from their location in the nation's capital. Other solutions to representing the District's population in Congress are available, such as a statute retroceding the District to Maryland[19] or a less radical constitutional amendment confined to providing voting representation in the House for District citizens. In any event, whatever the merits of the amendment, its failure hardly bulks large enough for the nation to suggest serious defects in the amendment process.

On balance, it is hard to argue on the basis of these six failed amendments that the nation would have been much better off if the amendment process had been less stringent. But for a nonoriginalist approach to interpretation, amendments that achieved the substantial objectives of a child labor amendment and an equal rights amendment would almost certainly have become law. The other amendments are, at best, of doubtful value.[20]

Amendments That Have Been Enacted

In contrast, the amendment process has not been too stringent to prevent very substantial changes in our system of political governance. The Sixteenth, Seventeenth, and Nineteenth Amendments made huge changes in the governance of our polity. It is difficult to say that an amendment process that allowed for such changes is obviously too strict. In particular, it should be noted that in enacting the Seventeenth Amendment, which permitted the direct election of senators, the state legislatures approved an amendment that eroded their power, and the Senate voted for an amendment that changed the method by which a significant portion of its members were elected.[21] In proposing and ratifying the Nineteenth Amendment for women's suffrage, many members of Congress and of state legislatures representing only men still approved an amendment that would dilute the power of those they represented.[22] Such amendments show that social and technological change can generate the consensus required by Article V to make necessary constitutional transformations even when they strike at interests powerfully vested in the amendment process itself. This provides compelling evidence that the amendment process is not too strict to make necessary changes.

The Civil War Amendments were even more transformative in character.[23] In fact, these amendments were so dramatic that they have been referred to as a Second American Revolution.[24] In Chapter 6, we argue that the failure of Congress and the federal courts to enforce the Amendments' original meaning was responsible for delaying the fundamental change they promised. But if enforced according to their terms, they would have helped usher in freedom for African Americans.

Any mention of the Civil War Amendments, of course, raises questions about the legitimacy of these amendments. There are two issues here: whether these amendments were legal and whether their enactment conformed to an appropriate supermajoritarian process. In particular, it has been suggested that their ratification may have been illegal because the state legislatures of the former Confederate states that ratified the amendments were not legally constituted and were, in any event, coerced into supporting ratification.[25] Here we discuss the Fourteenth Amendment, which has been the focus of the debate. While we cannot fully address this issue, we can suggest how these amendments are best understood to conform to the supermajoritarian approach.

Akhil Amar has responded to the questions about the legality of the Fourteenth Amendment by arguing that its ratification was legal on the theory that many of the former Confederate states were properly excluded from voting because they did not have the constitutionally required republican form of government. According to Amar, once the former slaves were emancipated, the southern states could no longer, consistent with having a republican form of government, disenfranchise such large portions of their populations.[26] With the exclusions of these states, the Amendment would have been legal, having passed with the requisite constitutional supermajorities of the states legally entitled to participate.[27]

If the exclusions were legal, we can then turn to the question of whether the supermajoritarian amendment process that excluded these states was a desirable one. One significant point is that the legality of the exclusions indicates that the original Constitution authorized these exclusions. And that authorization, by a constitution enacted by a supermajoritarian process, suggests that the exclusions were desirable. But the desirability of these exclusions is not merely based on an abstract argument. The republican form of government requirement that justified the exclusions was based on the idea that the nation needed a certain agreement on values in order to function—in particular, that all states needed to be republics. If they were not republics, then they might seek to impose problematic values on the rest of the union, particularly given the consensus requirements of a good constitution-making process. Thus, it would make sense to require that all states be republican and to exclude nonrepublican states from the constitutional amendment decision-making.

It is true that excluding some of the former Confederate states would lead to less of a consensus of the people living in the United States. But that cost in terms of consensus must be balanced against the benefits in terms of the republican values that were established as the basis for the union. Thus, one might reasonably conclude that excluding nonrepublican states was a desirable method of enacting constitutional amendments, despite the reduction in consensus.[28]

John Harrison also defends the legality of the Amendment, but on a different basis. Harrison argues that the state legislatures that consented to the amendment, but were not properly constituted, had de facto authority to consent even if they lacked de jure authority, because the law gives de facto authority to governments that exercise actual control over their territory for pragmatic reasons of stability. Moreover, Harrison argues that the alleged coercion of the ex-Confederate states was not a legal impediment. Unlike contract law, he maintains that the amendment process has no duress principle and thus even if Congress offered inducements for ratification, the ratification was still legal.[29]

As with Amar's argument, this approach may not simply justify the Amendment as legal, but also as having been adopted in accord with an appropriate supermajority enactment method.[30] It is true that many of the ex-Confederate state legislatures that ratified the Amendment had not been admitted to Congress, but these legislatures still had provisional or de facto authority to act for the state. When states purport to secede from the union, the process of bringing them back into normal relations with the union may take time. The constitutional amendment process may nonetheless need to operate during this period and the states may act through de facto authority, even though those states imperfectly represent the people within them. One might also argue that conditioning the readmission of the states into Congress on the state legislatures' ratification of the 14th Amendment was also justified. Employing a duress principle would create uncertainty about whether an amendment was enacted and therefore undermine the important purpose of allowing amendments to operate as political settlements. In both cases—recognizing de facto authority and excluding a duress principle—a mechanism that would have attempted to perfectly determine a state's preferences is replaced by one that serves to enact constitutional amendments in a timely and clear fashion.[31]

The Twenty-sixth Amendment, which lowered the voting age to eighteen years, is another more recent demonstration of Article V's continuing effectiveness.[32] In 1970, the Supreme Court, in *Oregon v. Mitchell*, invalidated a congressional statute insofar as it required the lowering of the voting age in state and local elections.[33] Congress immediately responded by proposing a constitutional amendment ending age discrimination in federal, state, and local elections for those over age eighteen. It was ratified in record time—107 days.[34] Thus, in the latter part of the twentieth century, the amendment process could not only effect substantial constitutional change, but could do so very rapidly when a consensus had crystallized.

The passage of the Eighteenth Amendment—instituting Prohibition— and its repeal by the Twenty-first Amendment—the Constitution's merriest—also shows that Article V is not too strict to permit other substantive changes. The rapid consensus that the Eighteenth Amendment was a mistake also supports our point that the amendment process is reasonable in its stringency. Article V is almost universally criticized as being too stringent rather than too permissive. Yet, as stringent as it is, the amendment process generated a provision that was quickly admitted to be a costly failure, illustrating the dangers of a less stringent amendment process.[35]

Nor has Article V been too strict by preventing less politically significant amendments that nevertheless advance good government. For example, the Twentieth Amendment shortened the duration of the lame duck portion of the president's term, and the Twenty-fifth Amendment improved the process of presidential succession.[36]

The most obvious rejoinder is that the amendment process has been too strict because other necessary changes—from the right to privacy, to greater power for the federal government to address economic and environmental problems—were not enacted by constitutional amendment and therefore had to be created by judicial decision.[37] This analysis, however, has the story backward.[38] As we will describe in Chapter 5 with examples like the Equal Rights Amendment, it has been the Court's attempts to enact amendments judicially that have frustrated the proper working of the amendment process. If the Court interpreted the Constitution in an originalist manner, this would allow the constitutional amendment process to develop, over time, consensus support for necessary changes.

In the absence of judicial updating, the nation would have a stronger culture of citizen participation in the amendment process. In contrast, the more the judiciary intervenes to create new constitutional rights and structures, the less democratic constitutional culture becomes. Without judicial updating, citizens would also have more confidence in constitutional amendments because they could assume more securely that the consensus crystallized in the amended text would be respected by the judiciary in the future. In Chapter 5, we describe in greater detail how the Court's updating undermines that confidence and seriously damages the future amendment process.

Comparative Analysis

It is sometimes argued that the United States has the most difficult consti-tution to amend in the world and that this comparison shows that it is too difficult to amend.[39] But the factual premise of the argument is not sup-ported by the evidence, and even were the premise true, it would not show that the US Constitution fails to fall within the reasonable range of strin-gency for an amendment process.

The only comparative study of which we are aware ranked the US Constitution as the second most difficult to amend at the time of its analysis of the thirty-one nations that the study considered.[40] But even under the study's own analysis, a variety of constitutions, such as that of Australia, came very close to the United States in difficulty of amend-ment.[41] Thus, even were the study's metric of measuring the difficulty of amendment sound, the process of amendment in the United States would cluster with that of other flourishing democracies in its formal difficulty. Given that culture as well as formal rules influence to some degree the ease of amending a constitution, on its own terms the study does not support the bald claim that the US Constitution is the most difficult to amend.[42]

But the metric on which the study relies is itself very dubious. The study estimates the difficulty of amending a constitution based on the author's own point evaluation of various formal aspects of the amendment process. That measure yielded a 5.1 difficulty score for the United States. The score was obtained by adding 1.6 points for the requirement of obtaining a two-thirds vote of both houses of Congress for proposing an amendment and 3.5 points for the requirement of obtaining ratification by three-fourths of the state legislatures. The claim underlying this point assignment for leg-islative passage of an amendment proposal was that requiring a vote of two-thirds of both houses of a legislature is twice as difficult as requiring the approval of only one house, which would add only 0.8 point of diffi-culty.[43] Unless the ideological distribution of the Senate is substantially different from that of the House, however, it is not likely to be twice as hard to obtain two-thirds support in both houses of Congress than to obtain two-thirds support in one.[44]

The 3.5-point value assigned to the difficulty of obtaining the approval of three-fourths of state legislatures is even more difficult to justify and is belied by the experience of Article V. This point total is almost twice as much as the value assigned to the requirement of passage by two-thirds of both houses.[45] This particular ad hoc evaluation is undermined by the evidence provided by the history of our amendment process. Because less than one-fifth of the amendments that have passed Congress have subsequently been blocked by the states, it does not appear that the three-fourths requirement imposes such a strong obstacle to amendments.[46] Precisely because the two-thirds congressional requirement is already substantial, it is a mistake to see the requirement of three-fourths of states legislatures as a factor that triples the difficulty of the amending process overall. Were the correct metric used, the constitutions of other nations, like those of Switzerland and Australia, might well be judged to be more difficult to amend than the Constitution of the United States.

Commentators also fail to note that many nations make substantial portions of their constitutions completely unamendable. Germany is a notable example.[47] In other nations, such as India, the highest constitutional court has declared portions of its constitution to be unamendable.[48] In contrast, the United States makes only one subject more difficult to amend than others—the equality of state representation in the Senate—and even in that case there is a substantial argument that this provision can be amended in a two-step process.

Even if it were true that the United States were the most difficult constitution to amend, it would not follow that its amendment process was too stringent. It might be that the other nations have processes that make their constitutions too easy to amend.

It has also been argued that the amendment processes of state constitutions are also less strict than that of the federal Constitution. But even if correct, that evidence would not prove that the federal amendment process is too strict. State constitutions exist within a federal system. Citizens can exit states more easily, and thus the need for consensus is less acute. The populations of states are also more homogeneous than those of continental republics and therefore there are less likely to be substantial outliers for which an amendment process needs to encourage buy-in. State constitutions have also often been criticized for being prolix, containing special-interest provisions, and creating dysfunctional governance (as when they divide executive power by creating multiple officeholders, like attorneys general and agricultural and insurance commissioners, who work at cross-purposes and may be vulnerable to special interests).[49] The substance of such constitutions is rarely held up as a model for fundamental law, and thus it seems odd to offer their less stringent constitution-making processes as a criticism of the federal process.

Defects of the Amendment Process

There is one way in which the US Constitution is definitely too stringent, but the problem is limited to the equal representation of states in the Senate. Article V states that this aspect of the Constitution cannot be changed without the consent of each state, which amounts to an excessively stringent unanimity rule. Although some have argued such equal representation might be eliminated by passing two amendments[50]—one to eliminate the requirement of each state's consent and another to change the representation—even if this were true, a two-amendment requirement would still be excessively stringent. Nevertheless, this defect may have been necessary to obtain passage of the Constitution, given concerns about the protection of state sovereignty at the time.[51] Moreover, as we show in Chapter 6, the contemporary Senate does not generally reach different results than it would with representation based on population.

There is another important defect in the constitutional amendment process, but it should not be confused with the claim that the amendment process is generally too stringent. Article V's process by which states seek a constitutional convention for proposing amendments—the alternative to the usual route of Congress proposing amendments—could certainly have been better structured. A process for passing amendments that bypasses Congress is necessary so that amendments can be enacted that constrain or are opposed by Congress.[52] Without this process, the amendment process would operate too strictly against such amendments. Unfortunately, this convention process appears to be broken: State legislatures have never invoked it in more than two centuries. State legislators appear reluctant to apply for conventions because the benefits of application are small and the costs are high. The benefits are small because the lack of coordination in the process makes it difficult for any specific proposal to secure the requisite votes for a convention. And the costs are high because there is a significant chance that if a convention does occur, it will end up being a runaway convention that proposes amendments that the legislators strongly dislike.[53]

There are two important caveats about this defect in the constitutional amendment process. The first is that there is a strong case that the principal obstacle to the operation of the convention process—the fear of a runaway convention—is the direct result of the failure to interpret the Constitution's original meaning properly and thus allow conventions limited to the subjects that state legislatures place in applications for a convention.[54] If this original meaning was widely accepted, then the convention method of amendment would work far better.

The second caveat is that the problems of the convention method are limited to certain types of constitutional amendment—mainly those that would constrain congressional power. Thus, the failing of the convention process does not extend to the inability to pass constitutional amendments that would extend congressional powers or restrict the states because there is no systematic reason why Congress would be unwilling to pass such amendments. The great bulk of the nonoriginalist actions taken by the New Deal and the Warren Court cannot be seen as responding to this defect of the amendment process.[55]

Thus, despite certain defects, the formal rules of the amendment process do provide a reasonably beneficial supermajoritarian process for entrenchment. They have permitted the polity to make substantial changes to its structure of governance, even over the opposition of powerful interests, while blocking many amendments that in retrospect seem ill advised.

Finally, we note that our claim about the reasonable stringency of the amendment process assumes that judges are in fact originalists. In these circumstances, the Article V supermajority rules reasonably balance the benefits of protecting political stability and limiting majority rule against the benefits of flexibility that allow for the accommodation of technological and social change. Because many modern judges, however, have not followed originalism and have instead rewritten constitutional provisions, the strictness of the amendment process gives them a wide policy space to construct norms according to their preferences. The stringency of the amendment process prevents the people from readily responding to judicial updating. Moreover, this very stringency may perpetuate judges' mistaken belief that they need to update the Constitution.

But to state this problem is only to underscore our basic thesis. It is originalism that is necessary to preserve the good constitution that the supermajoritarian structure for making the constitution creates. Even if one thought that a somewhat less stringent amendment process would better correct judges' intermittent infidelity, it would be impossible for the judiciary to make the Constitution better by introducing a less stringent process though its own decisions. Changing the voting procedures of the amendment process would be such a departure from the text of the Constitution that it would impair the judiciary's legitimacy. To our knowledge, no one has ever suggested that such a course would improve our constitutional system. The better course is for judges to adhere to originalism. As we discuss in Chapter 5, we have had a culture of originalism in the past, and we can imagine the re-creation of that culture today.

The Rough Symmetry between
Origination and Amendment Rules

As we discuss in Chapter 5, one important claim against following the Constitution's original meaning is that it permits the dead hand of the past to control the present. The idea is that the original enactors of the Constitution have disproportionate power over a constitution that is shared by generations through the ages. Here, we show that in at least one sense, this claim is untrue. The supermajority rules involved in enacting the original Constitution and amending the Constitution are roughly symmetrical. Thus, each generation is subject to the similar rules for placing their values into the Constitution.

Article V requires a two-thirds vote of both houses of Congress to propose an amendment and a three-fourths vote of the states either through legislatures or conventions to ratify one. For constitutional provisions passed through the amendment process, there is an obvious symmetry between the rules for passage and for repeal because constitutional amendments are the route to both.

The symmetry between the provisions for originating the Constitution in 1789 and amending it thereafter are not as clear on their face but become readily apparent on closer examination. Article VII itself required only a single vote for ratification of the original Constitution—passage by a supermajority of nine of the thirteen original states.[56] Considered in more detail, however, the enactment process for the original Constitution also required at least a double, and probably a triple, supermajority vote—and therefore was of at least comparable strictness to the double supermajority rule of the amendment process. The reason that Article VII, unlike constitutional amendments, required only one vote was that the Constitution was written in the middle of its own enactment process.

By the time the Constitution was sent to the states for ratification, supermajoritarian support had already been demonstrated for the constitutional enterprise at two stages. First, the Continental Congress approved the recommendation to hold a constitutional convention.[57] Then, twelve of the thirteen states sent delegates to the convention,[58] which was important because a strong consensus of the states was necessary to establishing an effective convention. By contrast, the previous Annapolis Convention had failed because it had been attended by only five states.[59] The substantial support evidenced by the states that chose to send delegates was considerably greater than the two-thirds supermajority required by the Constitution to propose an amendment or to call a convention. Second, the proposed Constitution also received a strong endorsement from the Philadelphia Convention itself. At the convention, all twelve of the attending states approved the final draft of the proposed Constitution and thirty-nine of the fifty-five delegates signed the Constitution.[60] Such a high level of support was probably necessary for the Constitution to proceed to and succeed at the ratification stage.[61] A bare majority would have signaled uncertain confidence in the wisdom of its provisions.

Third, the Constitution was initially ratified by eleven of the thirteen states, eventually receiving the support of all thirteen states. The nine-thirteenths requirement of Article VII for ratification is comparable to the three-fourths ratification requirement of Article V. Although nine-thirteenths is slightly lower than three fourths, the existence of thirteen states made it impossible to select a three-fourths requirement, and nine-thirteenths was one of the two closest ratios.

Moreover, it was reasonable that the Framers would have chosen the lower of the two proximate numbers because Rhode Island, the smallest state, seemed to be holding itself aloof from the entire process. It had previously vetoed amendments under the Articles of Confederation, refused to endorse the call for a convention, and declined even to send a delegation to deliberate at Philadelphia.[62] Thus, its fellow former colonies could have been legitimately uncertain about whether Rhode Island was any longer within the electoral pool.[63]

There are in the main four other differences between the origination and amendment rules, but we conclude that they do not significantly undermine the argument for symmetry.[64] The first is that, even with formally similar rules, large states wielded more power under the original process for making the Constitution than they do under today's amendment process. For instance, it is doubtful that the Constitution could have gotten off the ground if New York, Massachusetts, and Virginia had all refused to ratify, even if nine other states had formally approved the

Constitution. In contrast, today in our stable republic, amendments would be effectively ratified, regardless of the size of the states in the ratifying coalition. The effective additional weight of larger states at the time of the Framing, however, does not greatly undermine the parallel between the origination and amendment process. Indeed, the additional weight served as a corrective to the defect of voting by states rather than by people—a defect we discuss in Chapter 6.

A second difference is that, although there was strong supermajoritarian support both to hold the Convention and to approve the Constitution at the Convention, this support differs in one potentially significant way from that required to propose and ratify a constitutional amendment. Enacting a constitutional amendment requires surmounting two formal supermajority rules that have been previously established. By contrast, the proposed Constitution did not have to meet any preexisting supermajority rules because the Framers chose to depart from the amendment rules of the Articles of Confederation. This lack of preexisting formality is less than ideal, both because the votes of political actors may change depending on what the process is and because adopting a rule in midstream permits manipulation.[65]

Nevertheless, this problem is counterbalanced by the substantial supermajoritarian support at not two, but three stages of the process. Given the nearly unanimous endorsement of the call for the Constitutional Convention, the large supermajority for approving the Constitution at the convention, and the eleven out of thirteen states initially ratifying the Constitution, we are confident that the degree of support among the representatives in favor of the Constitution at the various stages of its making was at least comparable to that required to amend the Constitution.[66]

A third difference is that the Constitution was ratified in state conventions, but constitutional amendments are routinely ratified in state legislatures. Because all state legislatures (with one exception) are bicameral, this latter process potentially increases the difficulty of ratification by requiring a majority vote in two bodies rather than one. We do not regard this difference as significant because, under Article V, Congress has the choice of sending amendments to legislatures or conventions for ratification. Thus, it has the authority to dispense with the bicameral element of ratification, should it choose. Moreover, Congress's decisions to use state legislatures for every amendment it has proposed, except for the amendment repealing Prohibition, suggest that state legislatures, even with bicameralism, are not a more substantial obstacle to ratification than state conventions. State legislatures, while bicameral, permit vote trading, which can facilitate the passage of measures. State conventions, while unicameral, have only one item on the agenda and thus do not have access to the ready bargaining that can grease the wheels of legislative approval.

A fourth possible claim of difference is that the Philadelphia Convention faced a more urgent situation than proponents of amendments, because the nation needed a government. Because of this urgency, this argument would run, it was easier to obtain consensus for the original Constitution than for amendments. But the premise of this objection is false. In 1789, the nation did have a structure of government: the Articles of Confederation. People complained that the structure was defective, but so too did many citizens complain about fundamental defects of the polity before important structural amendments like the Sixteenth and Seventeenth were passed. Moreover, nothing prevented the convention from trying to enact a temporary constitution to provide time for more deliberation. Temporary constitutions were in fact known at the time.[67]

Having established the reasonable stringency of the origination and amendment process of the Constitution and their rough symmetry, we explore, in the next chapter, the relevance of these facts for constitutional interpretation today.

5

THE CONTINUING DESIRABILITY OF AN
OLD SUPERMAJORITARIAN CONSTITUTION

In this chapter, we discuss why it is desirable to interpret a supermajoritarian constitution based on its original meaning. It is the constitution's original meaning that secures the supermajoritarian consensus that makes the document likely to be beneficial. Thus, a constitution will be beneficial today only if it is interpreted according to its original meaning.

We recognize that one might question whether a constitution interpreted according to its original meaning would continue to be desirable over time. Supermajority rule might generate superior norms compared to majority rule during the years immediately following the constitution's enactment. But wouldn't the benefits generated by those norms decline over time as they become increasingly out-of-date because they no longer reflect modern circumstances or modern values? In fact, it is often argued that an especially old constitution, like that of the United States, remains desirable only because the Supreme Court has updated it by interpreting it as a living document.[1]

Our principal focus here is to show that this common understanding is mistaken. First, we argue that a constitution enacted pursuant to a strict supermajority rule is likely to remain desirable over a long period. We also contend that using the amendment process to update the Constitution is superior to relying on the courts to update it. The supermajoritarian process establishes as constitutional law only the provisions that can secure a consensus among a diverse citizenry, whereas judicial updating reflects the views of merely a majority of a single Supreme Court. Moreover, the judicial updating process cannot coexist with the stricter amendment process because judicial updating supersedes the latter process. Following the original meaning of an old supermajoritarian constitution simultaneously preserves the benefits of previous supermajoritarian constitution making processes and protects the opportunity to deploy such processes to improve our fundamental law in the future. Thus, originalism, while imperfect, still works better today than living constitutionalism.

Finally, we show how a supermajoritarian constitution resolves the dead hand problem—the complaint that through the constitution people long dead govern the political affairs of the living. We argue two points: (1) that a constitution enacted through supermajority rules subjects each generation to the same formal rules for enacting constitutional provisions, and (2) that if such a constitution, as a functional matter, provides the first generation with greater input, it also significantly compensates later generations for any resulting loss in control over their constitution.

Why a Supermajoritarian Constitution Should Be Interpreted According to Its Original Meaning

Our theory has clear implications for how a supermajoritarian constitution should be interpreted today. A good constitution enacted under supermajority rules should be interpreted according to its original meaning. The beneficence of the good constitution derives from the consensus support it gained among the enactors. In considering whether to support the constitution, the enactors would have voted for or against the constitution based on the meaning they attributed to it. Thus, it is the original meaning, not some other meaning, that has the beneficence conveyed by the supermajoritarian process. The constitution-making process catches that consensus and crystallizes it in a text, like the capture of lightning in a bottle.[2] Originalism then preserves that light for future generations.

In Chapter 7, we describe in more detail how originalist interpretation should be conducted. In our view, the meaning of the constitution that a supermajority of enactors approved as beneficial should be determined using the interpretive methods that the enactors would have deemed applicable to the constitution. These are methods through which the enactors would have understood the constitution. Thus, the appropriate mode of constitutional interpretation is "original methods originalism."

It is important to note that original interpretive rules followed by the enactors cannot be determined by inquiring as a matter of logic which rules today would be understood as revealing the original meaning. Rather, the content of the original interpretive rules deemed applicable by the enactors can only be determined as a matter of history. If the enactors believed that a living constitutional interpretive approach was applicable to the Constitution, that approach would be the proper way to determine the original meaning, even though it does not seem originalist. While it is theoretically possible that such an approach could have been held by the enactors of the US Constitution, we argue in Chapter 7 that the enactors employed interpretive methods that are similar to what passes for originalism as conventionally understood today. We also show why the original methods approach captures the meaning that reasonable people would ascribe to the Constitution and provide examples of how these methods can help fix meaning. Original methods thus help make originalism more accurate and determinate.

Here we would simply note that it seems improbable that enactors under a supermajoritarian procedure would embrace living constitutionalism as an interpretive method. Living constitutionalism would permit a constitution to regress from the beneficial protections that the enactors believed they bequeathed to subsequent generations. Enactors, like other citizens, are risk-averse. Embracing principles of a living or evolving constitution would carry a great deal of risk because such principles would not preserve the entrenchments that the enactors created as an anchor of the polity.[3] Instead, these principles would allow the Supreme Court discretion to substitute policies that the enactors did not choose and might even have rejected.[4]

Constitutional Enactors Can Design a Constitution to Endure

It might be argued that, while the discretion embedded in a living constitution approach has large costs, it avoids an even larger cost—originalism's inability to address the problems of a world that has changed dramatically since the Constitution's enactment. The problems of an old constitution, however, are overstated because a good constitution of the kind likely to be enacted through a supermajoritarian process can address legal change without requiring judicial updating. Moreover, the costs of such judicial updating are often understated because they ignore the costs of a judicial process that is not designed to forge consensus and that undermines the operation of a constitutional amendment process that is so designed.

It is certainly true that the benefits of legal norms—both constitutional provisions and ordinary laws—can decay over time. Such norms might be desirable initially but grow to be suboptimal or even detrimental. But a wise constitutional enactor, who desires an enduring constitution, has various means available to prevent its provisions from becoming outdated. If strict supermajoritarian procedures promote good constitutional provisions, then one would expect the constitutions enacted under such procedures, like the US Constitution, would have used these various means. As Chief Justice Marshall recognized, the Framers designed the Constitution to last indefinitely.[5]

Constitutional drafters can guard against constitutional decay in three main ways, and the enactors of the US Constitution used all of them. First, the Constitution does not decide most of the legal issues for the nation. Instead, it allocates the great majority of policy decisions to the states and to the federal government's political branches.[6] Most of federal and state law can be updated as often as the people's representatives decide that it needs to be.

Second, the enactors designed the constitutional constraints to endure. In particular, many constitutional provisions set out long-term principles that can be applied to changing circumstances and thus are entirely appropriate for long-term matters.[7] For example, assume that commerce among the states means trade or exchange across state lines.[8] Then the assignment to the federal government of the power to regulate interstate commerce will automatically expand (or contract) as circumstances change, causing additional (or fewer) matters to fall under the category of interstate commerce, even though the meaning of *interstate* and *commerce* does not change. Thus, the Commerce Clause will continue to identify a category of activities deemed especially appropriate for the federal government to regulate, for example, even though the specific activities covered by this category may change over time. If an exchange across state lines of a new type of goods, such as electronic books, were to be effected using the Internet, Congress could regulate the exchange. The Framers avoided anachronism when drafting constitutional provisions.[9]

Note that such general principles should not be confused with abstract principles that confer significant discretion on future decision makers. While interpreting interstate commerce as a general term would allow it to cover new activities, such as Internet sales, it would not allow the Supreme Court to change the meaning of *interstate* or *commerce*. By contrast, an abstract interpretation of "commerce among the states" might interpret it to cover any matter that could be better regulated by the national legislature than by its state counterparts. This abstract interpretation would confer discretion on the Court to classify almost any activity, even if it occurs solely within a state, as commerce among the states. The framers of an enduring constitution can thus employ general terms to cover unknown activities while still retaining the original structure and constraining the Court. The framers need not use abstract terms that allow the Supreme Court essentially to rewrite the constitutional provisions.

Finally, the Constitution also allows amendments that can change outdated provisions.[10] When constitutional provisions do occasionally become outdated, Article V includes what we have argued is a largely desirable amendment process.

Overall, then, a well-designed constitution should avoid becoming outdated. Its constitutional restraints should generally remain useful, and most of the updating necessitated by social change would be done by the legislature and the executive through ordinary politics. When constitutional provisions themselves did become outdated, one would expect that they would be amended. Of course, there might be other provisions that were undesirable but were not so sufficiently so to create support for a constitutional amendment. Those mildly undesirable provisions (an example may be the provision that requires presidents to be natural-born citizens) might be difficult to eliminate, and therefore some mildly undesirable provisions would remain. But that would be a small price to pay for a constitutional system that uses desirable procedures for enactment and amendment.

A Comparison with Judicial Updating

We have shown why a supermajoritarian constitution would likely remain desirable over time. But we do not have to rest our case on this relatively abstract claim because the ultimate question is a comparative one: whether it would be superior to follow the original meaning of the Constitution or to allow judges to depart from the Constitution in an effort to update it or establish new constitutional norms. In this section, we argue that judicial updating by the Supreme Court would be inferior to the supermajoritarian amendment process on the basis of the criteria for good constitution making that we previously identified. We also show that judicial updating cripples the functioning of the amendment process and therefore cannot be effectively combined with it.

The Judicial Updating and Constitutional Amendment Processes

One way to show that the constitutional amendment process is superior to judicial updating as a way of enacting constitutional norms is to compare the two processes. The constitutional amendment process ensures that the norms reflect a consensus by requiring strong supermajoritarian support from a widely dispersed range of legislative bodies throughout the nation. By contrast, Supreme Court decisions need not reflect a consensus. The decisions are made by a small number of officials (nine judges) who are relatively homogenous (elite lawyers who live around Washington, DC)[11] and are not accountable to the public (having life tenure).[12] Moreover, their decisions are rendered by a mere majority vote.[13]

The constitutional amendment process is also likely to lead to high-quality amendments. As we have shown, the supermajority requirement both reduces the partisanship involved by requiring bipartisan compromise and leads to constitutional enactments through a veil of ignorance.[14] The process of judicial updating does not share these features. While the justices are politically independent, they still have strong political ideologies that are reflected in their judicial decisions. The us-versus-them mentality that leads to ideological voting is alive and well at the Supreme Court.[15]

Indeed, judicial updating gives play to two tendencies that judges share with the rest of us and do not lose upon the donning of black robes. First, judges have a tendency toward self-aggrandizement.[16] Updating the Constitution gives judges more power than does strict adherence to original meaning. They can then become creators rather than implementers of the constitutional order. Second, judges have a tendency to view the law through their own preferences.[17] Judicial updating allows them greater freedom to write those preferences into law.[18] Both of these tendencies make it hard for a legal system to cabin the process of judicial updating and confine it to cases when a constitution is patently outdated.

Moreover, the Supreme Court does not make decisions behind a veil of ignorance. Although a constitutional amendment cannot easily be changed and therefore must be endured under changing circumstances, judicial decisions are much more easily revised. A decision today can be overturned in the future, either by those who disagreed with it when it was decided or by judges who initially agreed with it but subsequently changed their minds. Even more significantly, a judicial decision can be distinguished so that one based on a principle that benefits a group at one time need not be applied to impose costs on that group at a later time. For example, although conservative justices rejected a right to privacy based on penumbras, they later used analogous interpretive methods to ground state sovereign immunity.[19] Similarly, liberals criticized the theory of an unenumerated right to contract freely expounded in *Lochner*, but they later embraced that theory to establish the right to abortion in *Roe v. Wade*.[20]

The living constitution approach to interpretation transforms the nature of constitutional law, creating significant costs for society. First, the Constitution no longer has a fixed meaning that can be relied upon. Instead, the Court can develop new meanings that would have been strongly opposed in any constitutional enactment process. Thus, the security that the Constitution provides, including its constraint on government, is greatly reduced. Second, the dynamic nature of constitutional law means that it creates significant uncertainty, with people and government officials not knowing what a provision will mean in the future. This uncertainty undermines the rule of law.[21] Of course, judges recognize the costs of uncertainty in the abstract, but their interest in promoting their own importance and preferences is likely to make them unduly discount these costs.

Third, constitutional law will now be more open to obfuscation and dishonesty. If the Supreme Court was willing to admit openly what it was doing—employing norms that were not placed in the Constitution—then dishonesty would not be required. But the Court rarely admits that it is rewriting the Constitution and therefore its judicial opinions cannot be candid.[22] This dishonesty significantly impairs the Court's ability to debate the issues openly and thereby produces lower-quality judicial decisions.[23]

Of course, this analysis should not suggest that a Court applying the living constitution approach can reach any decision it likes. The power of the justices to update is circumscribed by their limited political capital. If the Court takes actions that provoke strong negative reactions from the Congress, the president, or the people, then it will be subject to attack and reprisal. The reputations of the justices will be harmed, and the political branches can begin to take actions that cut back on the Court's power. The political branches will also fill vacancies with justices who disagree with the Court's position.[24]

But even if the Supreme Court entrenched the constitutional principles favored by a majority of either the legislature or the people,[25] it would not likely generate beneficial entrenchments. Reflecting a majority legislative or popular opinion at a given moment does not generate the deliberative and crystallized consensus that is necessary for a good constitutional provision. Thus, the claim that the Court reflects the will of the majority of either the legislature or the people, even if true, is orthogonal to the conditions that we have shown to be necessary for a good constitution.

For similar reasons, a jurisprudence suggesting that the Court should simply defer to legislative interpretations of the Constitution would not maintain a good constitution over time.[26] As we saw in Chapter 3, legislative majorities would not entrench good constitutional principles. Indeed, we showed that if majorities could also repeal constitutional provisions, as they could if the Court deferred to whatever interpretations that legislatures embraced, constitutional provisions would not be entrenched in any meaningful way. Thus, a simple judicial theory of deference cannot substitute for fidelity to original meaning.[27]

Judicial Updating Undermines the Constitutional Amendment Process

THEORETICAL CONSIDERATIONS

The costs of judicial updating are not limited to the relatively low quality of such updating compared to supermajoritarian constitution making. Judicial updating also undermines the constitutional amendment process. Consequently, one cannot, to a significant degree, employ both judicial updating and constitutional amendments. One must choose between them.

The incompatibility of judicial updating with the constitutional amendment process is not generally appreciated, yet the explanation is direct and clear. The strict supermajority rules of the constitutional amendment process require a strong consensus to pass an amendment. That requirement means that an existing constitutional provision can be defective, albeit usually to a limited degree, without prompting the nation to enact a constitutional amendment reforming it. Only in situations where a provision is strongly defective—and therefore large numbers of citizens recognize that it needs to be changed—will a constitutional amendment be forthcoming.

Even if the nation is ultimately willing to enact such an amendment, it ordinarily takes a number of years during which a majority believes that a provision is undesirable before sufficient support can be secured to pass an amendment. During this period, supporters of the amendment will bemoan the Constitution and the strictness of its amendment process. Yet this period is essential to forming a consensus.

Now consider how judicial updating works. If the Supreme Court believes that it may update the Constitution, it is likely to attempt to correct defects during the period before a consensus emerges. Such a Court is likely to feel itself perfectly justified in attempting to make a correction on the ground that a significant percentage of the nation supports a change, but the unduly strict constitutional amendment process is preventing one from occurring.

Once the Supreme Court acts, however, the opportunity for the amendment process to work will likely be gone. Even if the process would have reached a somewhat different result, an amendment is not likely to be passed after the Supreme Court decision. Passing a new amendment changing a Supreme Court decision so that it captures the actual consensus is much less likely than passing an amendment that would have corrected the original constitutional defect. The consensus necessary to pass a constitutional amendment develops only if an existing constitutional provision is far from what the country regards as desirable. But if the Supreme Court has attempted to change the defective provision—to move it closer to the desirable result—then the necessary consensus is unlikely to be available to overturn the decision because the Court will have moved the provision closer to what the nation desires. An amendment will not be possible even if the nation would have enacted a different provision through the amendment process than the Court adopted in its decision.[28]

The fact that the Supreme Court rather than the constitutional amendment process has updated the provision is nonetheless harmful. The Supreme Court's updating decision may differ from the results of the constitutional amendment process in several ways. First, a constitutional amendment that would garner sufficient support to pass through the strict supermajoritarian process might differ substantially from the decision that the Supreme Court would have reached. The amendment would have likely been superior in quality to the decision because it would have reflected the various virtues of the amendment process, such as requiring a consensus and enactment behind a limited veil of ignorance. By contrast, the Supreme Court decision would lack these virtues and would often exhibit distinctive vices, such as creating uncertainty and failing to convey a candid justification.

Second, the proposed amendment might have failed to pass through the formal constitutional process. That is, apparently strong majority support might not translate into the requisite supermajoritarian consensus. If the constitutional amendment process is appropriately supermajoritarian, then this failure to produce an amendment suggests that it should not have been enacted.

Finally, even if judicial updating and the supermajoritarian process would have led to the same result, judicial updating would not replicate the virtues of the constitutional amendment process. The nation would not know that the judicial decision would actually have also been produced by the constitutional amendment process, which would deprive the decision of the acceptance that an amendment would enjoy. Moreover, a constitutional amendment would provide a more secure right than a judicial decision, which can be overturned more easily.

LOST AMENDMENTS: THE NEW DEAL, THE
ENVIRONMENTAL DECADE, AND THE EQUAL RIGHTS AMENDMENT

The differences between judicial updating and the constitutional amendment process can be illustrated with a couple of examples. First, consider the New Deal Supreme Court's series of decisions removing any real limitations on Congress's power under the Commerce Clause.[29] It seems quite likely that, during this period, the nation would have supported an expansion of the Commerce Clause.[30] But ultimately the Court's decisions later in the New Deal made the constitutional option unnecessary because it abandoned a long-standing originalist interpretation of the Constitution that limited the federal government to authority over interstate commercial matters, as opposed to manufacturing or agriculture.[31] In fact, by the end of the New Deal, the Court appeared to give the federal government essentially plenary power. Had the Court instead continued to follow the Constitution, the amendment process would likely have worked to provide the federal government with more substantial, albeit still circumscribed, power over economic matters.

It is hard to imagine a climate more favorable to a sustained campaign for constitutional amendment than the period following the 1936 election. President Franklin D. Roosevelt had been reelected by a landslide. Democrats had a 76 to 16 supermajority in the Senate[32] and a 334 to 88 seat supermajority in the House.[33] The picture in state legislatures was much the same. Of the forty-eight state legislatures, Republicans controlled only seven entirely, and they held one house in another seven.[34] The Democratic Party platform of 1936 in fact called for constitutional amendments if necessary to clarify that Congress had the power to pass legislation "to adequately regulate commerce, protect public health and safety and safeguard economic security."[35] Scholars have also suggested that, by 1936, the requisite supermajorities were available to pass amendments overruling Supreme Court decisions that had frustrated national legislation.[36]

President Roosevelt, however, did not choose to exploit this opportunity by mounting a campaign to amend the Constitution. Instead, he pressed for his famous Court-packing plan, an act that is often seen as at least partially responsible for the beginning of the Court's retreat from its prior constitutional interpretation—the "famous switch in time that saved nine."[37] Although this plan did not become law, Roosevelt's subsequent appointees to the Court soon gutted any remaining limitations on the federal government's power to regulate economic activities or establish economic programs.[38]

It is true that Roosevelt wrote a letter to state legislatures urging ratification of the Child Labor Amendment.[39] But a letter is very different from a sustained public campaign. Indeed, some historians believe that Roosevelt's letter represented an attempt to highlight the inadequacy of the amendment process rather than a genuine effort to pass the substance of the amendment.[40] Consistent with this view, Roosevelt gave no support to legislators who wanted to send a revised version of the Child Labor Amendment to state conventions, thus bypassing any recalcitrant legislatures.[41] In any event, the Child Labor Amendment had faced an uphill struggle for passage given that many states already had child labor laws, which they believed adequate.[42] Framing an amendment in terms of economic matters, as the Democratic Party platform suggested, would have better captured the political temper of the times. Consistent with this platform, members of Congress had introduced far-reaching amendments that would have permitted broad regulation of "agriculture, manufacture, industry, and labor."[43] They had also introduced amendments that would have permitted Congress to overrule Supreme Court decisions by a two-thirds majority, or even a mere majority if an election had intervened.[44]

Some have claimed that Roosevelt's attempt to pack the Court reflected his recognition that he was unable to pass the Child Labor Amendment through the supermajority requirements. But given his very substantial support in both Congress and state legislatures, the better explanation for Roosevelt's choice of Court-packing over the amendment process lies in his unwillingness to compromise. To pass a constitutional amendment, the president would have had to compromise to bring on board conservative

Democrats and moderate Republicans. Such a compromise would have expanded the federal government's powers but would not have provided the extraordinary powers that Roosevelt appeared to want.[45] His key legal adviser, Felix Frankfurter, opposed any constitutional amendment because he was an advocate of a flexible, living Constitution that could be adapted to encompass New Deal legislation.[46]

Thus, had the Court stayed firm and had Roosevelt thrown himself into the amendment process rather than focusing on Court packing, there likely would have been an amendment that authorized new regulatory powers for Congress but did not grant it the extremely broad power that the Court ultimately conferred. In the end, the New Deal is a sad story of judicial updating that undermined the amendment process.

If the New Deal had conferred only limited additional authority for economic legislation on Congress, it is also quite possible that another amendment would have been passed in the 1970s to address environmental matters. The Environmental Decade of the 1970s revealed strong, bipartisan support for federal action to address pollution.[47] Once again, a constitutional amendment might have been enacted that would have provided Congress with authority limited to addressing environmental problems, perhaps by focusing on interstate pollution.

Judicial updating, however, does not merely prevent specific constitutional amendments; it also changes the constitutional amendment process in ways that make future constitutional amendments less likely. Once the Supreme Court begins to displace or preempt constitutional amendments, this behavior provides the public with an additional incentive to avoid the time-consuming process of amending the Constitution. Political groups are less inclined to spend the effort necessary to mobilize support for a constitutional amendment if the Supreme Court is likely to take action during the process. Rather, they will change their focus and spend time attempting to influence Supreme Court nominations.[48] As time passes and fewer constitutional amendments are passed, people become unaccustomed to the amendment process, and it becomes even less likely to be used.[49]

Judicial updating also interferes with the process of constitutional amendment because people are less likely to use that process if the Supreme Court cannot be trusted to interpret amendments faithfully. This obstruction particularly harms the prospect of amending general provisions because scholars and judges now often claim that general provisions are intended to allow updating or judicial creativity.[50] Such provisions are unlikely to be used by those who seek to entrench a specific principle in the Constitution for fear the Court will update the Constitution to reflect its version of the principle rather than that of the enactors.

The harmful effects of judicial updating on the constitutional amendment process are illustrated by the failed attempt to enact the Equal Rights Amendment (ERA) during the 1970s. Although the Amendment secured the vote of thirty-five of the thirty-eight states required for ratification, it ultimately failed.[51] At least two factors contributed to its failure. During the period when the amendment was being considered, the Supreme Court decided cases that applied a heightened scrutiny standard to gender under the Equal Protection Clause, thereby reducing the need for the Equal Rights Amendment.[52] For instance, in 1971, before the amendment was even passed by Congress, the Supreme Court decided *Reed v. Reed,* which invalidated an Idaho law that gave preference to male administrators for estates.[53] Although *Reed* did not expressly endorse heightened scrutiny, it effectively provided more substantial scrutiny for sex discrimination than for ordinary economic legislation.[54] Indeed, a plurality in *Frontiero v. Richardson* later stated that *Reed* implicitly supported heightened judicial scrutiny of sexual discrimination.[55] Thus, even before the decision in *Frontiero,* state legislators could have rationally believed that sex discrimination was already subject to heightened judicial scrutiny and thus concluded that a formal amendment was unnecessary.

The willingness of the Warren and Burger Courts to depart from originalism generally was also an important cause of the failure of the Equal Rights Amendment. Many feared the amendment would be interpreted broadly to require unpopular measures and impose a more radical vision of sexual equality than was shared by its enactors. Many people worried that the amendment might be twisted to mandate same-sex bathrooms[56] and to eliminate the exclusion of women from combat. Given the history of the judicial activism prior to the proposed ERA,[57] citizens could not be confident that the Court would have interpreted the amendment's general language according to the meaning its enactors claimed to attach to it. By not enforcing the Constitution according to its original meaning, the Court thus reduces the effectiveness of the constitutional amendment process generally.

In short, had the Court not already updated the Constitution and had it been clear that the amendment would not be creatively interpreted, it is likely that the Equal Rights Amendment would have been enacted—either the version containing the general language passed by Congress or one with more specific limitations that might have been subsequently enacted.

In contrast to a Supreme Court engaged in judicial updating, a court that follows originalism would promote the use of the amendment process. During the period when recognition of a constitutional defect is growing, an originalist Court would decide cases under the original meaning and would make clear that it would not judicially correct the alleged defect. This unyielding fidelity would give political groups incentives to attempt to organize for a constitutional amendment. The Court's opinions might even state that the way to correct this defect is through a constitutional amendment, which would further promote such organization.

It is often argued that the Constitution's amendment provisions are too strict and therefore judicial updating is required.[58] Our examination suggests that this argument has the matter backward. It is not that the constitutional amendment process operates poorly and therefore nonoriginalism is required. Rather, it is that nonoriginalism prevents the constitutional amendment process from operating effectively.

It might be argued that our call for a return to originalism ignores the Supreme Court's incentive to take advantage of the supermajoritarian amendment process to maximize its own policy preferences within the large policy space in which judges cannot be overruled by a constitutional amendment. Although the Court has considerable power, the system still has resources to encourage originalism. Judges have been much more originalist in the past. Indeed, originalism was the overwhelmingly dominant jurisprudence before the Progressive Era.[59] There is no reason that it could not be dominant again in the future. If the legal culture strongly supported originalism, as it once did—and as it now does much more than a generation ago[60]—that would provide the courts with both a strong incentive and a desire to be originalist. As Richard Posner has noted, judges have a desire to play games by the rules.[61] Unfortunately, judicial updating destroys the rules of the game that generate a legal culture that helps enforce those rules.

The Theory of the Second Best

One particular kind of judicial updating consists in what have been called compensating adjustments.[62] A compensating adjustment is a nonoriginalist decision that the Court renders to compensate for a previous nonoriginalist decision. For instance, assume the Court's permissive stance toward delegations distorts the Constitution's original meaning. The Court might then compensate by permitting legislative vetoes—an additional means of controlling executive discretion—even though the legislative veto itself conflicts with the Constitution's original meaning.[63] It might be argued that the resulting structure created by two nonoriginalist doctrines is closer to the constraint on delegation imposed by the Constitution's original meaning than a structure created by the overly permissive nondelegation doctrine alone.[64]

In this sense, compensating adjustments represent an example of the theory of the second best. In its original economic context, the theory of the second best showed that a departure from the conditions for efficiency in one respect might actually lead to greater overall efficiency if the market already had departed from the conditions for efficiency in another respect.[65] So too a departure from originalism in a particular case might lead us to a result closer to the original structure of the Constitution if there were already a previous departure from originalism.[66] In either the economic or constitutional case, two wrongs might cancel one another out and make a right. But in both contexts, the theory of the second best shows only that this is a possibility, not that it has any degree of probability.[67]

The arguments for judicial updating through compensatory adjustments are no stronger, and may be weaker, than those for judicial updating in general. Although it is certainly conceivable that compensatory adjustments, like judicial updating in general, could reach a good result in a particular case, the Supreme Court is unlikely to regularly select the true second-best cases.[68] The core problems are the same as those outlined in our discussion of judicial updating. First, the Supreme Court faces substantial difficulties in accurately identifying compensatory entrenchments. Calculating the effects of compensating entrenchments is no easier and no less subject to ideological distortions than updating in general. Consider, for example, just a few of the many questions that a compensatory adjustment of the legislative veto would require answering. Because it is not defined in the Constitution, the very scope of the legislative veto is unclear. Does it extend to two-house vetoes only, or also to one-house vetoes? To committee vetoes? To vetoes by committees of one? Allowing a legislative veto would also encourage additional and broader delegations because the legislative veto allows members of Congress more power to control such delegations. As a result, it is difficult to know whether the legislative veto will increase or decrease the overall amount of executive discretion.

Furthermore, judicial updating to create compensatory adjustments interferes with the amendment process no less than other types of judicial updating. If a nonoriginalist precedent causes adverse consequences, a constitutional amendment can address the problem. But judicial compensatory adjustments will crowd out these amendments.

Updating through compensatory adjustments ensures that every nonoriginalist precedent has potential ripple effects, greatly magnifying the distortions that such precedent has on the Constitution's original meaning. Once a nonoriginalist precedent is accepted, compensatory adjustment theory urges judges to resolve other issues in a nonoriginalist manner. And then those other nonoriginalist resolutions can form the basis for compensatory adjustments in favor of further nonoriginalist decisions. In the real world, second-best originalism becomes the first best recipe for a feast of nonoriginalism. Finally, by providing an alternative to overruling precedents, the possibility of making compensating adjustments reduces the pressure for their reconsideration and therefore frustrates efforts to revive the Constitution's original meaning.[69]

Our conclusions are not materially changed by considering the strategic interactions of justices in another kind of second-best world—a world where an originalist justice has colleagues who are mostly nonoriginalists.[70] While it is logically possible that an originalist justice could do better by compromising with nonoriginalist justices in order to obtain results closer to those reached by originalism, once again there are strong reasons why originalists would do better in the long run simply by following originalism.

Departing from originalism undermines its public attractiveness and makes it difficult to generate an originalist legal culture, which is necessary to secure the greatest benefits from originalism. Inconsistency is a serious charge to be lodged against any constitutional approach, but it damages originalism much more for two reasons. Unlike other approaches, originalism possesses a transparent methodology, departures from which are often obvious. Moreover, rigorous consistency and clarity are two of its central proclaimed virtues.[71] Consequently, claims that originalist justices are failing to consistently follow originalism have become a familiar trope within critiques of originalism.[72] Second, it is unlikely that judges who cease to apply rigorous originalism will get sufficient payback in return from other judges' relaxation of their nonoriginalism. Most nonoriginalist judges lack a jurisprudential theory that has much public resonance.[73] Thus, there is an asymmetry between originalists discarding originalism and nonoriginalists discarding nonoriginalism.

An additional problem caused by compromising with nonoriginalist judges is that it is often difficult to determine what the long-run results of the compromise will be. Game theory, which models these interactions, confirms the difficulty of making these predictions.[74] Consequently, originalist judges may not even know whether their actions are likely to benefit originalism. Overall, then, the significant costs and reduced benefits from compromising with nonoriginalist judges suggest that originalist judges do better to stick consistently with their approach.

A Presumption of Originalism

It might be argued that the virtues of supermajority rules for enacting constitutional provisions can produce only a presumption in favor of originalism. Under such a presumption, judges would generally apply the original meaning unless they deemed that meaning seriously defective.[75] Clearly, this presumption would be superior to a general strategy of judicial updating because it would more often lead judges to follow the original meaning. This presumption would abandon originalism only in the cases when judges found constitutional provisions to be the most seriously problematic.

Nonetheless, presumptive originalism would be inferior to genuine originalism because the presumptive approach suffers from the same problems that afflict the more general judicial updating strategy. First, when the courts do update, the content of constitutional law suffers from the same infirmities discussed earlier, such as a lack of consensus, uncertainty, and not being enacted from behind a veil of ignorance. Perhaps most important, a presumptive approach would also undermine the constitutional amendment process. If it applied only to the worst provisions, it would tend to interfere with the proposed constitutional amendments that were the most likely to be enacted because the worst provisions are the most likely to be the object of a successful amendment. As a result, the presumptive approach would dishabituate the public from using the amendment process and vitiate the rich deliberative politics of constitutionalism that this process generates.

A presumptive approach also would prompt disagreements on the Court about which provisions justified updating. Although the standard would be more demanding than the standard for ordinary updating, the Court would still disagree about which provisions meet that more demanding standard. If liberals were to conclude that a provision satisfied the more demanding standard, conservatives might disagree and accuse liberals of failing to follow that standard (and liberals could not defend themselves in the open because this type of updating is not admitted publicly).[76] Such disagreements could easily lead the justices to descend from a presumptive originalism to a simple judicial updating arrangement. And presumptive originalism may in fact be more deceptive than a pure living constitution approach because it enables judges to mask their politically motivated decisions by pointing to other decisions where they followed the original meaning.

The Dead-Hand Problem

Another way to address the continuing desirability of our old Constitution is to focus on the dead hand problem.[77] The phrase refers to the following questions: Why, under the Constitution, the present-day majority is prevented from taking action that displaces the constitutional decisions of people who are long dead.[78] What justifies being ruled by the dead hand of the past? The supermajoritarian theory of constitutionalism has a powerful response.

In discussing the dead-hand problem, it is important to clarify what the problem actually is. Under one interpretation, any legal regime under which a current majority cannot change a rule passed by a prior generation is impermissibly ruled by the dead hand of the past. If this proposition is what is meant by the dead-hand problem, then the Constitution may indeed have one—but we do not regard that criticism as serious because this version is extreme and at odds with the essence of constitutionalism itself. It is inconsistent with any constitution that places limits on the powers of a current majority in order to prevent erroneous decisions driven by passion or external costs imposed by interest groups. A more useful version of the dead-hand problem would focus on narrower objections, such as whether a constitution fabricated by the dead continues to help the living, and whether the current generation can add provisions to the constitution on the same terms as previous generations.

Our supermajoritarian theory of constitutionalism provides strong reasons why restrictions imposed by a supermajority in the past can benefit the present. First, a supermajoritarian-enacted constitution likely generates desirable restrictions, such as the separation of powers, federalism, checks and balances, and the protection of individual rights. A supermajoritarian constitution that limits the current majority is not merely necessary to constitutionalism but can also be very beneficial to current majorities if it were enacted under appropriate supermajority rules. Under these conditions, the hand of the past is one that reaches out to steady the living.[79]

Second, while it imposes restrictions enacted in the past, a supermajoritarian constitution allows each generation to entrench values under the supermajority rules of similar stringency. Thus, a supermajoritarian constitution formally treats each generation equally. Moreover, appropriate enactment rules help to ensure that the values of the Constitution can be updated by each generation without compromising the other benefits generated by supermajority rules.

Of course, it might be argued that the Framers' generation still had a disproportionate influence on the Constitution, given that it enacted so many of the Constitution's provisions. Or to make a similar point, had the modern generation enacted the Constitution, it would probably look somewhat different than it does now. The Framers' generation might be thought to have a first-mover advantage.

But even if the enactors had more actual (as opposed to formal) input into the Constitution, that does not mean the current generation is necessarily disadvantaged. Once it is recognized that different generations affect one another—and, of course, the temporal relationship between generations cannot be changed—it is not surprising that different generations may have different advantages and disadvantages. While the Framers may have had more input into the Constitution, later generations have other advantages. We inherit the benefits of their system—a Constitution that is stable, desirable, and strongly supported by the nation. In fact, it seems evident that we are better off than the Framers were from this arrangement. After all, if we wanted to place ourselves in their position, we could simply junk the Constitution and draft a new one. But we do not do so; indeed, few of even our most adventurous thinkers entertain the prospect. We prefer the benefits of being constrained by the past.

6

SUPERMAJORITARIAN FAILURE, INCLUDING THE EXCLUSION OF AFRICAN AMERICANS AND WOMEN

So far, we have developed the theory that constitutions enacted pursuant to strict supermajority rules are likely to be desirable. And we have shown that the US Constitution conforms to this supermajoritarian theory to a remarkable extent. Yet we have also recognized that the Constitution has departed from the requirements of the desirable constitutional process in several important ways. Enactment and amendment, for instance, have been accomplished by states rather than by people, thereby giving greater weight to the votes of people in less populous states. Most importantly, African Americans and women were excluded from the original process of constitutional enactment and from the amendment process for many years afterward. This chapter explores the consequences of these departures. If the Constitution's supermajoritarian process has such defects, then what are the consequences of this supermajoritarian failure for our normative theory of the Constitution?

We maintain that only three responses to supermajoritarian failure are available. First, one can dispense with the existing constitution and attempt to establish a new one. Second, one can simply apply the original meaning of the imperfect constitution, even though it has defects. Third, one can purport to apply the original meaning of the imperfect constitution but then have the judiciary (or other government entity) depart from that original meaning in an effort to correct it—what we call judicial correction.[1] The concept of judicial correction is to be distinguished from judicial updating. Judicial updating changes the original meaning of a constitutional provision to improve it so that it fits better with contemporary norms or needs. Judicial correction changes the meaning of a constitutional provision to make it approximate more closely what the provision would have said had the proper supermajoritarian process of constitution making been followed.

Here we compare the three alternatives of (1) making a new constitution, (2) applying the original meaning of the existing imperfect constitution, and (3) engaging in judicial correction. First, we show that dispensing with an existing constitution is a drastic alternative because it creates very large uncertainty about the basic framework of government. It certainly is not justified for the United States because the US Constitution's defects are much less costly than the burden of dispensing with and replacing the document.

Second, we suggest that correcting these failures through judicial interpretation is generally problematic because such judicial correction shares many of the defects of judicial updating. Nonetheless, one cannot categorically reject judicial correction because it may be desirable in certain circumstances. But it should be deployed only if the defects in the supermajoritarian enactment process are so substantial and so reduce the desirability of a constitution that the benefits of judicial correction outweigh its substantial costs. We then apply our theory to the most important supermajoritarian failures of our own Constitution, including the exclusion of African Americans and women. It is our judgment that many of the defects of our Constitution have been solved and that judicial correction of any remaining defects clearly has greater costs than benefits.

The Theory of Supermajoritarian Failure

Replacing the Existing Constitution

The first response to supermajoritarian failure is simply to dispense with a constitution and to replace it with a new one that avoids the defect. In a way, this response is the most obvious and cleanest response to the defect. We could fully rectify the original exclusion of African Americans and women by simply discarding the Constitution and enacting a new one through a process that allows these groups to participate.

But there are powerful reasons why dispensing with a constitution is undesirable. First, enacting a new constitution involves a great deal of effort. The nation would have to concentrate tremendously on the issue, expending enormous political resources for a considerable period. Second, during that period of constitutional transformation, citizens would not know what the fundamental law might turn out to be. This uncertainty could have huge costs, as individuals and businesses might delay crucial decisions until they once again had a firm system of government. Third, the new constitution, even if its provisions were superior, would be unlikely, for a considerable period, to secure the same allegiance that the old one enjoyed. Finally, we cannot be confident that the new constitution would be better than the existing imperfect constitution. The supermajoritarian process has enough variability that even a perfect process could produce a worse result than an imperfect process did, particularly if the worst defects of that first process have been corrected over the years.

One other kind of uncertainty undermines the argument for getting rid of a constitution: How does one actually dispense with it? For the US Constitution, the question of replacing it can be quite difficult. It is not clear what method the nation could use to peacefully eliminate the Constitution. The least complicated way to enact a new constitution is to use the existing Article V mechanism to call a constitutional convention, which would then propose a new constitution. But in abandoning the whole Constitution, the convention might (whether legal or not) call for an entirely new system of ratification and disregard Article V, just as those who abandoned the Articles of Confederation dispensed with its unanimity requirement.[2] The uncertainty about the method of constitution making would be yet another cost of replacing the old Constitution with an entirely new one, and one could not be confident that the method selected would be a good one. The drafters of a new constitution might be more concerned with its substantive provisions than with creating the optimal process for ratification.

In the end, enacting a new constitution is a desirable option only in limited circumstances. We divide these circumstances into two different situations. First, assume that a constitution has a well-functioning amendment process. Getting rid of a constitution with such a process in place becomes very much less attractive because the amendment process permits large corrections without many of the uncertainties attendant upon eliminating an old constitution and writing a new one. Writing a new constitution under these circumstances would be a desirable option only if the old constitution had so many defects that amending the constitution was impractical, or if any amendments would suffer from lack of popular acceptance because of their being linked to previous fundamental law that was hugely defective.

On the other hand, if a constitution does not have a functioning amendment process, junking that constitution becomes more plausible, at least when it is not terribly popular. Even under these circumstances, the benefits of any such change must also be large enough to outweigh the uncertainty costs of creating a new constitution. In the case of the United States, the circumstances supporting a new constitution simply do not hold. Not surprisingly, only a very few scholars have ever suggested that replacement is a viable option.[3]

Judicial Correction

The other alternative to following the original meaning of an imperfectly enacted constitution is to have the judiciary attempt to correct the imperfection under the guise of interpretation. Under this approach, the judiciary would not update the constitution generally but instead would correct only problems that resulted from defects in the supermajoritarian process for enacting or amending the constitution. The judiciary would interpret the constitution so that it would provide for a provision that would have been enacted if the supermajoritarian process had followed the appropriate rules. For example, the Supreme Court would determine what constitutional provisions would have been enacted if blacks could have participated in the original enactment process.

We believe that judicial correction is an extreme course that is very unlikely to prove desirable for the present US Constitution. It suffers from many of the same infirmities of judicial updating. But unlike judicial updating, it is impossible to rule out judicial correction categorically. Here, we begin our analysis by outlining the principal hurdles that such judicial corrections must surmount to be beneficial. Given these significant hurdles, we then show that judicial corrections are unlikely to be justified when a constitution has rectified, as ours has, the worst consequences of the imperfections in the enactment process.

Judicial correction faces a number of obstacles. First, correction requires identifying the nature of the imperfection in the original constitutional enactment process. While some imperfections are obvious, such as the exclusion of African Americans, others are more subtle, like representation through states rather than individuals.

Second, correction requires identifying the substance of the constitutional provision that would have emerged but for the imperfection. Again, some consequences may be obvious. African Americans would have insisted on an antidiscrimination provision, ensuring their right to vote and participate in civil society. But other possible changes in the Constitution are harder to assess because it is difficult to determine what an excluded group would have wanted or whether its members would have had the leverage to get their desires translated into a constitutional provision.

Third, introducing such a corrective principle must advance the interests of those harmed by the exclusion and not be counterproductive. Before the Civil War, a constitutional correction that ended slavery would almost certainly have split the Union. Indeed, it is not at all clear that a retreat to sectarian regional governments would have left African Americans better off in the long run.

Fourth, the provision to be corrected must be important. Unless it has significant effects, it will not be worth the substantial costs of using the judicial correction method. Fifth, even if it is important, the judicial correction must not undermine the judiciary's legitimacy or the acceptance of the correction. A correction that blatantly rewrote the text of an important constitutional provision, like the Article V amendment process or the equal representation of states in the Senate, might so reduce respect for the Court as an institution that operates according to law that it is hard to imagine circumstances that would justify it.

These issues are all substantially more open-ended than determining the historical meaning of language. Some of the issues involved in judicial correction depend on an assessment not of history that happened but on history that has not happened. For instance, the content of judicial correction turns on counterfactuals, such as what provisions an excluded group would have wanted to place into the Constitution and whether it would have been able to obtain acceptance of those provisions in the supermajoritarian process. Assessing whether the judiciary harms itself by engaging in judicial correction requires the judiciary to be a judge both in its own case and in a case with very unclear metrics of decision.

As a result, judicial correction suffers from a variety of problems, many of which also plague judicial updating.[4] First, there is unlikely to be an agreement or consensus about the need for or the content of the judicial corrections. After all, wide agreement on these matters would likely prompt a constitutional amendment. Moreover, as we saw in Chapter 5, judicial updating lacks the institutional mechanisms to ensure accurate consensus, and the same is true of judicial correction. These disagreements could occur on all the issues discussed above.

If some judges seek to engage in judicial correction in a way that other judges view as improper, this behavior could lead to charges of judicial activism and illegitimacy. The offended judges might even attempt to fight fire with fire and use the judicial correction process as a cover for advancing their own policy views. Either result may lead to a downward spiral of dissension and politicization both in the courts and among the citizenry.

Second, disagreements about the need for, or the content of, appropriate judicial corrections would also surely lead to uncertainty, which would undermine the rule of law. It would be difficult for legislators and litigants alike to predict how the courts will decide cases that might be viewed as touching on issues involving supermajoritarian failure.

Third, judicial correction is likely to have a transparency problem because judges would be unlikely to acknowledge that they are engaging in the practice. The absence of transparency would have at least three unfortunate effects. It would undermine the rule of law because cases would be decided on factors that are not publicly revealed. It would hinder public deliberations among judges on the same court and among different levels of judicial hierarchy because they would not be able to discuss a key element of their reasoning. And it would create precedents that would distort the web of the law because they would be based on unacknowl-edged reasoning and thus would not be amenable to being distinguished on appropriate grounds.

This transparency problem would be avoided if the judges acknowl-edged that they were engaging in the practice, but such disclosure would have its own difficulties. Unless there was a consensus in favor of the prac-tice of judicial correction, many judges and citizens would think the rea-soning illegitimate and even strange. Its very novelty might then reduce respect for the courts and decisions made under the basis of the theory.

Finally, this judicial correction approach will also undermine the con-stitutional amendment process. The judiciary's attempts to correct the constitutional defects will effectively prevent the constitutional amend-ment process from doing so. Although it might seem that these superma-joritarian failures could not be corrected by constitutional amendments, our history shows that the beneficiaries of the current policies do not always refuse to agree to proposed changes. One clear example of a con-stitutional correction involves the passage of the Nineteenth Amendment guaranteeing women the right to vote, which received substantial support from men. By contrast, as we showed in Chapter 5, the Equal Rights Amendment was defeated at least in part because the Supreme Court had judicially corrected the Constitution when the amendment was being considered for ratification. Of course, not all defects may be correctable by constitutional amendment. But the fact that judicial correction interfered with this process must be regarded as another serious cost of using such corrections.

While judicial correction therefore has significant problems, we cannot categorically reject it as we do judicial updating. As discussed in Chapter 5, judicial updating allows the courts to revise the Constitution when they deem such a revision desirable, even when the Constitution is enacted pursuant to appropriate supermajority rules. But a constitution enacted pursuant to such supermajority rules is likely to be a good one—either a genuinely good one or at least a pretty good one—and therefore should be followed.

Although we categorically reject the judicial updating approach, two reasons make it much more likely that a judicial correction of a supermajoritarian failure might, under certain circumstances, be justifiable. First, although a constitution enacted under appropriate supermajority rules is unlikely to exhibit serious infirmities, one enacted through a defective supermajoritarian process might be so problematic that it requires correction through any means available.

Second, if there were a supermajoritarian failure, this failure would provide a greater focus on the defect and the way to correct it. We have emphasized that there may be significant disagreement about what aspect of the supermajoritarian process failed, as well as the content of the appropriate correction. Nonetheless, there is still likely to be more agreement about it than there would be about what provisions happen to be outdated or undesirable. Although judicial correction might theoretically turn out to be the best option, we argue that this is not the case at present.

Three Supermajoritarian Failures

Here we address the consequences of process defects in the Constitution's supermajority enactment rules. First, and most importantly, the original Constitution allowed African Americans and women to be excluded from participation in its enactment. Moreover, in 1787 and even today, the ratification of the Constitution and amendments takes place through the approval of states, and thus individuals wield different amounts of influence depending on where they live. We apply our theory of supermajoritarian failure to show that, despite these defects, judicial correction of the

Constitution currently would be worse than enforcing the amended Constitution according to its original terms.

Exclusion of African Americans

The exclusion of most African Americans from the constitutional enactment process was undoubtedly an enormous failure of the supermajoritarian process. We show that there is a strong case to be made, however, that this failure was corrected through the enactment of the Reconstruction Amendments.[5] Moreover, even if those amendments did not fully resolve the original supermajoritarian failure, they still came close enough to render additional judicial correction inadvisable.

The exclusion of the vast majority of African Americans from substantial participation in the drafting or ratification of the Constitution represents the most serious departure from the conditions conducive to generating a good constitution.[6] The exclusion goes to the heart of how supermajority rules produce a desirable constitution. Supermajority rules have the virtue of creating consensus solutions, but if a group of voters is excluded from the process, their absence casts doubt on the existence or content of that consensus. Thus, the constitutional enactment process depends for its beneficence on representation of the entire population. The supermajoritarian process is designed to protect minorities, but it will have difficulty doing so if those minorities cannot participate. Hence the original sin of America—slavery—and its consequent exclusion of blacks from political participation are also the greatest challenges to the beneficence of the supermajoritarian process for creating the Constitution.[7]

The consequences of this exclusion for nineteenth-century constitutionalism were quite severe. The Constitution did not guarantee African Americans civil or political rights, nor did it dismantle the system of slavery. Given the slaves' exclusion from the enactment process and their harsh treatment under laws not prohibited by the Constitution, our argument for the binding nature of the Constitution probably did not even apply to the slaves. Their exclusion also raises a real question about the appropriate way to have interpreted the Constitution in the antebellum period, particularly the constitutional provisions that involved slavery.[8]

But the question of whether judges should correct the Constitution differs today because the supermajoritarian failure has largely been rectified by a supermajoritarian correction through constitutional amendments. The Thirteenth Amendment ended slavery.[9] The Fourteenth Amendment prohibited state infringements of civil rights.[10] The Fifteenth Amendment forbade racial discrimination in the protection of voting rights.[11]

If enforced according to their terms, these amendments would have contributed substantially to a "new birth of freedom" for African Americans that would have provided them with largely the same rights that white males enjoyed in 1789.[12] Under this view, the Reconstruction Amendments have added the provisions that African Americans in 1789 most obviously would have demanded had they been part of the enactment process. Congress has also passed substantial laws preventing discrimination under these amendments.[13] Thus, there is a strong, although not uncontestable, argument that the Reconstruction Amendments fully correct the supermajoritarian failure: They provide African Americans with the provisions they would have been able to obtain in 1789 if there had been no supermajoritarian failure and they had fully participated in the enactment process.[14]

It is true that one might argue that the Reconstruction Amendments did not fully correct the original supermajoritarian failure on the ground that the original inclusion of African Americans might have resulted in additional changes to the Constitution. For instance, some might say that African Americans' participation in the process would have led to provisions in favor of affirmative action. But our theory of supermajoritarian failure suggests that the courts should not attempt to insert such a provision into the Constitution.

First, the case for concluding that the Constitution would have included an affirmative action provision had African Americans been able to participate in the constitutional amendment process is relatively weak. It would be ill-considered to extrapolate from the preferences of African Americans today what measures they would have supported 100 or 200 years ago. Even if African Americans would have desired affirmative action, it is not at all clear that they would have secured this benefit, given that it would have been less important to them than antidiscrimination provisions and would have been more strongly opposed than such provisions. Thus, affirmative action provisions likely would not have garnered the consensus support necessary for constitutional entrenchment.

In addition to the low probability that affirmative action would have been included, there are, of course, the additional costs of engaging in judicial correction on this issue. These costs include the absence of long-term decision making, the superseding of the constitutional amendment process, and the possibility of partisan decisions. In particular, disagreements on elusive counterfactuals, such as whether African Americans would have secured affirmative action, could easily be caught up in ideological disagreement about what provisions are desirable. Such divisions on fundamental issues, particularly framed in emotional terms about the effect of exclusion on African Americans, could easily lead to a spiral of dissension threatening the integrity of the Constitution.

Despite the passage of the Reconstruction Amendments, African Americans still faced practical exclusion for almost a century. While the constitutional document conferred rights on blacks, these rights were often ignored until the 1960s. Because the focus of our analysis is originalism today, this prior failure by all three branches of government to enforce the Constitution is not our principal concern. It is worth discussing briefly, however, for the light it sheds on originalism.

It is sometimes thought that the plight of African Americans during the Jim Crow era was the fault of the Constitution's original meaning. On the contrary, however, it was principally the result of a failure to enforce the Constitution's original meaning.[15] In other words, the failure of the Reconstruction Amendments to protect African American rights and welfare during the Jim Crow era was the result of nonoriginalism, not originalism. Although the original meaning of the Reconstruction Amendments would have provided blacks with substantial, if not complete, protection against discrimination, the three branches of the federal government failed to respect that original meaning, to the great detriment of African Americans.

This nonoriginalism included a massive failure of the three branches to enforce the constitutional provisions that prevented racial discrimination in voting rights. The Supreme Court largely ignored, and sometimes even sanctioned, state legislation that effectively precluded blacks from participating in the political process. During Reconstruction, African Americans voted in large numbers in the South.[16] By the 1890s, however, their participation had faded to insignificance as a result of discriminatory voting regulations.[17] Some statutes, for instance, required new voters to be literate but grandfathered in people whose ancestors voted at a time when African Americans could not vote.[18] The Court's response to these regulations was wholly inadequate to enforce the antidiscrimination requirement of the Fifteenth Amendment.[19]

Whatever the Court's failures, Congress should have acted against these schemes to enforce the Reconstruction Amendments. One particularly glaring act of neglect was the failure to reduce the South's proportion of representation to reflect the exclusion of African Americans from the franchise—a reduction required by Section 2 of the Fourteenth Amendment.[20]

Beyond voting rights, the Supreme Court also failed to enforce the civil rights guaranteed by the Constitution. *Plessy v. Ferguson* exemplifies the denial of the equal right to contract guaranteed by the Fourteenth Amendment.[21] The Court failed to invalidate state laws that denied African Americans and railroad companies the opportunity for African Americans to contract to sit in coaches otherwise reserved for whites.[22] The law represented a denial of the equality to contract and thus of a privilege or immunity guaranteed by the Fourteenth Amendment because African Americans were denied the same right to contract to sit in particular coaches as whites.[23] The response that whites were also denied the right to contract to sit in other coaches (those restricted to blacks), and thus that each race had equal rights (to sit in coaches with their own races), is not compelling. First, as John Harrison has argued, the Fourteenth Amendment was designed to constitutionalize the Civil Rights Act of 1866, which stated that all citizens should have the same rights as white citizens and that "if the rights are different under any description, they are not the same."[24] Moreover, if one had to choose between a description of rights in race-neutral terms (the right to sit in a particular coach) and race-infused terms (the right to sit with one's own race), the first description is to be preferred. After all, a core purpose of the Fourteenth Amendment was to eliminate caste legislation, and permitting a description of rights in caste terms is at odds with that purpose.[25] Finally, it is not at all clear that symmetrical rights to discriminate could be equal for whites and African Americans when whites were so much more numerous and wealthy.

The reasoning of *Plessy* permitted states and localities to extend this apartheid regime to a variety of important contractual services.[26] The Supreme Court's distortion of the Fourteenth Amendment thus became a legal foundation for Jim Crow. Moreover, Congress never used its Section 5 authority to rectify this situation until well into the twentieth century.

Thus, if one believes, as we do, that the treatment of African Americans remains the greatest political evil in the history of the US polity, the greatest indictment of constitutional interpretation during this era is not that the Court did not correct the Constitution to reflect some set of additional provisions that the inclusion of African Americans might have prompted. Instead, the root of the tragedy is that the government, including the Court, often failed to enforce the original meaning of the corrections enacted through the amendment process. The legacy of John Bingham and Jacob Howard was encapsulated in these amendments,[27] and yet the federal government, including the courts, too often abandoned their understanding of the words for that of officials like Charles Crisp,[28] who, as Speaker, led the Congress to repeal most of the statutes enforcing the Reconstruction Amendments.[29]

This perspective suggests that the emphasis on *Brown v. Board of Education* in discussions of civil rights jurisprudence has obscured a salient truth about the history of civil rights and constitutional interpretation.[30] We believe that *Brown*'s holding extending the equality guarantee beyond common law rights to public schooling can be defended on originalist grounds, even if the opinion's reasoning was not originalist.[31] But whether or not originalism is compatible with *Brown*, the world would likely have been so different, had the Reconstruction Amendments not been nullified for generations by the refusal of all the branches to follow the Constitution's original meaning, that it is not even clear that *Brown* would have been necessary to secure educational equality for blacks. That is, the greater economic and voting power that would have come with a fair enforcement of the Reconstruction Amendments would likely have eroded the caste system of public education in the South. Before we simply celebrate *Brown*'s nonoriginalist reasoning, we should reflect on the great suffering and injustice that nonoriginalism caused for so many for almost a century.

The Exclusion of Women

The exclusion of women from the constitutional enactment process constitutes another serious supermajoritarian failure.[32] This failure directly led to the failure to guarantee voting rights to women until early in the last century. But like the exclusion of African Americans, the exclusion of women has been substantially corrected. In 1920, the nation passed another supermajoritarian correction to a supermajoritarian failure: The Nineteenth Amendment guaranteed women the right to vote, ensuring that women from that time forward could fully participate in the constitutional amendment process.[33] Women now also have been granted constitutional protections against state discrimination. It is true that these rights were the result of Supreme Court decisions, but absent those decisions and the fear of nonoriginalist interpretation by the Supreme Court, they would have come about through the amendment process. As we saw in Chapter 5, an equal rights amendment would likely have been passed if the Supreme Court had not engaged in judicial updating, including judicial enactment of a version of the amendment. Thus, the failure of an equal rights amendment is a prime example of the costs of judicial updating rather than an argument for the practice.

It might be thought that even the passage of the Nineteenth Amendment and these Supreme Court precedents do not provide full correction. But, as with African Americans, it is extremely speculative to assess how the Constitution would have been further changed, if at all, by the earlier inclusion of women in its making. For instance, it is sometimes argued that the inclusion of women would have prevented statutes against abortions, but the current views of women provide reason to doubt this conclusion: The proportion of women who oppose abortion today is close to the proportion of men.[34]

Women have now had almost a century to contribute to the enactment of additional corrective measures. And unlike African Americans, their right to vote was not undermined by state practices. Thus, it seems that the courts should be less willing to correct for the exclusion of women than for the exclusion of African Americans. But as with judicial attempts to correct for the exclusion of African Americans, similar attempts on behalf of women would lead to divisions and lack the discipline for sound long-term decision making provided by the amendment process.[35]

Representation Based on States Rather Than People

Another supermajoritarian failure involves the Constitution's decision to base representation in the constitutional enactment process on states rather than individuals. Consequently, individuals wield different levels of influence on the Constitution depending on where they live, with the relatively few individuals in small states having greater proportional influence than the relatively many individuals in large states. Despite the absence of a supermajoritarian correction, our theory of supermajoritarian failure would not justify judicial correction of the provisions that base representation on states.

Both the enactment and the amendment processes relied on the approval of states rather than individuals. The original constitution-making process set the stage for such imperfections. The delegations voted at the Philadelphia Convention by state, and the original Constitution was ratified by equally weighted state conventions.[36] The Constitution itself requires that amendments be proposed by two-thirds of each house of Congress and therefore by a Senate in which states have equal weight.[37] The ratification of amendments is also achieved by obtaining the support of three-quarters of the states.[38] This pervasive representation of states, rather than individuals, permits some individuals to have more influence in shaping the document than others. This process departs from the desirable conditions for constitution making because it is a consensus among individuals, rather than among states, that ultimately helps to ensure the beneficence of the Constitution. Individuals, rather than states, ultimately have value and therefore it is important to ensure that the Constitution has their consensus support.

Given this defect in the process for constitution making, it is no surprise that the resulting Constitution establishes a structure for ordinary politics that also relies in part on state representation, permitting some individuals potentially to wield more influence there as well. Most notably, the structure of the Senate provides individuals in different states with widely different levels of influence not only on legislation but also on appointments and treaties because the Senate approves these presidential decisions.[39] The officials appointed include Supreme Court justices, who in turn influence the Constitution's interpretation.

The Electoral College also creates a system of state rather than individual representation and makes the votes of some individuals weightier than others. On its face, the Electoral College, like the Senate, puts people in large states at a disadvantage and benefits individuals in small states, but this appearance is deceiving. The Electoral College, however, may improve rather than exacerbate the problem of equality of representation. As long as states retain the unit rule (which awards all electoral votes to the statewide winner), the large states are the most advantaged because large states have a greater chance of being decisive in the Electoral College.[40]

Having described the pervasiveness of the problem of representation through states, we first explain why this defect is not as serious in practice as it might seem in theory. Second, we show that this defect is impossible to correct without radically rewriting the Constitution.

State representation in the constitution-making process likely did not substantially distort the results that individual representation would have provided.[41] First, as we noted in Chapter 4, in the original enactment process, larger states may have effectively wielded greater influence than the formal rules contemplated, thus compensating in some measure for this defect. Second, the danger that a large group of small states representing a minority of the population could pass a constitutional amendment is small.[42] In the only constitutional amendment process that has ever been used, proposed constitutional amendments still need the approval of two-thirds of the members of the House of Representatives as well as the Senate, and the House representation is based on population.[43]

The opposite danger—that a small number of states can block a constitutional amendment—is more substantial. This danger potentially undermines sound constitutionalism because the individuals living in small states would have more blocking power than individuals living in big states. For the most part, however, this danger is unlikely to occur because policy views are not substantially correlated with the size of states. Ideologically speaking, there are conservative big states, like Texas and Florida, and liberal big states, like New York and California. There are liberal small states, like Hawaii and Rhode Island, and conservative small states, like Wyoming and Alaska. As a result, the number of states supporting a policy measure is not necessarily a bad proxy for the number of individuals supporting it. We recognize that there are some important exceptions where support for certain measures is indeed substantially correlated with population size: For instance, states with small populations disproportionately represent farmers.[44] Nevertheless, in deciding whether judicial correction is advisable, it is important to recognize that the extent of the problem is not as pervasive as might be initially thought. One statistic in particular suggests that our politics would not differ dramatically if representation were proportionate to population: The ideological median member of the Senate has closely tracked the ideological median member of the House for the last seventy years.[45]

The problem of state representation is unlikely to be corrected in the foreseeable future. As we already discussed in this chapter, the Constitution prohibits passing an amendment that deprives any state of its equal representation in the Senate without its consent.[46] Nor is judicial correction of the state representation problem justified. While the costs of the state representation defect are circumscribed, the costs of addressing it through judicial correction are enormous. To be sure, it is possible to isolate the provisions responsible for providing representation to states rather than people. The most important provisions are the structure of the Senate and the state ratification of constitutional amendments. But departing from the basic political structures that the Constitution establishes in clear terms would cast doubt on the legitimacy of the Supreme Court's actions and on the entire document.

Indeed, although many scholars have defended departures from originalism in matters that are not the result of evident constitutional enactment defects and that involve unclear terms, such as equal protection, few have argued for judicial correction of state representation at the federal level to fit a constitutional vision of one person, one vote. This anomaly underscores the weak case for judicial correction.

We conclude, then, that judicial correction is not a desirable cure for any of the defects flowing from the imperfections of the original supermajoritarian process of the US Constitution. Judicial correction has costs and these costs are not worth paying at the current time because there has been supermajoritarian correction of the worst defects wrought by the exclusion of African Americans and women. Other defects in the supermajoritarian enactment process that derive from the representation of states rather than individuals are relatively small and are significantly smaller than the costs of judicial correction, especially the costs to judicial legitimacy. Thus, the most desirable solution is to follow the imperfect, but good US Constitution.

7

ORIGINAL METHODS ORIGINALISM

In Chapter 5, we argued that our normative justification for originalism calls for interpreting the Constitution using the interpretive methods that the enactors would have deemed applicable to it. Using the enactors' interpretive methods ensures that the provisions have the meaning that the enactors expected and thereby reflects the costs and benefits of the provisions that the enactors would have calculated. It is the balance of such expected costs and benefits that obtained the consensus support that is the mark of the Constitution's beneficence.

Although the original methods have a close connection to the normative justification for following the Constitution's original meaning, such methods are also crucial for engaging in the positive task of determining the actual meaning. In this chapter, we argue that the actual meaning of its Constitution requires an application of the original interpretive methods. In our view, many of the key questions that arise about constitutional interpretation—such as whether intent or text should be its focus, whether legislative history should be considered, and whether words should be understood statically or dynamically—are answered based on the content of the interpretive rules when the Constitution was enacted. We also say more about the actual content of those original methods. If our previous chapters have set forward a normative defense of originalism, this chapter fills in the positive content of originalism by showing how the enactors understood the interpretive rules that they would have applied to the Constitution to determine its meaning. Our normative and positive theories converge because they are linked by an insistence that both positive meaning and the normatively desirable interpretation of the Constitution are generated by the interpretive rules obtaining at the time the Constitution was enacted.

We begin by showing how a focus on the original methods helps resolve the debate among the two leading approaches to originalism: original intent and original public meaning. If properly understood, the premises of both these approaches lead to the view that the Constitution should be interpreted based on the enactors' original methods. To find the original intent of the Constitution's enactors, one must look to the interpretive rules that the enactors expected to be employed to understand their words. Similarly, to find the Constitution's original public meaning by determining what an informed speaker of the language would have understood that meaning to be, one must also look to the interpretive rules that were customarily applied to such a document. Therefore, under both original intent and original public meaning, the Constitution's meaning should be interpreted based on the applicable interpretive rules of the time. We then present additional evidence from the time of the Framing to show that enactors did indeed understand and interpret the Constitution through the prism of the interpretive rules of the time.

While the original methods approach requires that the Constitution be interpreted using the original interpretative rules, nothing guarantees that those rules were originalist in the sense that originalism is understood today. For instance, the rules at the time could conceivably have required that the Constitution be interpreted as a living document. Although we do not engage in a comprehensive review or defense of particular interpretive rules, we nonetheless provide strong evidence that the original interpretive rules were essentially originalist in that they tried to discover the meaning of a provision at the time of its enactment.

Interpretive Theories and Interpretive Rules

Positive and Normative Interpretive Theories

In this chapter, we consider the interpretive approach necessary to determine the positive meaning of the Constitution. It is important to distinguish between positive and normative theories of the constitutional interpretation. A positive theory seeks to understand the meaning of the Constitution without reference to whether that meaning is desirable.[1] Originalist interpretive theories argue that the actual meaning of the Constitution is fixed as of the time of its enactment.[2] The two leading positive originalist theories are original intent and original public meaning.

A normative theory of constitutional interpretation, in contrast, tells us the most desirable way to interpret the Constitution. Originalist normative theories maintain that following the original public meaning or intent of the Constitution is desirable. For example, Randy Barnett defends originalism on the ground that the Constitution's original meaning is consistent with substantive ideas of justice.[3] Keith Whittington argues that interpreting the Constitution based on original intent is justified as a means of enforcing popular sovereignty.[4] Nonoriginalist normative theories, such as the living constitution view, maintain that it is desirable to change or evolve the Constitution's original meaning over time.[5]

Our positive interpretive approach differs from the leading positive interpretive theories. Original methods originalism does not attempt to provide a comprehensive positive theory of interpretation. Rather, it insists on a single core idea: that determining the meaning of language requires reference to the interpretive rules and methods that were deemed applicable to the Constitution at the time it was enacted.

Our argument here does not attempt to defend originalism in general or to advocate a particular version of it as a positive approach. Instead, we assume in this section that original intent or original meaning—or some combination of them—is the correct interpretive theory. We argue that either of these approaches, when properly applied, requires using the original interpretive rules. In short, under a positive interpretative approach, original methods originalism is the foundation for both original intent and original meaning.

Our normative interpretive approach, however, is more comprehensive. We have argued in Chapters 3 and 4 that the Constitution's original meaning is likely to be beneficial because it was enacted through a strict supermajoritarian process. But, as we argued in Chapter 5, the Constitution will produce the beneficial effects resulting from this supermajoritarian process only if it is given its original meaning because the enactors would have supported or opposed it based on that meaning. This argument also suggests that the document should be interpreted using the original interpretive rules. If the enactors read the document employing those interpretive rules, then giving effect to the document they approved requires using those same rules.[6] Thus, while the arguments for our positive and normative approaches differ, they both maintain that the enactors would have interpreted the document based on the interpretive rules at the time.

Interpretive Rules—Nonlegal and Legal

Much of this chapter is devoted to our claim that the relevant interpretive rules that existed at the time of the Constitution's enactment are necessary to determining the actual meaning of the document. While our main arguments for this claim are presented in the next two parts of this chapter, a brief discussion of interpretive rules and their relationship to the meaning of the document is helpful at this point.

Originalists argue that the Constitution's meaning was fixed at the time of enactment. Originalists—both of the original intent and original meaning variety—argue that modern interpreters should be guided by the word meanings and rules of grammar that existed when the Constitution was enacted.[7] But word meanings and grammatical rules do not exhaust the historical material relevant to constitutional interpretation. There are also interpretive rules, defined as rules that provide guidance on how to interpret the language in a document. It is our position that originalism requires modern interpreters to follow the original interpretive rules used by the enactors of the Constitution as much as the original word meanings or grammar rules.

Consider an interpretive rule that was used at the time of the Framing and is still in use today: a reader should avoid interpretations that render words to be redundant or surplusage.[8] This interpretive rule is not a word meaning or grammatical rule. Instead, it derives from a regularity of language used in formal documents—that when people write carefully about a matter, they tend to eliminate redundancies. Given this regularity, it makes sense for readers of formal documents to prefer interpretations that do not render words redundant. Moreover, the existence of this interpretive rule provides future writers with additional reason to eliminate redundancies in their language.

Of course, this interpretive rule is not absolute. While it provides weight in favor of one interpretation, it can be overridden by other considerations. After all, writers do not single-mindedly pursue the goal of eliminating redundancies. As a result, the correct interpretation may sometimes involve more redundancies than other, inferior interpretations. Nonetheless, redundancies created by an interpretation increase the probability that the interpretation is incorrect.

The anti-redundancy interpretive rule has continued to exist since at least the time of the Framing. But imagine instead that the rule had changed over time: It was followed when the Constitution was enacted but has fallen out of use in the last century. Even if the rule had fallen out of favor, we argue that it would bind modern interpreters as much as original word meanings and grammatical rules.

There is a wide variety of interpretive rules, and the applicability of each turns on context, such as the subject matter of the writing and the type of document involved. Some interpretive rules apply generally. For instance, the anti-redundancy rule appears to apply to all formal documents. Even more generally, the interpretive rule that requires an ambiguous term to be construed in accordance with the subject matter of the communication applies to all forms of communication, including oral and informal language.[9] Other interpretive rules apply only to narrower areas. For example, different types of documents follow different patterns of usage so that an interpretive rule that applied to a scientific chapter might not apply to a recipe.

The discipline of law is filled with interpretive rules. Some of these interpretive rules apply inside and outside the law, such as *ejusdem generis*.[10] Other interpretive rules, however, are more specific to the law, like the rule of lenity.[11] And still other interpretive rules apply to specific documents or areas of law, such as interpretive rules for wills or treaties.[12]

It is important to distinguish between legal interpretive rules and the legal meanings of words or provisions. Some words have both an ordinary and a legal meaning. Thus, the term *ex post facto law* has an ordinary meaning that covers retroactive laws that are either civil or criminal, whereas its legal meaning covers only retroactive criminal laws.[13] Legal interpretive rules, like the rule against redundancies, in contrast, are the rules that govern how to interpret a legal document.

The legal interpretive rules, however, do not necessarily select the legal meaning of a word. Instead, they establish how the meaning should be ascertained. The interpretive rule that governs how to interpret a word in a legal document that has both an ordinary and legal meaning generally requires that the meaning be chosen based on context.[14] Thus, the legal interpretive rule often requires the selection of the ordinary meaning rather than the legal meaning.

While it is common to view legal interpretive rules as involving subtle or technical matters, such as canons of interpretation, these rules actually extend to some of the core issues of interpretation. Most fundamentally, they can inform the focus of an interpreter's inquiry. The rules can tell interpreters whether to look to public meaning or intent and whether to focus on original or dynamic meanings. Such rules can also inform interpreters about what evidence to consider when determining meaning, such as requiring or forbidding the use of legislative history.[15]

The Constitution is a formal, legal document, and therefore its interpreters must follow the original interpretive rules applicable to a document of this type. This argument is not simply definitional. It is also based on the view that the enactors would have regarded these interpretive rules as applying to the Constitution.

The Positive Theory of Interpretation

The two leading positive theories of originalist interpretation—original intent and original public meaning—both, when properly applied, lead to the original methods approach. Original intent requires applying the original interpretive rules because the enactors likely intended only the meaning that would be generated by the relevant contemporaneous rules, and applying those rules is the most accurate way of discerning a single intent. Original public meaning also leads to original methods because an informed and reasonable speaker of the language would have understood the Constitution to be subject to the interpretive rules applicable to such a document.

Original Intent

The theory of original intent is part of a more general and comprehensive theory about language and meaning. The theory holds that the intent of the author of words or language determines the meaning of those words. Applying this theory to the Constitution, Richard Kay argues that judges should apply the rules of the Constitution "in the sense in which those rules were understood by the people who enacted them."[16] Other prominent contemporary intentionalists include Larry Alexander, Raoul Berger, Sai Prakash, and Keith Whittington.[17]

Defenders of original intent contrast it with more text-oriented theories. Thus, Kay argues that purely textualist theories fail to account for how we think about or treat texts. He argues that readers do not understand texts independently of real or presumed human intentions. "Words are only meaningless marks on paper . . . until we posit an intelligence which selected and arranged them."[18] Rather, meaning is fundamentally connected with a human agent who intended to communicate something.

This insight has much to be said for it, especially when the author of the language is a single person. An important connection often exists between the intent of the speaker and the meaning of words. But whatever the advantages of original intent in the case of a single author, it is much more problematic in situations where multiple authors are involved, as is the case with legislative and constitutional enactments.

The presence of multiple authors creates a serious problem of defining and determining the intent of an utterance. This problem has at least three facets. First, and most important, it is not clear how to define the collective intent of the group of authors when the individual intents of each author might differ. It is quite possible that there is simply no joint intent, which would suggest, problematically, that the document had no meaning. While some have argued that an agreement by a mere majority of the body is sufficient to demonstrate a collective intent,[19] this claim is controversial because it is not clear why a majority's view about the statute decides its meaning. Although the majority's view certainly determines whether a statute is enacted, the majority's power in this regard does not indicate, without more evidence, that the majority determines its meaning.[20] In any event, even if a majority were adequate to determine meaning, this view still leaves the strong possibility that a legislative body might vote for a measure that did not have a single meaning because a single meaning was shared only by a plurality. Any such measure would presumably be void.

Second, apart from whether adequate agreement existed, an audience addressed by multiple authors faces serious problems determining what the intent behind the document might have been. The existence of multiple authors (and thus multiple intents) might lead to shifting interpretations based on the political beliefs of the interpreters. In particular, the people for whom the Constitution is written may be misled and subsequent interpreters may be confused by reliance on intent. Most legislators do not explain their votes, and those who do may be speaking strategically.

Finally, the problem of determining intent and meaning extends beyond interpreters to the legislators themselves. If legislators cannot easily determine the meaning of a provision upon which they are voting, then their vote is less likely to reflect a shared legislative intent.

Problems related to the intent of multiple authors or legislators can be addressed, however, through background interpretive rules. The possibility of multiple meanings can be significantly reduced or even eliminated if legislators understood that the words of a provision would be interpreted in accordance with applicable rules, such as accepted word meanings, proper grammar, and interpretive rules. In this situation, the legislators would intend to enact a law that had the meaning determined

by these rules. Not only would the background rules promote the enactment of laws with a single meaning, they would also facilitate the determination of that meaning. Thus, the benefits of interpretive rules come both
ex ante and ex post: These rules enable legislators to determine the
meaning of a measure before voting on it, and they allow courts to interpret it accurately after its enactment.

These background rules are not simply a hypothetical means of
addressing the problem of multiple intents. It is our view that the best way
to understand the enactment of the Constitution under the original intent
approach is to assume that the enactors understood that the Constitution
would have a meaning based on background rules. The Anglo-American
legal tradition has long interpreted laws based on word meaning, grammatical rules, and interpretive rules. Moreover, we are not aware of a single
instance where anyone has argued—or even raised the issue—that a formally passed law had no meaning because the requisite common intent
was missing. Yet one would expect this argument to be made if the original intent approach without background rules had been employed.

This understanding of original intent strongly suggests that the Constitution should be interpreted using the interpretive rules that were
deemed applicable at the time. These rules help solve the problem of multiple intents and therefore should be considered by interpreters. Hence,
the original intent approach requires the application of the original
methods approach.

Original Public Meaning

Theories of original public meaning, in contrast to original intent, interpret the Constitution according to how the words of the document would
have been understood by a competent and reasonable speaker of the language at the time of the document's enactment.[21] Original public meaning
is now the predominant originalist theory, with contemporary adherents
including Randy Barnett, Gary Lawson, Michael Paulsen, and Larry
Solum.[22]

The original public meaning approach should also employ the original
interpretive rules because this approach focuses on the understanding of a
competent and reasonable speaker at the time of the Constitution's enactment. Just as such a person recognizes that his understanding of the language depends on conventions for word meanings and grammatical rules,
he also recognizes that his understanding depends on widely applied

interpretive rules. And just as such a person recognizes that there are specialized word meanings, so he recognizes that specific documents may be subject to specific interpretive rules.

The reader of a legal document knows that documents are often subject to legal methods that may affect their meaning. While this is true of legal documents, it is not less true of other specialized documents. For example, the reader of a postoperative report would recognize that the interpretive conventions of the medical profession govern its meaning. Similarly, the reader of the US Constitution would recognize that its meaning depends on interpretive rules that were generally deemed applicable to written constitutions of this type.

Some advocates of original public meaning are open to the possibility of treating interpretive rules as part of original public meaning analysis, but others oppose it.[23] It is not clear, however, how a principled original public meaning analysis could exclude the applicable interpretive rules. The meaning of a document is not merely a function of the word definition and grammatical rules, but also of generally accepted rules for interpreting the document. Of course, interpreters may disagree about what the applicable rules were and how much evidence is needed to establish them. But if the authors and readers of a document know that certain interpretive rules are generally deemed applicable to a document, then it is hard to understand how one could believe these rules are not essential for determining the original public meaning.

Professor Randy Barnett denies, however, that the applicable interpretive rules are needed to determine meaning.[24] Although Barnett has offered a variety of explanations for the content of original public meaning,[25] we do not see how any of his analogies or arguments show why interpretive rules should be less relevant than other rules like grammar or word meanings. In his book *Restoring the Lost Constitution*, Barnett compares original public meaning theory to the objective theory of contractual interpretation, in which the objective meaning of the words rather than the subjective intent of the parties is relevant.[26] Barnett observes that "the Constitution is a written document and it is its writtenness that makes relevant contract law theory pertaining to those contracts that are also in writing."[27]

Barnett's analogy to the objective theory of contract, however, also leads to a focus on original methods as a necessary means to determining objective meaning. Contractual terms often are derived from legal methods, such as precedents or interpretive rules specific to contract law. It is true, of course, that many contractual terms should be interpreted according to their ordinary meaning, but it is a legal interpretive rule that determines whether a term should receive its ordinary or legal meaning.[28]

Barnett also argues against use of the original interpretive rules on the ground that the assumptions of the Constitution are not binding, only its original public meaning is.[29] But this argument begs the question of whether the public meaning can be divorced from the original interpretative rules. Although the public meaning cannot be divorced from grammar rules, Barnett never explains why the interpretative rules should be treated differently from grammatical rules. It is true that the content of legal interpretive rules is disputable, but so is the content of grammatical rules.[30]

The binding nature of the applicable interpretive rules can be seen more clearly by contrasting them with a nonbinding assumption that Barnett provides. He argues that even if it were widely assumed when the Constitution was enacted that the South's population would grow faster than the North's population and therefore would allow the South's political power to protect slavery, that assumption would not be binding.[31] We agree. Constitutional provisions usually do not make factual assumptions binding. The Constitution establishes rules regarding representation that cannot be read as in any way requiring that southern representation be increased over time. If one asked the enactors whether that assumption were legally binding, we have no doubt they would say no. By contrast, interpretive rules that were regarded as applying to the Constitution are binding. If one asked the enactors whether a legal interpretive rule that was widely accepted as applying to the Constitution—say, perhaps, *ejusdem generis* or the rule of lenity—we have no doubt that the enactors would have regarded it as binding.[32]

Professor Larry Solum admits the possibility that the original methods might determine the original meaning because a community could understand interpretive rules, including legal interpretive rules, as contributing to that meaning.[33] He appears to doubt, however, that in the context of the US Constitution, the relevant community regarded interpretive rules in this way. We believe that the correct application of Solum's theory should result in the application of original methods as part of the way of determining the Constitution's original meaning.

Solum himself acknowledges that one might argue in favor of using legal interpretive rules on the ground that it is the actual linguistic practice of the general public to always defer to meanings derived from legal interpretive rules.[34] Solum questions this argument, claiming that it is unlikely that the actual linguistic practice is to always defer to meanings so derived.[35] But we believe Solum is mistaken about linguistic practice. A competent speaker of the language would know that certain interpretive rules apply to all formal written documents. Moreover, a competent speaker would also believe that legal documents receive—at least for legal purposes—a legal interpretation that employs legal methods.[36] It is a common, if not universal, reaction for a layperson to read a legal document, whether a contract, a statute, or a constitution, and have the following reaction: "Well, it seems to mean X to me, but I am not a lawyer. To be sure of its meaning, I will need a lawyer to read it."

Significantly, the lawyer's interpretation of the document is understood to be better than, and to take priority over, the layperson's. In part, this is because legal interpretive rules govern how to construe the document, and these rules are only known by those with legal knowledge.[37] This example suggests that the linguistic practice of the community would give priority to legal interpretive rules and to the lawyer's understanding of legal documents, such as the Constitution.

Original Methods: Additional Evidence and Answers

While both original intent and original public meaning support the original methods approach as a positive theory of interpretation for the Constitution, additional evidence also supports original methods. This evidence derives from the Constitution's text and early historical understanding. We also address two complications for our view: the source of the legal interpretive rules and an objection based on the popular nature of the Constitution.

TEXT AND HISTORICAL UNDERSTANDING

The text of the Constitution suggests that it is properly interpreted in accordance with the applicable interpretive rules. In the Supremacy Clause, the Constitution defines itself as the "supreme Law of the Land."[38] The status of the Constitution as a legal document was not simply left to implication by the enactors but was set forth explicitly within the Constitution itself. This suggests that the enactors intended it to be interpreted according to the specific rules applied to contemporary legal documents of this kind.

The Ninth Amendment also provides strong evidence that the enactors believed the Constitution would be understood in light of interpretive rules.[39] While there is disagreement about what the amendment means, everyone agrees that it focuses primarily on forbidding an interpretive inference: inferring from the enumeration of rights that the people do not enjoy other rights.[40]

One understanding of the Ninth Amendment is that it was intended to foreclose an inference that Alexander Hamilton had mentioned in opposing a bill of rights.[41] Hamilton had noted that, if the right to freedom of the press had been listed, even though Congress did not have an enumerated power to regulate the press, that enumeration might lead an interpreter to conclude that Congress actually possessed that regulatory power. As Hamilton said, a bill of rights "would contain various exceptions to powers not granted; and, on this very account, would afford a colorable pretext to claim more than were granted. For why declare that things shall not be done which there is no power to do?"[42] Hamilton is here anticipating that interpreters might employ the interpretive antisurplusage rule to expand Congress's enumerated powers.

Other commentators view the Ninth Amendment as protecting against not merely the enlargement of enumerated powers but also the retraction of individual rights.[43] Again, this understanding of the Ninth Amendment assumes that it was designed to address an inference based on interpretive rules. The fear here is that interpreters would assume that a listing of rights meant that unlisted rights were not protected. This interference would have been based on the rule of *expressio unius est exclusio alterius*.[44] Thus, the two leading approaches to the Ninth Amendment assume that the Constitution was written with interpretive rules in mind. The purpose of the Ninth Amendment clearly shows that the Constitution's original meaning cannot be understood without reference to interpretive rules.

Other parts of the Constitution also depend on the existence of interpretive rules. For instance, the Second Amendment provides: "A well regulated Militia, being necessary to the security of a free State, the right of the people to keep and bear Arms, shall not be infringed." The provision contains both a prefatory clause and an operative clause. The relation between a prefatory clause and an operative clause, like those in this amendment, could easily be a source of confusion to the interpreter. But the law has resources to dispel such confusion in the form of interpretive rules.

The recent case of *Heller v. District of Columbia*, perhaps the most important originalist opinion in several generations, turned on the question of just such a clarifying interpretive rule.[45] The majority found that the relevant canon of interpretation at the time posited that a prefatory clause could clarify an ambiguity, but it could not otherwise limit or expand the operative clause.[46] Relying on the canon, the majority then held that the operative clause—the right of the people to keep and bear arms—was unambiguous and therefore could not be limited by the militia preamble. Our point here is not to defend the Court's historical analysis of the content of this particular canon. For our purposes, what is important is that the decision is clearly premised on the view that an interpretive rule was binding on modern courts.[47]

Early historical understanding also supports the applicability of interpretive rules, including legal interpretive rules, to the Constitution. As discussed below, there is substantial evidence that legal interpretive rules were employed in the early years of the Constitution, but we focus here on one of the most important and contested issues—the nature of the new Union and the proper way to understand the federal government's powers. This issue would have prompted the opposing sides to deploy their most persuasive arguments.

In contesting the nature of the new Union, both advocates of states' rights and nationalists employed legal interpretive rules to reach their preferred conclusions. Eminent lawyers like St. George Tucker and Thomas Jefferson argued, for instance, that the Constitution was a compact of the sovereign states.[48] This characterization of the Union allowed them to employ the traditional common law interpretive rule that grants of powers by a sovereign should be narrowly construed. In contrast, the nationalists argued that the Constitution was simply the fundamental law of the nation. As John Marshall maintained, it involved a delegation of power by the national people to their representatives.[49] This fundamental law did not receive a strict construction, but instead was to be interpreted neither strictly nor broadly, but reasonably.[50] What is significant for our discussion is that neither side argued that legal interpretive rules were inappropriate in construing the Constitution. Rather, their disagreement focused only on the proper interpretive rule to apply.[51]

THE SOURCE OF THE
INTERPRETIVE RULES FOR THE CONSTITUTION

We have argued that the proper positive interpretive approach for the US Constitution requires reference to the interpretive rules, including the legal interpretive rules, that were applicable to that Constitution. But that raises an important question: Because the Constitution was a new document, what was the source of these interpretive rules? Statutes were to be interpreted based on statutory interpretive rules, but which rules applied to the Constitution in a world with limited constitutional experience? This complicated issue cannot be answered fully in the limited space available here. It is possible, however, to provide the outlines of an answer and to suggest how the details could be filled in.

Ultimately, the interpretive rules applicable to the US Constitution are those that people at the time would have regarded as applicable to a document like the Constitution.[52] Examining the particular interpretive rules that early interpreters of the Constitution actually applied provides some evidence of these rules. Other evidence turns on the interpretive rules in legal documents that the enactors thought were most like the federal Constitution. Here we discuss three sets of interpretive rules that are important for the Constitution: rules that applied to all legal documents, rules that applied to state constitutions, and rules that applied to statutes.

First, there is strong evidence that the constitutional enactors would have assumed that the interpretive rules that applied to all legal documents would also apply to the Constitution. These rules were applied generally to legal documents, and it is hard to believe that they would not have been applied to the Constitution as well, particularly to a document that describes itself as "Supreme law." Second, a strong case can also be made that the enactors would have assumed that many of the interpretive rules applied to state constitutions would be applied to the federal Constitution. As the use of the term *constitution* suggests, the enactors modeled the federal Constitution on the preexisting state constitutions.[53] While the federal Constitution differed in certain respects from the state constitutions, these differences are more political than legal. But one area where the differences are important involves the increasing legalization of constitutions between 1776 and 1787. Much more than the earlier state constitutions, the enactors modeled the federal Constitution on written legal enactments that were applied judicially, like statutes.[54]

The enactors assumed that the interpretive rules that were applied to statutes would also be models for the constitutional interpretive rules.[55] Like statutes, the Constitution was the product of deliberation by representatives of the people, and its provisions were written enactments designed to govern until amended or repealed.[56] Of course, the statutory interpretive rules differed from the federal constitutional interpretive rules in certain respects. Chief Justice Marshall articulated one famous distinction—that the Constitution was a concise document, not like a statutory code.[57] Certainly, statutory interpretive rules that had been employed when interpreting the state constitutions were prime prospects for application to the federal Constitution.

A LEGAL DOCUMENT ENACTED IN THE NAME OF THE PEOPLE

One possible argument against the positive version of original methods is that it neglects that the Constitution claims to speak in the name of "We the People," not "We the Lawyers." Thus, one might infer from this language that the Constitution's authors would have used only ordinary interpretive rules and ordinary meanings rather than the legal interpretive methods and legal meanings. This objection is mistaken. First, that the Constitution was written in the name of the people does not mean that only ordinary language and ordinary interpretive rules were employed. It is a common occurrence, both today and when the Constitution was written, for a client to have his or her lawyer draft documents that speak in the client's name.[58] That the document is drafted in the client's name does not transform the legal meanings of the document into ordinary meanings. In fact, the client often benefits from the precision and clarity of legal language that he cannot fully understand.

Second, the ratification process itself belies the view that the Constitution used ordinary language because the Constitution was written in the name of the people. As with other legal documents, the people decided whether to ratify the Constitution based on an explanation of its meaning by those with legal knowledge. Pamphleteers with legal knowledge wrote lengthy explications of the Constitution precisely so that the people could be informed.[59] It is not too much to say that they translated the condensed, sometimes technical language of the legal document into familiar language that was more easily accessible to the electorate as a whole. The people did not vote directly on the Constitution, just as they did not vote directly on the passage of statutes. They instead relied on their representatives, who were more likely to have legal knowledge or to be able to consult colleagues who did.

To be sure, we recognize that some people employ the Constitution as a statement of political principles or as a document of political aspiration.

We agree that one might interpret the Constitution as a political document without using legal interpretive rules. Our argument for the application of legal interpretive rules is confined to its positive, enforceable meaning, which is a direct corollary of a fundamental premise of judicial review. As Chief Justice Marshall in *Marbury* and Alexander Hamilton in the *Federalist* both recognized, judicial review is premised on the idea that the Constitution is law and must be applied in a specific case.[60] Thus, it would be inconsistent with the premises of judicial review to eschew the legal nature of the Constitution by enforcing a nonlegal interpretation of the document.

An expansion of this objection would argue that ordinary meaning, rather than a meaning derived from original methods, better preserves constitutional legitimacy because the Constitution draws its legitimacy from a popular and not a lawyerly consensus. While this claim is normative rather than positive, we address it here for convenience. First, it is easy to exaggerate the extent to which the meaning derived from original methods differs from the ordinary meaning of the Constitution. Legal interpretive rules often require that the ordinary meaning of the language be employed. They also use many of the same techniques as ordinary language rules for resolving ambiguity and vagueness.

Thus, the ordinary constitutional language usually gives the public a general sense of the constitutional meaning under the legal interpretive rules. Although those rules may be necessary to determine the details of a clause, the general meaning of the clause is often transparent to the public. Any reader understands that the enactors designed the language of the Eighth Amendment to prohibit some very bad punishments. This understanding is communicated to the public even if lawyers are needed to assess precisely its scope and limits in a particular case. Therefore, the meaning of the Constitution, as derived from original methods, is continuous with the ordinary meaning of the document.[61]

Second, even to the extent that the legal meaning of a provision differs from the ordinary meaning, this does not mean that the public will be misled. Citizens with legal knowledge can explain the legal meaning of the provisions to the public so that they can make an informed decision on whether to adopt the provision.

Rejecting original methods for fear of distancing constitutional law from the people is a romantic delusion. Like a mechanical clock constructed during the same period, the Constitution was a complex mechanism of government, and lawyers, like clockmakers, had a comparative advantage in understanding the details of how that constitutional mechanism worked. Ignoring the movements of that mechanism would distort its operation. It is better to use the expertise of lawyers to allow the constitutional clock to run on time, while allowing those with legal knowledge to explain its operation to the public at large.[62]

ORIGINAL METHODS AND EXPECTED APPLICATIONS

A focus on the original interpretive methods should also provide an answer to the recently debated question of whether the enactors' expectations about how a provision would be applied should influence its meaning.[63] Some originalists discount such expected applications on the ground that it is only the Constitution's words that are binding, whereas others argue that these applications provide important evidence of the original meaning or intent.

This question about expected applications can be discussed in the abstract. Yet we believe that the answer lies, as with almost all interpretive questions, in the enactors' interpretive rules. If the original interpretive rules forbade reliance on expected applications, then, of course, those rules would preclude us from doing so today. By contrast, if the interpretive rules indicated that such expected applications were strong evidence of the original meaning then that rule would be binding. In the latter case, the claim that the expected applications were not binding because they were not part of the text would be mistaken because the text would have been drafted with the understanding that the expected applications would be used to explicate it. Although more scholarship is needed on the matter, we are not aware of any evidence that the original interpretive rules forbade reliance on expected applications.

Even if the interpretive rules did not seem to credit expected applications as direct evidence of meaning, later interpreters might still be able to use them as indirect evidence of meaning. Expected applications of the meaning of a provision often provide evidence of what people at the time thought were the word meanings, the legal landscape, the interpretive rules, or the values of the society. Because knowledge of these matters is necessary to interpret the Constitution under the interpretive rules at the time, modern interpreters can mine expected applications for information about them (unless the original interpretive rules somehow barred all consideration of expected applications).

Toward the Content of the Original Interpretive Rules

In this part of the chapter, we briefly discuss the content of the original methods for interpreting the US Constitution. We do not have space to provide a comprehensive account of the original interpretive rules. Our purposes here are much more limited. First, we illustrate the type of inquiry needed to establish the original interpretive rules. The approach we employ here focuses on the interpretive rules used at the time of the Constitution's enactment. Second, we show that the original methods were broadly originalist in the modern sense of the term. Nothing guarantees that the interpretive rules that the enactors deemed applicable reflected either of the prevailing modern approaches to originalism. Some evidence suggests the original interpretive methods were intentionalist and some evidence suggests they were textualist. But we find no strong evidence that the rules were dynamic or otherwise nonoriginalist. Thus, while we do not argue here for a particular type of originalism, we do believe some form of originalism—whether intentionalist, textualist, or some combination—is the correct approach.

Discovering the Original Methods

The interpretive rules of the enactors can be derived in two possible ways. First, one can derive them from the constitutional text either directly or by implication.[64] For example, one might conclude that the Constitution incorporated the interpretive rules that were then deemed appropriate at the time for a constitution of the sort enacted at the federal level.[65] Second, if the constitutional text does not indicate the correct interpretive rules, one can look to the interpretive rules that the enactors would have deemed applicable to it. Discovering these rules requires an examination of the interpretive rules at time of the Constitution's enactment. Here, we focus on the second method, looking to the interpretive rules that would have been deemed applicable when the Constitution was enacted.

The content of the original methods is crucial for determining how to interpret the Constitution. The original methods determine whether interpreters should look to the text, intent, or some combination thereof. While other theorists have argued for a particular approach based on policy or philosophical considerations, we maintain that the correct approach turns on the methods that the enactors would have deemed appropriate to a Constitution.[66] Even if a particular interpretive theory could be shown to be the best philosophical account of meaning, this account would not show that that theory should be employed. If that philosophical approach were not followed by the enactors, then employing it to interpret the Constitution would produce a different positive meaning than the one the enactors expected. Relying on a different meaning could, in turn, undermine the normatively beneficial effects derived from the supemajoritarian process.

The original methods even determine whether the Constitution should be interpreted in the manner that originalism, as it is conventionally understood, requires. Although the original methods approach is an originalist interpretive theory—because it requires that one look to the *original* methods—it will only require that judges interpret the Constitution based on original meanings if that is what the original methods required. If, for some reason, the enactors had deemed dynamic constitutional interpretation applicable to the Constitution, then the original methods approach would require this type of interpretation. But we argue here that, whatever the precise content of the interpretive methods, they were originalist rather than dynamic or policy-oriented.

The Content of Original Methods
Originalism under Our Constitution

This section briefly discusses the original methods of the US Constitution. This is a vast subject and we cannot discuss it here comprehensively. Our main goal is to suggest that the original methods were within the family of what is today conventionally understood as originalism. Thus, we argue that the interpretive rules that would have been deemed applicable to the Constitution conformed to original public meaning originalism, original intent originalism, or something between the two. These principles do not encompass dynamic interpretation or living constitutionalism.

To determine what interpretive rules the enactors intended, we consider various pieces of evidence. First, we examine the interpretive rules used to interpret analogous written laws at the time. These written laws include not only state constitutions but also statutes because statutes were both familiar to the enactors and similar in character to the Constitution. Second, we consider not merely American but also English practices because the American practice often regarded the prior English practice as setting forth the proper rule. Finally, we also examine the practice that developed soon after the Constitution was enacted as further evidence of what the applicable interpretive rules were thought to be.

We suggest that all of these roads lead to Rome; in other words, the bulk of the evidence points to some form of originalism. In both the statutory and constitutional areas, there is some evidence that interpretation was primarily textualist and some evidence that it was intentionalist, although we believe that textualism was more strongly supported at the time of the Constitution's enactment.[67] But whether or not the evidence supporting textualism is stronger than that supporting intentionalism, the key point is that there is little or no evidence supporting dynamic interpretation or living constitutionalism.

STATUTORY INTERPRETATION

Both intentionalism and textualism in statutory interpretation have evidentiary support. The traditional view, laid down in Blackstone, was that interpreters should look to the intent of the framers of a statute. As Blackstone states, "[the] fairest and most rational method to interpret the will of the legislator, is by exploring his intentions at the time when the law was made, by signs the most natural and probable."[68] Blackstone here clearly indicates that it is the original intentions—the "intentions at the time when the law was made"—that are relevant.

In listing the methods of determining the legislature's intent, Blackstone gives pride of place to text, mentioning first that interpreters should look to the "usual and most known" meaning of the words of a statute. While Blackstone's intentionalism thus has a textualist component, he also authorizes interpreters, especially when the words are "dubious," to look to other considerations, such as context, subject matter, and effect.[69] Most important, Blackstone states that judges should look to the reason and spirit of the law—that is, "the cause which moved the legislator to enact" the law.[70] Under this last approach, judges can depart from the language of a statute if they believe it is necessary to further the legislature's intent.[71] Thus, Blackstone's approach is thus broadly consonant with original intent originalism, although it has a strong textualist component.

Scholars have shown that this intentionalist approach to statutory interpretation was widely followed in England and America in the years leading up to the Constitution.[72] For instance, in 1736, the treatise writer Mathew Bacon declared: "Such a Construction ought to be put upon a Statute as may best answer the Intention which the Makers of it had in View . . . Every Thing which is within the Intention of the Makers of a Statute is, although it be not within the Letter thereof, as much within the Statute as that which is within the Letter."[73]

The support for intentionalism continued on this side of the Atlantic and right up to the Framing of the Constitution. No less an authority than James Wilson declared: "The first and governing maxim in the interpretation of a statute is . . . to discover the meaning of those . . . who made it."[74] He was echoing the sentiments of a treatise well known to the colonists, Thomas Rutherforth's *Institutes of Natural Law*, which stated: "The end, which interpretation aims at, is to find out what was the intention of the writer; to clear up the meaning of his words."[75] Thus, Blackstone's view of the salience of intent was by no means isolated or confined to England.[76]

There is also evidence, however, of a more textualist approach to statutory interpretation, even in England. Some of the evidence suggesting an intentionalist approach is actually ambiguous because references to intent could mean not the intent of the author but the intent expressed in the text.[77] If the intent of the text is the touchstone of interpretation, such intent could not be used to modify the plain meaning of the text. Moreover, in the years leading up to the Constitution, it is significant that statutory interpretation came to place greater emphasis on the text of the statute. This occurred first in eighteenth-century England and then in the United States, culminating in the Marshall Court.[78]

This increasing emphasis on statutory text was due in part to the emergence of a stricter separation of legislative and judicial powers. As legislative power was separated from judicial power, the significant discretion that the traditional intentionalist theory appeared to provide to judges seemed inconsistent with a nonlegislative, constrained judicial role.[79] So, in England, following the Glorious Revolution and the increased separation of powers, departures from the text began to decline.[80] Similarly, in the United States, with the enactment of the Constitution and its separation of legislative from judicial power at the federal level, the federal courts significantly increased their reliance on text.[81] Because people reading the Constitution would see that it separates legislative from judicial power, they would recognize that the interpretive rules appropriately applied to the Constitution would be more likely to be those textualist rules associated with the separation of powers.

Although there is evidence both for intentionalism and for textualism, the interpretive rules may also combine these two different approaches. For example, Philip Hamburger has written: "Common lawyers ended up with a two-tier approach" to interpretation.[82] One tier reflected "an initial presumption that the intent could be discerned from the words."[83] The other tier reflected "a recognition that when the words remained unclear it was necessary to inquire more broadly about the act's intent."[84]

CONSTITUTIONAL INTERPRETATION

The evidence concerning constitutional interpretation is also primarily originalist, with substantial support for textualism but some support for intentionalism.[85] Alexander Hamilton, in his bank opinion, argued for interpreting the Constitution's words in their "obvious and popular sense." He rejected evidence from the Philadelphia drafting convention because the "intention of the framers . . . is to be sought for in the instrument itself, according to the usual and established rules of construction."[86] Similarly, Chief Justice Marshall wrote of the Constitution (and statutes): "[A]lthough the spirit of an instrument, especially of a constitution, is to be respected not less than its letter, yet the spirit is to be collected chiefly from its words. It would be dangerous in the extreme, to infer from extrinsic circumstances, that a case for which the words of an instrument expressly provide, shall be exempted from its operation."[87] Indeed, the constitutional opinions of the Marshall Court largely articulated an original meaning approach.[88] While Jefferson Powell's famous work attacked original intent originalism on historical grounds, his evidence largely comports with original public meaning originalism.[89]

But there is also some evidence of intentionalist interpretation of the Constitution—evidence for considering the intent of the ratifiers and drafters. The strongest evidence is for considering the intent of the ratifiers, who were said to actually enact the Constitution into law.[90] Robert Clinton has gathered evidence that members of Congress and others in the early Republic, including James Madison, used material from state ratifying conventions to support constitutional interpretations.[91] But there is evidence too for considering drafter intent. Again, Robert Clinton reports many examples of high officials using either their own recollections of the Philadelphia Convention or the actual journals of the convention to support their positions on a question of constitutional interpretation.[92] For instance, several references were made in debates about the power of the national government to assume state debts and incorporate a bank.[93]

Perhaps the most important example was President Washington's use of the journals of the Philadelphia Convention in the debate over the Jay Treaty to show that a treaty had force of law without action by the House.[94]

This brief discussion suggests substantial evidence both from the statutory and constitutional context that the enactors in 1789 deemed originalist interpretive methods applicable to the Constitution. While the evidence is conflicting as to whether original intent or original meaning provides the proper interpretive method, our key point here is that there is little or no evidence to support a living constitution interpretation. Consequently, it is safe to conclude that the original methods approach to constitutional interpretation argues for some form of originalism.[95]

We recognize that we have provided evidence only about the originalist nature of the interpretive rules applicable to the Constitution of 1789. If enactors of subsequent amendments deemed other rules applicable to those amendments, those interpretive rules would apply. But as Howard Gilman has shown, originalism was the standard mode of constitutional interpretation until the Progressive Era.[96] More historical work needs to be done on this question, but we have not yet seen substantial evidence that contradicts Professor Gilman's thesis.[97]

8

ORIGINAL METHODS
VERSUS CONSTITUTIONAL CONSTRUCTION

Our original methods approach stands in sharp contrast to the theories of constitutional construction. Such theories are a central part of what is sometimes called the new originalism, but which we believe is more accurately called constructionist originalism.[1] The constructionist originalist theorists believe that original meaning controls the interpretation of provisions that are not ambiguous or vague, but that constitutional construction allows judges and other political actors to resolve ambiguities and vague terms based on extraconstitutional principles.

For instance, Randy Barnett, a leading constructionist, argues that a clear provision, such as the requirement that the president be thirty-five years of age, needs no construction, but provisions, like the Equal Protection and Due Process Clauses, do "because some choice must be made between possible ways of putting them into effect."[2] Barnett then suggests that such construction requires the judge or other official to appeal to extraconstitutional principles—that is, principles that are not in the Constitution.[3] As Barnett's examples show, construction can operate on some of the most important and disputed provisions of the Constitution.

As Larry Solum has suggested, these extraconstitutional principles can encompass a wide variety of considerations.[4] Construction can be effected, for instance, through principles of substantive justice, deference to the political branches, or the methods of the common law, including precedent. The common premise of these methods of construction is that additional principles beyond interpretation are necessary to resolve ambiguity and vagueness in the Constitution. Only then, the constructionists claim, can the Constitution as ratified be transformed into a constitution for governance.[5]

In this chapter, we offer a critique of the distinction between interpretation and construction offered by the new originalists—both on positive and normative grounds—and show that original methods originalism is superior to constructionist originalism. As a positive critique, we first show that the original meaning need not run out when constitutional language is ambiguous or vague, as constructionists often assert. Even when the meaning of terms is ambiguous or vague, interpretive rules can provide a resolution to that ambiguity or vagueness. Because the language would have been enacted in the shadow of those interpretive rules, the meaning selected based on those rules would be properly regarded as the original meaning.

Further, we find no support for construction, as opposed to interpretation, at the time of the Framing. Indeed, the constructionists have not supplied evidence that the constitutional enactors contemplated construction. Rather, the evidence suggests that ambiguity and vagueness were resolved by considering interpretive rules that resulted in a single interpretive meaning. Whether or not construction has a philosophical justification, the Framers' generation does not appear to have known about it.

Original methods originalism is also normatively superior to constructionist originalism. Constitutional construction discards valuable information from the beneficial supermajoritarian enactment process about how ambiguity and vagueness should be resolved. The enactors would have expected such matters to be interpreted based on the original interpretive rules, but constitutional constructionists substitute extraconstitutional principles for their resolution. Moreover, a dichotomy between interpretation and construction that allows extraconstitutional norms undermines the stability of original meaning because, under this view, the Constitution would not govern many constitutional issues. Constitutional construction also exacerbates agency costs because it allows interpreters to employ discretion rather than requiring them to follow the guidance furnished by the original constitution-making process.

Constitutional Construction—Its Problems as a Positive Theory

The original methods approach doubts that the distinction between interpretation and construction is a proper part of the account of how the Constitution's meaning should be determined. As we have noted, constructionists—theorists who adhere to the distinction between interpretation and construction—believe that interpretation governs situations when the original meaning of a constitutional provision is clear, whereas construction governs situations when the original meaning is ambiguous or vague.[6]

We have two objections to construction as a positive matter. First, we believe there is a more plausible alternative to construction when constitutional language appears ambiguous or vague. The alternative is to choose the most probable interpretation of the available alternatives and measure the probability of an interpretation with reference to the interpretive rules the enactors deemed applicable to the Constitution—norms internal rather than external to the enterprise of originalism. Second, advocates of construction have not provided evidence that anyone embraced construction at the time of the Constitution's enactment, and we have been able to find none. On the contrary, the evidence that we have found suggests that interpreters believed that ambiguity and vagueness could be resolved through the applicable interpretive rules and thus through originalist methods.[7]

The Interpretive Rules Addressing Ambiguity and Vagueness

Constructionists argue that the Constitution's original meaning sometimes runs out. While they believe that the Constitution's language sometimes has a clear meaning, they also believe that the language is often ambiguous or vague so that there is no way to determine the meaning of this language. As a result, they argue there is no alternative but to decide these questions based on extraconstitutional norms.

We argue here that the constructionist claim that ambiguity and vagueness necessarily cause the original meaning to run out is untrue. There can be background interpretive rules that provide sufficient resources for resolving ambiguity and vagueness. If the Constitution were written with the assumption that these interpretive rules would be applied, then the resolutions of ambiguity and vagueness that these rules effect would be properly deemed part of the original meaning. Moreover, the evidence that we have uncovered suggests that the original interpretive rules are of the type that can resolve ambiguity and vagueness and therefore avoid the need for construction.

To understand how the original interpretive rules could resolve ambiguity and vagueness, we must examine the definitions of the words *ambiguity* and *vagueness*. The theory of construction itself is ambiguous about what constitutes ambiguity and vagueness. One possible meaning of ambiguity is limited to the case where two proposed meanings are absolutely in equipoise. Another could encompass situations where there are two (or more) reasonable interpretations, but there is stronger evidence for one over the other.

If the definition of ambiguity is limited to the situation of equipoise, then ambiguities should not occur very often—because exact equipoise seems very unlikely—and therefore would not be very important. By contrast, if ambiguity encompasses the second kind of situation, there is a strong argument that there is no real ambiguity. Instead, one might conclude that the language should be understood according to the more probable meaning.

A similar problem exists with respect to defining vagueness. Vagueness might be limited to situations when it is equally likely whether a term extends to a proposed application. By contrast, vagueness might be defined as encompassing situations in which there are plausible arguments that a term both extends and does not extend to an application, even though the evidence for one of the positions is stronger. As with ambiguity, the definition of vagueness that encompasses any plausible vagueness seems weak because plausible vagueness need not be regarded as real vagueness. This analysis still leaves the equally likely definition of vagueness as a possibility, but this situation of equipoise, again, seems unlikely to occur often and therefore is relatively unimportant.

The analysis of ambiguity and vagueness is important for two reasons. First, constructionists need to specify which of these views they hold and then present an argument for their position. Unless they adopt the wider definitions, construction will have very little practical applicability.

Second, and more important for our purposes here, the narrow view points the way toward an alternative method for resolving ambiguity and vagueness. Under this method, an interpreter would be required to select the interpretation of ambiguous and vague terms that had the stronger evidence in its favor. When the interpretation of language was unclear, the interpreter would consider the relevant originalist evidence—evidence based on text, structure, history, and intent—and select the interpretation that was supported more strongly by that evidence. Thus, in contrast to the scope given to ambiguity and vagueness within the theory of construction, this interpretive approach would avoid ambiguity and vagueness unless the evidence in favor of two meanings was exactly equal.

This approach would represent the original meaning, if there were an interpretive rule that adopted it, that was deemed applicable to the Constitution when the document was enacted. Under this interpretive rule, there is no legal ambiguity or vagueness, regardless of whether there is ambiguity or vagueness in ordinary language or according to a philosophical theory,[8] unless the two best interpretations are equally supported.

Moreover, even if the evidence for the two interpretations were exactly equal, ambiguity and vagueness that require judicial construction could still be avoided with an interpretive rule that resolved the question when there was a tie. One such rule is to provide that, in cases of a tie, the interpretation offered by the legislature should prevail. This rule might be justified on the ground that the legislature is entitled to deference as to its interpretation of the Constitution.[9]

An interpretive rule that gives a stronger preference to the legislature would also avoid ambiguity or vagueness.[10] Even if this stronger interpretive rule allowed the legislature's interpretation to prevail in some cases when that interpretation was a bit worse than the other interpretation (as opposed to the two interpretations being tied), that would still eliminate ambiguity and vagueness under the narrow and more appropriate definitions of ambiguity and vagueness.[11]

So far, we have argued that there are interpretive rules that could resolve ambiguity and vagueness and therefore prevent the original meaning of the Constitution from running out. We also believe, however, that the original interpretive rules—the rules that were actually deemed applicable to the Constitution—include interpretive rules of this sort. Although we have not engaged in a comprehensive study, our understanding of the original interpretive rules suggests that they employed a combination of the two rules already discussed in this chapter to resolve ambiguity and vagueness.

To begin, the original interpretive rules appear to have resolved close questions by selecting the interpretation that was supported by the stronger evidence. Part of the support for this conclusion derives from our discussion in the next section showing that no one has yet uncovered evidence that the Framers' generation applied construction. But part of the support also comes from the fact that, in close cases, judges appear to resolve constitutional questions simply by determining which interpretation is supported by stronger evidence.[12] They do not generally apply sources of law extrinsic to the Constitution or a policy calculus to come to their constitutional decisions.[13]

There is also evidence that courts sometimes deferred to the legislature's interpretation of the Constitution. One interpretation of these historical examples of deference is that they simply applied when the other evidence was in equipoise. But another possible interpretation is that they applied a stronger version of the rule that sometimes allowed the legislature's interpretation to prevail even when the weight of the other evidence was against it.[14]

The absence of construction is also supported by other considerations. Rational enactors would likely have embraced some method to resolve ambiguity and vagueness.[15] Without such a method, ambiguity and vagueness would leave enormous discretion to subsequent interpreters, even when one interpretation resolving such ambiguity or vagueness was the better one. Such discretion is particularly problematic because it would allow subsequent interpreters to choose constructions that would override legislation without surmounting the substantial hurdles of the Article V amendment process.[16]

The Constitution contains no provision delegating the power to fill in possible gaps. Given the substantial power that construction would confer on judges, this dog that did not bark is a significant omission. Judges had at the time a duty to decide cases according to law—a power from which judicial review's preference for the Constitution over ordinary law can be inferred. But the discretion to make decisions based on extraconstitutional considerations is another matter that cannot be so easily inferred.

The Lack of Evidence for Construction

Given the anomalous nature of construction from the perspective of both Article V and the judicial function, advocates of construction must provide strong evidence from the Constitution itself or from the original methods to show that construction was indeed part of positive law. If construction existed at the time of the Framing, one would expect that such evidence would exist because the Constitution (as well as statutes and state constitutions) was both ambiguous and vague on important issues. But in the absence of such evidence, constructionism remains an ahistorical originalism—one that does not reflect the original methods of the enactors and thus cannot capture their positive meaning.

William Blackstone, the leading legal theorist before the Constitution's enactment, did not recognize any power of construction or a process resembling it. On the contrary, he believed that interpretive rules were necessary to resolve ambiguity and vagueness. In his discussion of interpretation, Blackstone listed a variety of rules for interpreting laws when the words were unclear, including reference to context, subject matter, effect, and the reason and spirit of the law.[17] This discussion strongly suggests that construction was not part of traditional interpretation. Not only does Blackstone fail to mention construction, but his discussion of the variety of interpretive rules gives the impression that they are all that is needed to resolve interpretive questions. This resolution could be achieved, however, only if the interpreter is required to select the interpretation that has the greater degree of support.

Justice Joseph Story presents the most comprehensive discussion of legal interpretive rules in the early Republic. If there had been any serious discussion of construction or a similar process during this era, he would surely have recorded it. But like Blackstone, Story does not recognize the existence of any such process.[18] This absence is all the more striking because, as the advocates of construction themselves argue, the Constitution certainly contains unclear language that was in dispute in the early Republic.[19] Yet we know of no instances where protagonists in those early disputes suggested that the ambiguous or vague language could not be resolved using ordinary interpretive rules.[20] It seems scarcely conceivable that a recognized dichotomy as fundamental as the difference between interpretation and construction would not have been at least mentioned and most probably substantially discussed.

Certainly, the evidence offered by the advocates of constitutional construction does not begin to show that such a concept existed at the time of the Framing. Professor Solum quotes a passage from *Gibbons v. Ogden* where Chief Justice John Marshall argues against "strict construction" of the Constitution.[21] But there is no evidence that Marshall used the term *construction* to mean a method of deciding cases other than by reference to original meaning, as informed by interpretive rules. In fact, there is no indication that Marshall explicitly or implicitly contrasted construction with constitutional interpretation. On the contrary, in *Gibbons*, Marshall rejected one interpretive rule (strict construction) proffered as a means of discerning the Constitution's original meaning in favor of another interpretive rule (reasonable construction) that he saw as more in keeping with the nature of the Constitution.[22] Far from supporting a theory of construction, this passage is consistent with Marshall's search for the Constitution's original meaning and the correct interpretive rules to aid him in this search.

Professor Barnett relies on a passage from a speech by James Madison in which Madison argued that the Constitution's enumerated powers for the federal government do not include the power to establish a national bank.[23] At one point, Madison stated: "In admitting or rejecting a constructive authority, not only the degree of its incidentality to an express authority is to be regarded, but the degree of its importance also; since this will depend on the probability or improbability of its being left to construction."[24] It is true that Madison, like Marshall, used the term *construction*. But there is no suggestion that Madison used it in the sense that Barnett uses it—as a term for a different and more discretionary process than legal interpretation.

Rather, Madison used the term *construction* to distinguish between express and implied authorities in the Constitution. The gravamen of Madison's speech on the unconstitutionality of the national bank is that the Constitution does not expressly authorize the establishment of a bank and that the power to establish one is too large to be left to implication. Authorities of limited scope can be granted by implication, but large powers must be expressly granted. Thus, according to Madison, one cannot construe this power's existence from the express authorities, such as the authority to tax or spend or to regulate commerce among the several states.[25] In short, only an incidental power of relatively small importance can be left to implication, or in his phrase, "construction." Madison was therefore discussing the difference between express and implied authority, not the difference between interpretation and construction.

Professor Barnett also relies on a statement by Thomas Jefferson as support for construction, offering this quote: "When an instrument admits of two constructions, the one safe, the other dangerous, the one precise, the other indefinite, I prefer that which is safe & precise. I had rather ask an enlargement of power from the nation; when it is found necessary, than to assume by a construction which would make our powers boundless."[26] Barnett seems to be making two claims here: that Jefferson's use of the term *construction* signals that he is engaged in a distinct enterprise from interpretation, and that enterprise focuses on extraconstitutional or normative values rather than original meaning or intent. We disagree with both claims.

To see that Jefferson is engaged in the task of interpreting the original intent of the Constitution, it is useful to consider the language both preceding and subsequent to the words Barnett quotes. Jefferson is discussing whether the constitutional language authorizing Congress to admit new states allows it to do so from new territory or only from the existing territory of the United States at the time of its formation. He writes, "But when

I consider that the limits of the US are precisely fixed by the treaty of 1783, that the Constitution expressly declares itself to be made for the US, I cannot help believing the *intention* was to permit Congress to admit into the Union new States" only if "formed out of" existing territory.[27] Clearly, this language indicates that Jefferson is seeking to determine the intent of the enactors of the Constitution. This is interpretation, not construction.

Jefferson's discussion of intention then follows with the language that Barnett quotes. Why would he use that language if he is concerned with intention? The sentences immediately following this language provide the answer. Jefferson is attempting to resolve an ambiguity in the Constitution's language. In resolving the ambiguity, Jefferson considers the purpose and character of the Constitution—that it is a constraint on government power. He writes: "I had rather ask an enlargement of power from the nation [through a constitutional amendment], where it is found necessary, than to assume it by a construction which would make our powers boundless. Our peculiar security is in possession of a written Constitution. Let us not make it a blank paper by construction."[28] The language from Jefferson that Barnett quotes is not concerned with normative values, but instead with the character of the Constitution and its ability to resolve ambiguity in a way that furthers the intention of the enactors.

This interpretation of Jefferson's argument is reinforced by his use of the term *construction* in his famous opinion on the Bank of the United States. There he argued that the phrase "to provide for the general welfare" was not a freestanding power but was part of the power to lay taxes.[29] Jefferson's reasoning for this conclusion was based on a rule of what he calls "construction": "It is an established rule of construction where a phrase will bear either of two meanings, to give it that which will allow some meaning to the other parts of the instrument, and not that which would render all the others useless."[30] This rule of construction is similar to the one Jefferson uses with regard to the power to admit states—in both cases, an ambiguity is resolved in favor of the narrow interpretation to preserve the structure or character of the Constitution. And in both cases, it is clear that Jefferson's task of "construction" is to determine the intent or meaning of the Constitution rather than to pursue extraconstitutional or normative values.

Keith Whittington also argues that construction is a permissible way to implement the Constitution. As his sole example of constitutional construction from the time of the early Republic, Whittington offers the contending views of what constituted high crimes and misdemeanors during the impeachment trial of Justice Samuel Chase.[31] Chase argued that only violations of positive law constituted "a high crime and misdemeanor."[32] The more radical Republicans maintained that the term included all political offenses, including egregiously wrong opinions of the Constitution.[33] The more moderate Republicans contended that "a high crime and misdemeanor" did not have to be a crime but could include violations of the duties of an office, such as the judicial office.[34]

We do not believe these debates reveal evidence of construction. First, Whittington does not show that any of the participants in these debates thought they were exercising discretion to fill in an ambiguous or vague term. On the contrary, all argued as if they were interpreting the Constitution as determinate law. It is true that they appealed to constitutional principles in addition to textual arguments,[35] but appeals to constitutional principles that are actually written into the Constitution (such as the separation of powers) or that are implied by constitutional provisions (such as the long-term character of the Constitution) are legitimate ways of determining the original meaning of ambiguous and vague terms. Even if one regarded this discussion as departing from legal interpretation, it would not be surprising if the methodology of some of the participants was not pristine or careful. The context was a bare-knuckle political fight in the Senate where all the participants were advocates, not careful deliberations by judges in court.[36]

Supermajority Rules and Constitutional Construction

A possible objection to our position is that construction is inevitable because the Constitution is filled with ambiguity and vagueness. Indeed, it is argued that this uncertainty is unsurprising because the Constitution was enacted through supermajority rules. Since such rules require the approval of a wide variety of people, they generally lead to language that papers over disagreements.[37] Thus, according to this argument, the nature of the constitution-making process leads directly to the need for construction.

One problem with this argument is that even if supermajority procedures led to indeterminate provisions, that development would not necessarily require construction if the original interpretive rules resolved ambiguity and vagueness in the manner we have discussed. But there is an additional problem with the argument: It has not been shown that supermajority rules are likely to lead to unclear provisions. Supermajority rules are unlikely to lead to constitutional delegations to the future. The main reason is that citizens are risk-averse when it comes to constitutional provisions[38] because a great deal is at stake in the choice of important entrenchments that cannot be easily repealed.[39] Thus, embedding provisions that might lead to bad results as perceived by the Framers' generation would have particularly large costs.[40] Even if a majority were willing to take the risky action of delegating to the future, it would be extremely difficult to secure the supermajority necessary to do so.

This risk aversion is likely to be expressed in the constitutional enactment process because opponents of the proposed constitutional provision can play on the fears of citizens in this regard. Our discussion of the Equal Rights Amendment (ERA) in Chapter 5 exemplifies this point. One of the reasons the ERA failed to be enacted was that the broad language, combined with nonoriginalism interpretive methods at the time,[41] caused people to question what the amendment would cover. People were concerned that the amendment would be construed to require unisex bathrooms and women in combat, results that many found repugnant.[42]

Given the risk of delegating to the future, what supermajority rules encourage are not broad delegations to the future, but determinate principles about which there is a broad consensus. Such widely supported, determinate principles are exactly the type of provisions that can pass through the consensus requirements of the supermajority process.[43] Of course, this process would fail to produce these widely supported, determinate provisions if no such provisions were available. But it would be surprising if, at any time, there were not various provisions about which a very substantial majority of people agreed. These they would enshrine into the Constitution through consensus.

The Bill of Rights provides an excellent example of how widely accepted provisions can be enacted. To be sure, the Antifederalists demanded these provisions. But James Madison and the Federalist Congress eliminated the provisions that they deemed improper.[44] As a result, the Bill of Rights did not focus on deeply contested matters. Rather, it incorporated rights that colonists had fought for and deemed the birthrights of British citizens.[45] One measure of the consensus was the reaction of the Federalists to the initial Antifederalist proposal to put these rights in the Constitution. They did not object by disputing their importance or by quibbling about their content. Instead, they argued that the rights were already implicitly protected against federal encroachment by the enumeration of powers and that including the Bill of Rights might undermine that protection.[46] Again, the evidence of the Constitution itself militates against the insistence that construction is necessary.

Original Legal Methods versus
Constitutional Constructivism: The Normative Perspective

Interpretive methods raise important normative issues because the manner of interpreting a constitution is such a central part of the process of giving it meaning. We argue here that the original methods approach is superior, from a normative perspective, to the constructionist originalist approach for two basic reasons. First, the original methods approach uses the interpretive rules that were deemed applicable to the Constitution by the constitutional enactors. Because the enactors expected these rules to be applied, the meaning they produce is accurately described as having gone through the beneficial supermajoritarian process for constitution making. Thus, the results that the original methods produce, including their resolution of ambiguity and vagueness, are likely to be more desirable than the results produced by other interpretive methods.

Second, because these interpretive rules were fixed at the time of the Constitution, applying them raises fewer issues than interpretive methods that are not predetermined. An interpreter following a predetermined rule does not choose a rule that produces a policy result that he desires. Instead, he applies the preexisting interpretive rules. As a result, the original methods approach reduces the agency costs of subsequent interpreters and helps to impose a consistent approach to constitutional interpretation.

Constructionist originalism operates differently. Although there are different versions of constructionist originalism, here we address constructionist originalism in the abstract and then discuss two versions of the theory. In the abstract, constructionist originalism requires that judges follow the original meaning, but does not impose any constitutional or legal requirements as to construction. Because there is no legally required or even accepted method for determining how to resolve questions of construction, judges are likely to determine how to engage in construction based on their own views. There are two problems with this aspect of construction that correspond to the two advantages of the original methods approach.

First, judicial discretion to resolve matters of construction is less likely to produce good results than the supermajoritarian constitution-making process.[47] As we saw in Chapter 5, the Supreme Court is less likely than the constitutional amendment process to generate norms that represent a national consensus. The Supreme Court has a small number of members who have limited knowledge and are not very representative of the country.[48] By contrast, the supermajoritarian amendment process involves large numbers of people who collectively possess enormous amounts of information and who are representative of the country as a whole.[49]

The second problem with constructionist originalism is that it is likely to reach inconsistent and ad hoc results. Because there is no accepted method for construction, some judges will choose one way to resolve constructions, whereas others will choose another. Moreover, some judges may not commit to one way of resolving constructions, but instead may use different methods in different cases. As a result, the construction process is likely to be less consistent and coherent than resolving ambiguity and vagueness by reference to the applicable interpretive rules. Because it is less consistent or principled, construction is likely to reduce the consensus support for courts. And because it is less coherent, construction will make for a less understandable and integrated Constitution.

We now turn from constructionist originalism in the abstract to two specific versions of the theory—those of Randy Barnett and Jack Balkin. While the former argues that constructions should be resolved with a particular theory of justice, the latter maintains that constructions should respond to the actions of successful social movements.

Barnett argues that the Constitution's original meaning should be followed, but that the original meaning does not fully resolve many questions. As a result, there will be many possible constructions of the Constitution that are not inconsistent with the original meaning.[50] Barnett believes that interpreters should select constructions of the Constitution based on a libertarian theory of constitutional legitimacy.[51] He also believes that this approach furthers the legitimacy of the Constitution.[52] And given his libertarian views, it is not surprising that he finds that this libertarian construction of the Constitution would be attractive. But it is not clear how the application of these extraconstitutional constructions can be justified to those who do not accept libertarianism.

One way to develop this point is to view constructionist originalism as a combination of law and political morality. Under constructionist originalism, a portion of constitutional decision making is decided by the original meaning and a portion is decided by construction or political morality.

Our question, then, is: Why is that mixed approach more attractive than one based entirely on the original meaning of the Constitution?

If someone were to propose that constitutional decision making be based entirely on political morality, originalists, including Barnett, would reject this approach. Originalists would argue that, under this approach, there would not be agreement on the content of constitutional law and the government would not be subject to locked-in or fixed constitutional constraints. But if basing constitutional decision making entirely on political morality is defective, then why is basing it partially on political morality not also defective for the same reasons? And why would it not be better to base constitutional decision making entirely on the original meaning that the original methods generate? In short, if originalism views a constitution that imposes fixed, legal constraints on the government as normatively attractive, then originalism should reject watering down that constraint through extralegal construction.

Jack Balkin also presents a prominent theory of constitutional construction, giving pride of place to social movements in making important constructions.[53] Social movements, however, can constitute less than a majority of the population and thus may be even worse than majorities at obtaining the information to resolve ambiguity and vagueness in a way that leads to consensus and good entrenchments. Moreover, only the products of social movements approved by the Supreme Court would ever become part of the Constitution, and judicial choice in this context poses the same problems that we have already identified. Balkin's process for resolving ambiguities and vagueness therefore has a particular elite bias. In fact, nonoriginalist interpretation throughout Supreme Court history has reflected the views of the elites of their day. When elites were sympathetic to economic rights, the Supreme Court ruled in their favor, as in *Lochner v. New York*,[54] and when they became sympathetic to the rights of sexual autonomy, the Court ruled in their favor, as in *Roe v. Wade*.[55]

Thus, original methods originalism offers a critique of the various versions of constructivist originalism. Our approach legitimates the Constitution through its supermajoritarian constitution-making process and thus take pains to retain the full benefits provided by that beneficial process, including its resolution of ambiguity and vagueness. In contrast, constructionist originalism uses other methods to resolve ambiguity and vagueness. Barnett offers a particular version of justice, and Balkin relies on social movements. Because they do not use the original supermajoritarian process to resolve ambiguity and vagueness, constructionist originalists leave much of the beneficial information from this process on the table. And because they lose that information, they leave it to subsequent interpreters to resolve ambiguity and vagueness based on information the interpreters themselves generate. As a result, constructionist originalists lose most of the advantages of originalism: the advantage of reaching presumptively good results endorsed by the beneficial constitution-making process and the advantage of reaching those results through a rule-like process that preserves the political and ideological neutrality of the judicial process.

Of course, we are not arguing that the constitution-making process never results in ambiguity or vagueness. Original methods originalism, however, offers its own distinctive resources to address indeterminacy in the actual instances it occurs. As we have noted, one way of resolving such issues is to recognize that the presence of good arguments on both sides of a question still allows an interpreter to conclude that one argument is stronger than another. Another corollary of original methods originalism is that interpretative conventions and rules at the time of the Framing provide additional information to resolve such ambiguities and vagueness. Original methods originalism thus addresses ambiguity and vagueness in a fundamentally different way than construction. Rather than restricting the scope in which originalism operates, it provides additional tools to improve the operation of constitutional interpretation.

Everyday language can be a slippery thing. One important contribution of law is to create mechanisms to pin down meaning. This enterprise helps generate more certainty and reduces the discretion of political officials, including judges, so that citizens can rely on norms around which to build their lives. Over time, the law has developed such distinctive methods to resolve ambiguity and vagueness. Constitutional provisions are generally not created ex nihilo, but rather against the background of a complex and reticulated legal tradition, which provides more information about their meaning than can be gleaned from a naïve reading of the text. Original methods originalism thus takes full advantage of the legal capital that has been built through the centuries and that enactors expected would be used to cash out the Constitution's meaning.

9

PRECEDENT, ORIGINALISM, AND THE CONSTITUTION

Originalism is often thought, by both its advocates and its critics, to be inconsistent with precedent. But if originalism cannot be reconciled with precedent, it becomes a theory of limited appeal and usefulness. Originalism would then require ignoring precedent even when doing so has enormous costs. It would also conflict with the practice of almost every justice and judge in the nation's history. As a result, originalism would be extremely unlikely to be followed.

In this chapter and the next, we challenge this common view of originalism. We argue that nothing in the Constitution forbids judges from following precedent. Rather, the Constitution allows for precedent in two ways. First, the Constitution, as a matter of judicial power, incorporates a minimal notion of precedent. While this minimal incorporation has important theoretical implications—because it indicates that a no-precedent position is unconstitutional—it is so minimal that it does not have significant practical consequences for current judicial disputes about precedent. Second, the Constitution treats precedent as a matter of federal common law that is revisable by congressional statute. Thus, the courts initially and Congress ultimately possess significant discretion over which precedent rules should be adopted. The Constitution thereby allows either extremely weak or extremely strong precedent.

Although the argument that precedent violates the Constitution's original meaning has largely been based on the constitutional text, the view of precedent offered here is entirely consistent with the constitutional text. The key ground, however, for preferring the compatibility of originalism and precedent is historical. Precedent was an important part of Anglo-American law for centuries before the enactment of the Constitution, and the Founding generation expected precedent to apply to, and continue after, the Constitution. Therefore, there is a strong presumption for interpreting the Constitution in a way that permits precedent.

Historical arguments have previously been made to justify precedent, but they have been used to prove a different point—to justify a relatively strong modern approach to precedent as deriving from the grant of judicial power. This argument is hard to make. By contrast, our argument is easier because it is more closely tied to the historical practice regarding precedent. We show that judges consistently accepted at least a weak view of precedent from the time of Coke until after the ratification of the Constitution. This evidence strongly suggests that the Constitution does not reject precedent and that it authorizes the use of precedent in the two ways we describe.

Having established that the Constitution's original meaning does not forbid precedent, in the next chapter, we address what is the normatively best approach to precedent under originalism. Employing a consequentialist perspective, we argue that an intermediate approach to precedent is best. A precedent doctrine should consist of rules that require precedent to be followed when doing so would produce net benefits and that require original meaning to be applied instead of precedent in other cases.

Our position is thus intermediate between scholars like Michael Paulsen[1] and Gary Lawson,[2] who believe that precedent is illegitimate, and scholars like Thomas Merrill[3] and Henry Monaghan,[4] who believe that precedent has a strong presumption in favor of being followed. In response to the first group of scholars, we argue that it is both constitutional and wise to follow rules that mandate the use of precedent when abandoning a prior decision would likely be more costly than beneficial. Against the second group of scholars, we argue that precedent is not as presumptively beneficial as the Constitution's original meaning because the judicial process is not as well suited to creating constitutional entrenchments as the supermajoritarian constitution-making process. It is therefore a mistake to generally privilege precedent over the original meaning and to employ a general presumption in its favor rather than following the more carefully circumscribed precedent rules we recommend.

Our argument on precedent is divided into two parts. In this chapter, we argue that the original meaning of the Constitution is compatible with precedent. We initially explore the history of precedent to show

155

that history strongly suggests that the Constitution does not forbid the use of precedent. We then offer a constitutional interpretation that, consistent with history, authorizes precedent. In the next chapter, we develop the normative argument in favor of an intermediate approach to precedent.

This chapter examines Gary Lawson's widely discussed theory, which argues that following precedent is inconsistent with the Constitution's original meaning, and shows that Lawson's argument largely depends on an account of the history of precedent. The chapter then turns to the history of precedent in England and the United States and shows that some form of precedent had been a consistent part of Anglo-American law from at least the time of Coke. This history strongly suggests that precedent is not unconstitutional. The chapter concludes by offering an interpretation of the constitutional text that is supported by our historical account.

The Supposed Conflict between Originalism and Precedent

Although many scholars believe that originalism is inconsistent with precedent, Gary Lawson's argument was one of the first in the modern era to this effect, and it remains the most arresting, powerful, and persuasive. In two articles published over a fifteen-year period, Lawson eloquently argues that the Constitution's original meaning prohibits precedent in constitutional cases.[5] Lawson's argument is both simple and elegant. He notes that the Supremacy Clause makes the Constitution, federal statutes, and federal treaties the supreme law of the land. It does not include prior judicial decisions. Thus, if a judge believes that a prior judicial opinion misconstrued the Constitution's original meaning, the judge is obligated to follow the Constitution, not the precedent. The use of precedent is therefore unconstitutional in constitutional cases.[6]

The simplicity of this argument should not lead us to ignore its radical implications. First, this interpretation does not merely allow judges to disregard precedent; rather, it actually *forbids* them from following precedent.[7] Thus, following mistaken precedent is unconstitutional, regardless of the consequences.[8] Second, this interpretation also appears to prohibit following precedent in statutory cases. If federal statutes are the supreme law of the land, then they should be applied rather than a mistaken precedent.[9]

Importantly, Lawson's interpretation conflicts with traditional Anglo-American practices. In particular, our historical review indicates that precedent was a consistent and valued part of Anglo-American law at least for nearly two centuries before the Constitution's enactment. The review also provides evidence that the Founders' generation expected precedent to apply to the Constitution. Given this history, a strong presumption exists against any constitutional interpretation that prohibits following such a valued and consistently employed practice. Ideally one would require an express provision prohibiting such a practice, or at least the absence of any plausible reading of the text that would permit it. As shown later in this chapter, neither of these conditions holds.

Lawson is aware, as he puts it, that "the doctrine of precedent was certainly familiar in the Founding era," but he does not believe this fact has significant force.[10] This is due in part to Lawson's belief in the strength of his own textual argument, but it is also due to the weakness of the claim that he seems mistakenly to believe is the sole alternative to his interpretation—that the judicial power establishes "a general obligation to prefer judicial decisions to the Constitution in at least some cases."[11] To support such a claim, one would have to find evidence for a relatively strong view of precedent under the judicial power. This claim would thus require both evidence of a relatively strong kind of precedent and evidence that such a view was so consistently adhered to that it became bound up with the concept of judicial power itself. Our historical review does not reveal evidence for any such claim. Thus, it is no surprise that Lawson concluded that precedent at the time of the Founding was "not so well established and developed to be a part of the 'judicial power' in the superstrong sense that would be necessary to give judicial decisions preference over the Constitution."[12]

But the view that the judicial power incorporates a relatively strong notion of precedent is not the sole alternative to Lawson's no-precedent interpretation. We argue that the Constitution treats precedent rules as a matter of common law that is revisable by congressional statute. We also argue that the Constitution incorporates a very weak notion of precedent as judicial power. As we show later in this chapter, precedent rules had been employed since at least the time of Coke. While the rules for precedent varied at different times and in different courts, judges at the very least consistently applied and valued a weak version of precedent during this period. This history strongly cuts against Lawson's view that the Constitution does not permit precedent, and it supports our interpretation of the Constitution.[13]

A Short History of Precedent

Our historical discussion begins with a focus on the English legal system. We then turn to the American experience, first in the colonies, then in the independent states and during the ratification debates, and finally in the Supreme Court under the new Constitution. In all of these periods, we find evidence for three general claims. First, precedent existed in all of these periods.[14] Although precedent was generally weaker (in the English and early American legal systems) than in modern times, the precedent rules varied over time and in different courts. For example, in some courts, significant weight was conferred on an individual decision, whereas other courts placed significant weight only on a series of decisions. Next, precedent rules conferred greater weight on a series of decisions than on any single decision. And finally, precedent rules placed more weight on decisions involving property and contract rights because they involved greater reliance interests.

Precedent in England

In England, support for precedent goes back many centuries, with one prominent statement by Bracton endorsing precedent in the thirteenth century.[15] For present purposes, it is necessary to go back only to the time of Coke, when there were many statements supporting precedent.[16] Coke himself wrote that "our book-cases are the best proofs what the law is."[17] His support for precedent is no surprise because the artificial reason of judges, which Coke emphasized, consisted largely of knowledge of precedent.[18] Coke's emphasis on precedent as an essential ingredient of the common law[19] was continued by the next English legal giant, Mathew Hale, who in 1713 announced:

> The Decisions of Courts of Justice, tho' by Vertue of the Law . . . do not make a Law properly so called, (for that only the King and Parliament can do); yet they have a great Weight and Authority in Expounding, Declaring, and Publishing what the Law of this Kingdom is, especially when such Decisions hold a Consonancy and Congruity with Resolutions and Decisions of former Times. . . . [20]

Hale's view was then developed further by William Blackstone in the 1760s. Blackstone, who was the most widely read English legal commentator in the United States at the time of the Constitution, noted:

[I]t is an established rule to abide by former precedents, where the same points come again in litigation; as well to keep the scale of justice even and steady, and not liable to waiver with every new judge's opinion; as also because the law in that case being solemnly declared and determined, what before was uncertain, and perhaps indifferent, is now become a permanent rule, which is not in the breast of any subsequent judge to alter or vary from, according to his private sentiments; he being sworn to determine, not according to his own private judgment, but according to the known laws and customs of the law; not delegated to pronounce a new law, but to maintain and expound the old one. Yet this rule admits of exception, where the former determination is most evidently contrary to reason; much more if it be contrary to divine law. But even in such cases the subsequent judges do not pretend to make a new law, but to vindicate the old one from misrepresentation. For if it be found that the former decision is manifestly absurd or unjust, it is declared, not that such a sentence was *bad law*, but that it was *not law*; that is, that it is not the established custom of the realm, as has been erroneously determined. . . . The doctrine of the law then is this: *that precedents and rules must be followed, unless flatly absurd or unjust*: for though there reason be not obvious at first view, yet we owe such a deference to former times as not to suppose they acted wholly without consideration.[21]

Several aspects of Blackstone's discussion deserve emphasis. His analysis provides further evidence that precedent had an important role to play in the English legal system. It also reveals that there were various reasons for following precedent, including that it promoted judicial consistency and constraint as well as clear and predictable law. Finally, while Blackstone makes clear that precedent is important, he also indicates that it is not an absolute rule because there is an exception for decisions that are "flatly absurd or unjust," or, as he alternatively puts it, "most evidently contrary to reason" or divine law.

This exception, however, is not one that can swallow the precedent rule by allowing judges to ignore precedents by finding them unreasonable. Many precedents do not implicate matters of reason at all. For example, there may be several ways to resolve a matter within the limits of reason.

While a prior decision might not employ the next judge's preferred analytical method, it still may not fairly be characterized as contrary to reason.[22] Moreover, even if the resolution does seem to be unreasonable, Blackstone states that it must be "flatly absurd or unjust" or "most evidently contrary to reason." Thus, earlier decisions are seen as being presumptively correct as a matter of reason "because we owe . . . a deference to former times as not to suppose they acted wholly without consideration."[23]

Although Blackstone, following Coke and Hale, obviously had an influential view, his stance does not mean that every judge followed precedent to the same degree. While some judges emphasized precedent less (or more), no evidence exists that judges rejected precedent entirely. Blackstone's contemporary, Lord Mansfield, is sometimes characterized as eschewing precedent, but that is not correct. Mansfield may have placed less value on precedent, but he still recognized its force.[24] As the noted legal historian C. K. Allen wrote: "Many dicta might be quoted to illustrate Mansfield's insistence, even against some of his own contemporaries, on the necessity of adhering to settled principles, provided that they were established by clear evidence . . . in the form of reliable precedents or well-known practice."[25]

Although the general precedential approach applied by English judges may seem relatively weak, they applied precedent more strongly in two situations. First, English judges gave much greater weight to a series of decisions than to a single decision.[26] Second, English law also placed greater weight on decisions involving property and contract rights. In these cases, reliance interests were deemed to be especially important.[27] Thus, while precedent existed in all areas to some extent, it was stronger in certain circumstances.[28]

This brief review of English law indicates that judges gave precedential weight to decisions from at least the time of Coke. Yet it is sometimes said that historians cannot agree on when precedent became established in England, with some dating it to the nineteenth century and others to an earlier period.[29] If that were true, one might then argue that precedent was not a clearly established part of English law when the Constitution was written at the end of the eighteenth century. This argument has been made by numerous opponents of precedent.[30]

But the argument rests on a point of confusion. While historians do differ about when precedent emerged, their disagreement relates to the question of the emergence of the *modern* English view of precedent, under which a single judicial decision established an absolute (or at least very strong) obligation for future courts to follow.[31] Our question is not whether a single judicial decision had absolute or significant weight, but whether prior judicial decisions could lead judges to decide cases differently than they otherwise would have. If a series of prior judicial decisions had significant precedential weight, then such cases would influence judicial decisions, even though the modern theory of precedent had not been adopted. While it may be unclear when the modern English view of precedent emerged, it *is* clear that a significant precedent practice existed since at least the early seventeenth century, and probably for centuries before that.

Precedent in Colonial America

The English approach to precedent was transplanted to America when the English established colonies there. Of course, the Anglo-American approach changed over time as the Americans developed from colonies to a confederation of republican states and finally to a nation under the Constitution. But the developing US legal system continued to use precedent in a manner that exhibited significant similarities to its English counterpart.

During the colonial period, the American colonies developed from informal outposts to the political communities that would successfully rebel against the British. As British subjects, the colonists were largely governed by the English system of law.[32] Their judiciaries were filled with persons selected by English governors and their councils, with the governor himself serving in the judiciary.[33] Colonial judicial decisions were sometimes subject to judicial review in England.[34] Thus, it is no surprise that English rules of precedent were applied in American courts.

As the colonies developed into mature political communities, they increasingly employed English common law.[35] By the eighteenth century, commentators suggest that a practice of giving respect to precedent was generally followed in America.[36] The legal historian Morton Horwitz believes that the colonists held a strong view of precedent: "[T]he overwhelming fact about American law through most of the eighteenth century is the extent to which lawyers believed that English authority settled virtually all questions for which there was no legislative rule."[37] Consequently, there was "a strict conception of precedent."[38] William Nelson has a similar view.[39] Even if one disagrees with these historians and believes that a weaker view of precedent prevailed in the colonies, that would still allow a significant role for precedent, similar to that in England at the time.

Statements supporting precedent came from the bar as well as the courts. John Adams wrote during the colonial period that "every possible Case [should be] settled in a Precedent, leav[ing] nothing to the arbitrary Will or uniformed Reason of Prince or Judge."[40] Similarly, judges emphasized that the courts were not free to depart from "the known rules of the common law."[41] In the Maryland case of *Somerville v. Johnson,* for example, the court followed precedent, stating that it otherwise would have reached the opposite result.[42]

There is also evidence that colonial courts followed the two additional aspects of the English precedent doctrine.[43] First, the courts recognized that a series of decisions was entitled to greater weight than a single decision. The Massachusetts Supreme Court stated that when a "Usage had been uninterrupted . . . the Construction of the Law [is] thereby established" and the court "therefore would make no Innovation."[44] Second, the courts acknowledged that precedents were entitled to greater weight in cases involving property because of the reliance interests involved.[45]

Precedent in the Independent States

After independence, the colonies became states. Although they were no longer formally subject to the English legal system, the states in the period before the Constitution and in the early years afterward largely continued to employ the Anglo-American legal system, including the precedent rules. The courts used precedent, with some courts applying stronger rules and other courts applying weaker ones. They also followed the two additional precedent rules: They gave greater weight both to a series of decisions than to a single precedent and to decisions concerning property.[46]

Statements by important judges and commentators from this period illustrate the use of precedent. James Wilson, a leading participant at the Philadelphia Convention and in the ratification debate, as well as a Supreme Court Justice and author of a legal treatise, wrote that:

> Judicial decisions are the principal and most authentic evidence, which can be given, of the existence of such a custom as is entitled to form a part of the common law. Those who gave such decisions, were selected for that employment, on account of their learning and experience in the common law. As to the parties, and those who represent the parties to them, their judgments continue themselves to be effective laws, while they are

unreversed. They should, in the cases of others, be considered
as strong evidence of the law. As such, every prudent and cau-
tious judge will appreciate them. He will remember, that his
duty and his business is, not to make the law, but to interpret
and apply it.[47]

Wilson here seems to follow the Blackstone approach, which treats precedent as entitled to strong, but not absolute, weight.

Thomas Jefferson also appears to have expected and approved of the use
of precedent. In 1776, the Virginia legislature set up a committee, chaired
by Jefferson, to codify the laws. Jefferson, supported by a committee
majority, tried not to change the language of certain "ancient statutes," in
part because "the meaning of every word [had been] so well settled by
decisions."[48] Jefferson and the majority did not try to reduce the entire
common law to statutes because "every word and phrase in [the new stat-
utes] would become a new subject of criticism and litigation, until its sense
should have been settled by numerous decisions."[49] Clearly, then, Jefferson
and the committee majority expected precedent to apply to statutory interpretation, and they appeared to believe it had desirable qualities in terms
of clarity and predictability.

Chancellor James Kent also approved of precedent. In his widely read
treatise, Kent noted:

> A solemn decision upon a point of law, arising in any given case,
> becomes an authority in a like case, because it is the highest
> evidence which we can have of the law applicable to the subject,
> and the judges are bound to follow that decision so long as it
> stands unreversed, unless it can be shown that the law was mis-
> understood or misapplied in that particular case. If a decision
> has been made upon solemn argument and mature delibera-
> tion, the presumption is in favor of its correctness; and the com-
> munity have a right to regard it as a just declaration or exposition
> of the law, and to regulate their actions and their contracts by it.
> It would therefore be extremely inconvenient to the public, if
> precedents were not duly regarded and pretty implicitly fol-
> lowed. . . . If judicial decisions were to be lightly disregarded,
> we should disturb and unsettle the great landmarks of prop-
> erty. . . . [W]hen a rule has been once deliberately adopted and
> declared, it ought not to be disturbed, unless by a court of appeal

> or review, and never by the same court, except for very cogent
> reasons; and if the practice were otherwise, it would be leaving
> us in a state of perplexing uncertainty as to the law.[50]

Thus, Chancellor Kent too seemed to follow the Blackstone approach[51] of treating precedent as strong evidence of the law.[52]

The evidence from this period is also important because it reveals that the dominant approach to precedent was not limited to the common law but was also applied to decisions construing written laws. Many decisions invoked what were regarded as the ordinary rules of precedent when construing written laws.[53] Moreover, judicial opinions did not state that different precedent rules should apply to written laws. This is important because it might otherwise be thought that the precedent rules were special to the common law. Under that view, judicial decisions might be accorded weight, not because that is how judicial decision making operates, but rather because the common law consists of precedents or judicial custom. That precedent was applied to written law strongly indicates that this latter view of precedent as part of the common law was not the full understanding of precedent. Even if precedent first originated on the understanding that judicial custom was part of the law, the precedent practice became so deeply entrenched that it came to be understood as an aspect of judicial decision making that also applied to written laws.

One factor that complicates the experience within US states after the Revolution is that of English precedents. While the Americans were operating within an English common law framework that was often deemed to extend beyond national boundaries, they had declared independence and therefore were no longer subject to English law. Consequently, some of the states adopted a two-level approach to precedent, giving English precedents less weight than state precedents. Because the states treated American precedents with greater respect, the treatment of English precedents does not indicate a change in precedent rules generally, but only a reduced authority for English law in an independent nation.[54]

Precedent during the Ratification Debates

This Anglo-American tradition of precedent was also recognized during the constitutional ratification debate. The question of precedent arose in several different criticisms of the proposed Constitution by Antifederalists. Yet defenders of the Constitution did not deny that precedent would be employed.

In fact, comments about precedent and the Constitution suggest that commentators believed that the Constitution did not prohibit precedent.

The Federal Farmer, an Antifederalist critic of the Constitution, both expected and approved of the development of precedent. The Federal Farmer was concerned about the lack of precedents to guide the federal courts concerning equity: "[W]e have no precedents in this country, *as yet*, to regulate the divisions in equity as in Great Britain; equity, therefore, in the supreme court *for many years* will be mere discretion."[55] While he was thus critical of the absence of precedent, he clearly believed that precedent would emerge over time.

Another Antifederalist critic of the Constitution who expected precedent to be employed was Brutus. Brutus wrote that the federal judiciary

> will be able to extend the limits of the general government gradually, and by insensible degrees, and to accommodate themselves to the temper of the people. Their decisions on the meaning of the constitution will commonly take place in cases which arise between individuals, with which the public will not be generally acquainted; one adjudication will form a precedent to the next, and this to a following one. These cases will immediately affect individuals only, so that a series of determinations will probably take place before even the people will be informed of them.[56]

This analysis shows that, while he was displeased about how it would operate, Brutus believed that precedent would be applied to constitutional adjudications.

In "Federalist No. 78," Alexander Hamilton responded in part to Brutus's criticisms of the judicial power under the proposed Constitution. Hamilton defended the judiciary, not by denying that precedent would apply, but by asserting it:

> It has been frequently remarked with great propriety that a voluminous code of laws is one of the inconveniences necessarily connected with the advantages of a free government. To avoid an arbitrary discretion in the courts, it is indispensable that they should be bound down by strict rules and precedents which serve to define and point out their duty in every particular case that comes before them.[57]

Thus, Hamilton defended precedent, and the context indicates that such precedent would apply as to written laws.

James Madison also expected and approved of precedent, writing in "Federalist No. 37" that "[a]ll new laws, though penned with the greatest technical skill and passed on the fullest and most mature deliberation, are considered as more or less obscure and equivocal, until their meaning be *liquidated* and ascertained by a series of particular discussions and adjudications."[58] During the ratification period, Madison noted in a letter that, "[a]mong other difficulties, the exposition of the Constitution is frequently a copious source, and must continue so until its meaning on all great points shall have been settled by precedents."[59] This evidence demonstrates that Madison believed precedent would apply to constitutional decisions. Moreover, he adopted the traditional view that a series of decisions was entitled to greater weight than a single decision.[60]

Precedent in the Supreme Court

The early Supreme Court also followed precedent.[61] While it is less clear whether it followed a weak or strong form of precedent, our major interest is not in establishing the kind of precedent it followed, but rather that its actions suggest that following precedent is legitimate. To that end, we first present evidence that it followed a relatively strong form of precedent, then offers evidence that it followed a weaker form, and finally reject any suggestion that the early Court opposed the use of precedent.

On the one hand, the early Court took many actions consistent with a strong adherence to precedent.[62] First, the Marshall Court overruled almost no decisions, and its few overrulings had special justification.[63] Second, the justices sometimes made clear that they felt confined by precedent: in *Ex parte Bollman*, Chief Justice Marshall relied on two prior decisions to conclude that an issue was no longer open, even though the issue had not been raised by counsel or addressed by the Court in those two decisions.[64] Third, the justices sometimes announced that they were following a precedent, even though they disagreed with it.[65]

On the other hand, in *Ex parte Bollman*,[66] Justice William Johnson contested Marshall's reliance on prior cases. While Johnson rejected a strong view of precedent,[67] he adopted a weaker view. Johnson noted that

> this court has been imperatively called upon to extend to the prisoners the benefit of precedent. I am far, very far, from

denying the general authority of adjudications. Uniformity in decisions is often as important as their abstract justice. But I deny that a court is precluded from the right or exempted from the necessity of examining into the correctness or consistency of its own decisions, or those of any other tribunal. . . . Strange indeed would be the doctrine, that an inadvertency once committed by a court shall ever after impose on it the necessity of persisting in its error.[68]

Johnson is merely denying that two individual cases that did not even address an issue constitute precedent sufficiently powerful to resolve the matter. Thus, he is not rejecting the concept of precedent generally, but arguing for circumscribing its principal force to a series of decisions.[69]

We also disagree that Marshall's failure on occasion to cite a prior case suggests that precedent had no place in his jurisprudence. Indeed, it seems that Marshall sometimes neglected precedent because of the poor digest system available to the Court. In *McCulloch v. Maryland*,[70] for example, Marshall did not cite *United States v. Fisher*,[71] which had also construed the Necessary and Proper Clause fourteen years earlier.[72] But none of the attorneys in the case mentioned it either, suggesting that the precedent was simply overlooked.[73] In *McCulloch*, Marshall himself suggested that legal precedent and practice from all three branches—legislative, executive, and judicial—were important determinants of his decision.[74] Thus, Marshall's occasional neglect of precedent should not be understood as a rejection of that concept.[75]

We know that precedent was supported by the leading Founders of the country, including James Madison, Alexander Hamilton, Thomas Jefferson, James Wilson, and John Adams, as well as by leading legal giants, including Coke, Hale, Blackstone, and Kent. This represents a veritable who's who of Founders and legal giants. Perhaps equally powerful is the absence of writers who explicitly or even implicitly rejected the use of precedent. We can conclude that precedent was a long-standing, important, and valued part of Anglo-American law. It is thus extremely unlikely that the enactors would have prohibited precedent in the Constitution,[76] and one should not conclude that they intended to do so absent either an explicit prohibition or no alternative way to read the text. Fortunately, there are two ways to find precedent recognized under the Constitution.

The Consistency of Originalism and Precedent

The powerful history of the use of precedent raises the question of whether the constitutional text can accommodate it. In fact, the Constitution allows for precedent in two distinct ways. First, it incorporates a minimal degree of precedent under the judicial power. Second, apart from this minimal degree of precedent, the Constitution treats precedent as a matter of common law that is revisable by congressional statute.

Judicial Power as a Basis for Precedent

Article III vests the judicial power of the United States in the federal courts.[77] The judicial power can be understood as requiring judges to deploy a minimal concept of precedent—a concept of precedent that was followed widely and consistently from at least the time of Coke until the enactment of the Constitution. This minimal concept requires that judges give some weight to a string of judicial decisions on an issue over a substantial period of time. Under this view, the Constitution allows the common law or Congress to establish stronger precedent rules, but establishes a floor below which precedent cannot be eliminated.

The term *judicial power* in Article III is, at least on its face, ambiguous. It might be understood narrowly to mean the power to say what the law is in a particular judicial proceeding. But it might also be understood more broadly to include certain traditional aspects of the judicial office that were widely and consistently exercised. Such core aspects of an office often come to be identified with the power that the officer exercises. One prominent example is the view of many originalists that executive power is not simply the narrow power to execute the law but also includes many of the traditional powers of executives, such as the foreign affairs power.[78]

There are strong reasons for concluding that the Framers' generation would have understood the judicial power to include a minimal concept of precedent, which requires that some weight be given to a series of decisions. The concept of precedent that we would attribute to "judicial power" is, to be sure, a very narrow one. Indeed, this concept is actually slightly weaker than the weakest one that was followed historically. While we have found evidence of judges placing *substantial* weight on a series of decisions, the minimal precedent concept requires only that *some* weight be given. The narrowness of this definition makes it more likely that the concept was universal and would be regarded as part of the core of judicial power. Consequently, it is likely that, when the Constitution was enacted, a judge refusing to give any weight to a series of cases all decided in the same way would have been deemed not merely to have been mistaken, but to have improperly exercised judicial authority.

This incorporation of minimal precedent under the judicial power would also have promoted the important values associated with precedent, such as predictability and judicial constraint. Even more significant is that the incorporation of minimal precedent helps ensure the beneficence of Congress's power to establish precedent rules. Congress's power is potentially sweeping, but the minimal degree of precedent contained in the Constitution restrains Congress by preventing it from eliminating precedent.

It is true, of course, that the fact that judges deployed a legal concept at the time of the Framing does not necessarily make it a requisite element of Article III's judicial power.[79] Judges employed many legal rules, but the federal courts are not required to deploy them now to exercise judicial power properly.[80] Widely followed precedent rules differed from particular common law rules, however, in that they were more centrally connected with judicial decision making. The minimal concept of precedent was followed not just in one area of the law, but in all of them, and it involved the method of judicial decision making rather than simply the application of certain legal rules.[81] Thus, giving weight to a series of precedents would have been seen as an aspect of judging, not simply as one of a multitude of rules judges happened to apply.[82]

The constitutionally required precedent rule just outlined is so narrow in scope that it is unlikely to have any practical import in a world where precedent is accepted as a value. Rather, its most important contribution is theoretical: The rule indicates that the Constitution's original meaning embraces at least some precedent. This rule shows that the no-precedent position is unconstitutional. The bulk of precedent rules, however, derive from another source: These rules are a matter of common law that is revisable by congressional statute.

Common Law as a Basis for Precedent

There are two basic arguments for treating precedent as a matter of common law. First, it is difficult to view precedent rules as other types of law, including constitutional law, statutory law, or state law. Second, precedent has the characteristics of common or general law. But before making these arguments, it is useful to briefly discuss the concept of federal common law, or more accurately, the general law. In recent years, scholarship has begun to recover the idea of general law that existed in the early years of the Republic.[83] This general law was unwritten, and it was not the product of a single sovereign, but instead originated in both private and judicial custom. Yet, where applicable, this law was deemed authoritative, and courts were therefore bound to apply it. Examples of general law include admiralty law, interstate law, and the law applied when the Supreme Court exercises original jurisdiction.[84]

Typically, general law would apply when it was not displaced by some superior law issued by the federal or state governments.[85] The general law would then bind the courts. An important feature of the general law is that it is not, as the federal common law is conceived today, the supreme law of the land under the Supremacy Clause.[86] Two important implications follow from the general law not being the supreme law of the land: The general law is inferior to written federal law, and the general law cannot, on its own force, displace state law.[87]

In examining the arguments for understanding precedent as part of the general law, we follow the groundbreaking work of John Harrison, who first articulated this understanding.[88] The first argument obtains by a process of elimination. The alternative ways for viewing precedent are not sustainable.[89] The main alternative source of precedent rules—the Constitution—cannot establish any more than a minimal portion of those rules. While the judicial power can be fairly read to require a minimal precedent rule that was widely and consistently followed and was connected to judicial decision making, other precedent rules do not satisfy these criteria. Rather, there has been a diversity of precedent rules, both horizontal and vertical, that has governed judicial decisions both before and after the Constitution was enacted.[90] It is hard to see how one could derive a single precedent approach from this diversity. One would have to select a particular precedent rule and then show how it was incorporated into the term *judicial power*, despite the existence of diverse precedent approaches. One would also have to explain why the Constitution's enactors would have sought a single precedent approach that did not change even as circumstances did. Nor can precedent be viewed as federal statutory law or state law. Congress has not passed any statutes that directly address precedent, especially at the Supreme Court level.[91] State laws also cannot be viewed as the appropriate source of precedent for the federal courts throughout the nation.[92]

The second argument for treating precedent as general law is that precedent has the characteristics of general law.[93] As our historical review has shown, precedent norms existed across different jurisdictions in the Anglo-American legal world. Thus, there was a general law to apply. Moreover, that law was unwritten, originated in judicial custom, and was deemed authoritative. Finally, while commentators are not as explicit about the nature of precedent as one might like, they did indicate that precedent was a common law doctrine.[94]

Furthermore, the history recounted in this chapter perfectly fits the view that precedent is a matter of common law. While this history strongly suggests that the Constitution does not prohibit precedent, the historical variability of precedent rules also indicates that the Constitution does not enact most of the rules. Treating precedent as a matter of common law allows for precedent to operate under the Constitution without requiring identification of a single, unchanging approach. Thus, given the absence of an alternative source of law and its conformity with the history, the argument for treating precedent as a matter of common law is compelling.

Although precedent rules have been treated as a matter of common law, a strong argument exists that Congress can revise these rules. Congressional power to establish or revise precedent rules for constitutional cases in federal courts is found in Congress's authority to pass laws that are necessary and proper for carrying into execution the judicial power. This power allows Congress to pass laws that permit the judiciary to perform its job more effectively. If a law can be viewed as enabling the judiciary to perform more effectively, then the Constitution gives Congress the discretion to decide whether to pass it.[95] Precedent rules involve questions such as how judges would best balance conflicting values of the judicial enterprise, like accuracy and predictability? Such rules are therefore easily classified as helping the courts perform their function more successfully. Thus, Congress is given the authority to decide which precedent rules courts should follow. Just as Congress can use this power to legislate rules of procedure for the federal courts, so too can it use this power to enact rules of precedent.[96]

One might object that permitting judges and legislatures to shape precedent rules delegates too much power to ordinary officials to change the Constitution, exacerbating agency costs in a manner the constitutional enactors would have avoided. But precedent does not allow subsequent actors to change the meaning of the Constitution.[97] Rather, it governs the internal operations of the judiciary by telling judges how to balance values such as accuracy and predictability when deciding whether to follow potentially erroneous decisions. Moreover, the Necessary and Proper Clause permits Congress to frame only genuine precedent rules, not subterfuges for reaching particular results—that is, to exercise legislative, not judicial, power. Consequently, these precedent rules must be relatively general in scope and application. Judges and legislatures cannot pick and choose certain rules to protect the authoritative value of cases they like, while applying different rules to overturn the cases of which they disapprove. Instead, they are permitted to make general decisions, such as to what extent society should value the benefits of original meaning compared to predictability and constraint. Furthermore, because judicial power incorporates a minimal concept of precedent, there are additional limits on Congress's power to use its authority to legislate precedent rules to decide particular cases.

We do not understand precedent ever to replace the Constitution's original meaning. Originalism remains the sole route to establishing its meaning. But precedent is authorized by the Constitution's original meaning. Indeed, there is nothing strange about the Constitution authorizing decisions that depart from its original meaning. For example, the Constitution clearly requires the executive to enforce court judgments in specific cases, even if it believes these judgments have misconstrued the Constitution. The Constitution establishes this rule presumably because it sometimes regards other values as taking priority over following the original meaning. Similarly, the Constitution should be understood as authorizing that precedent be followed, rather than the original meaning, because it sometimes confers greater weight on other values, such as predictability, clarity, and stability.

An ideal theory of precedent would balance these values against the benefits from preserving the Constitution's original meaning. Of course, this ideal theory need not be the one courts previously struck, either today or historically. We have used traditional precedent practice to show that precedent was an essential part of the law at the Framing, not to argue that the balance it struck was necessarily optimal.

Interpreting the Supremacy Clause to Allow Precedent

Having seen the two ways in which the Constitution allows precedent—as a minimal constitutional requirement of judicial decision making and as common law that it is revisable by statute—we can return to Lawson's theory of the unconstitutionality of precedent. Under Lawson's view, the Supremacy Clause indicates that the courts must treat the Constitution, not precedent, as supreme law. But we are now in a position to see that this view is not correct. The Supremacy Clause and a vibrant precedent doctrine can coexist under the Constitution.

In our view, the Supremacy Clause is ambiguous. On the one hand, it could have the broad meaning that Lawson ascribes to it, requiring that courts both apply the Constitution in preference to federal or state law and apply the Constitution's original meaning instead of nonoriginalist precedent. On the other hand, the Supremacy Clause could have a narrower meaning, requiring only that the courts apply the Constitution rather than federal or state law. This narrower meaning would not prevent the courts from following nonoriginalist precedent.

Under this narrower meaning, the Supremacy Clause would tell the courts to follow the Constitution's original meaning, but to do so in the way that courts traditionally apply the law—by applying the governing law in accordance with applicable precedent doctrine. In Anglo-American courts, for the 200 years prior to the Constitution, the judicial power was exercised in accordance with some form of precedent. Consequently, instructing a court to follow the Constitution's original meaning would plausibly be understood as instructing it to apply that original meaning, but to follow precedent when precedent rules require it. In fact, given this tradition of precedent, an instruction to the courts to ignore precedent would seem odd, and therefore Framing era interpreters might require a clear statement to that effect before concluding the Constitution had required it. But the Supremacy Clause does not contain such a clear statement, even though it does contain a clear statement (that would otherwise be redundant) regarding other matters.[98]

The existence of this narrower interpretation of the Supremacy Clause and the case for adopting it as the correct interpretation are supported by various considerations. First, in addition to the fact that precedent was a traditional and fundamental characteristic of the legal system, the practice of applying precedent to statutory interpretations is extremely instructive as to how supreme law was understood to be applied by courts. The history of precedent shows that judicial decisions interpreting statutes were given effect as precedents. Statutes, however, would have been regarded as supreme law. Therefore, under Lawson's understanding of supreme law, these precedents should not have been given effect. That precedent doctrine was applied to statutory interpretations supports our narrower interpretation of the Supremacy Clause: that the clause instructs the courts to follow supreme law in the manner that courts traditionally apply law—by taking into account applicable precedent rules.

Second, the narrower interpretation of the Supremacy Clause is supported by the fact that precedent can be found in other parts of the Constitution. We have argued that the judicial power incorporates a minimal notion of precedent and that the Constitution leaves room for a common law of precedent that is revisable by Congress. That precedent is sanctioned by other parts of the Constitution provides further support for reading the Supremacy Clause as allowing precedent.

Third, the narrower interpretation is also supported by significant differences between following supreme law and following precedent. The ordinary case of treating something as supreme law involves following one body of law rather than another, such as constitutional law rather than federal law, or federal law rather than state law. By contrast, nonoriginalist precedent does not involve a body of law in the ordinary sense. The Constitution does not authorize courts to issue nonoriginalist precedents. Instead, precedent is the way that the courts deal with mistaken decisions that have previously been made. Allowing precedent law does not involve making precedents supreme law, but instead is orthogonal to the normal situation of making something supreme law.

Finally, the narrower interpretation derives support from the fact that people at the time of the Framing expected that precedent would apply to the Constitution. By contrast, we are not aware of anyone who argued that precedent would be unconstitutional or that the Supremacy Clause would prevent the application of precedent.[99]

We believe that the Supremacy Clause is wholly consistent with the deployment of precedent in constitutional decision making. Moreover, we think that the phrase *judicial power* contemplates a requirement of minimal precedent. Beyond this minimum, the decision about what precedent to follow is a matter of common law revisable by statute. In the next chapter, we turn to the content of the optimal doctrine of constitutional precedent.

10

THE NORMATIVE THEORY OF PRECEDENT

Because precedent is not significantly constrained by the Constitution but instead is largely a matter of common law and statute, it is useful to discuss the optimal precedent approach in constitutional cases. In the first instance, the Supreme Court can apply such rules as a matter of common law. Should Congress become dissatisfied with the rules that the Court applies, Congress can legislate such rules through statute. In this chapter, we offer a framework for formulating sound rules of precedent, propose two such rules, and tentatively suggest a third.

We initially examine the relative benefits of following the original meaning and of following nonoriginalist precedent. The following several sections then begin to distill desirable precedent rules. We identify two specific rules for when precedent should be followed: when following precedent is necessary to avoid enormous costs and when precedent has been entrenched. We next identify several factors or circumstances when precedent would be relatively more or less beneficial—factors from which additional precedent rules could be constructed. We then use those factors to construct a third possible precedent rule. After contrasting our approach to precedent with that of other scholars and with the Supreme Court's approach in *Planned Parenthood v. Casey*, we conclude by applying our two proposed precedent rules to some important Supreme Court cases.

The question is how to fit precedent into our normative theory of originalism. When precedent departs from the Constitution's original meaning, the Supreme Court must decide whether to follow the precedent or the original meaning. We answer this question by comparing the benefits of following the original meaning with those of following precedent. One advantage of a consequentialist theory is that it treats both originalism and precedent as having commensurable effects that can be compared.

The Relative Benefits of Original Meaning and Precedent

The Benefits of Following Original Meaning

The benefits of original meaning are threefold. In the first place, our supermajoritarian theory shows that the Constitution's original meaning is likely to be desirable because it was enacted through a strict supermajoritarian process. Thus, enforcing the original meaning of this desirable Constitution is likely to be beneficial.

A second benefit derives from the clarity, predictability, and judicial constraint that originalism is likely to produce. Justice Antonin Scalia, among others, has emphasized this benefit.[1] While the original meaning of the text does not always yield clear rules, it usually provides clearer guidance than an approach that allows a majority of judges to interpret provisions based on their policy views. Although this benefit may be insufficient to justify originalism on its own, it is nonetheless significant and adds to the substantive benefits of a constitution produced by supermajority rules.

A third benefit of originalism emphasized in Chapter 4 is its preservation of the constitutional amendment process. An effective supermajoritarian amendment process allows the Constitution to be updated without undermining the benefits produced by a fixed constitution enacted through a supermajoritarian process. However, nonoriginalism, especially when it attempts to update the Constitution, prevents that amendment process from operating effectively.

Thus, originalism enforces desirable constitutional provisions, promotes clarity, predictability, and judicial constraint, and protects the constitutional amendment process. These benefits suggest that originalism should be followed in cases of first impression, and all the more so in cases when there is a precedent that accords with original meaning. But when there is a precedent that conflicts with the original meaning, the benefits of departing from that meaning and following the precedent must also be considered.

The Benefits of Following Precedent

Several benefits ensue from following precedent. We summarize them here only briefly because, unlike the virtues of originalism from a consequentialist perspective, these benefits are well known. The first two of these benefits overlap with some of the benefits of originalism. Precedent can often make the law more predictable by increasing its clarity. Especially if a constitutional provision is ambiguous or vague, a judicial decision can resolve the uncertainty. By clarifying the meaning of provisions, precedent can also serve to constrain judges in the future.[2] An important aspect of this constraint advances a core value of the rule of law—helping to ensure that like cases are decided alike.[3] Finally, precedents protect important reliance interests.[4] When precedents are overturned, people who took actions in reliance on them may incur significant costs. Following precedents in these circumstances not only avoids such costs, it also reduces uncertainty in the law.[5]

The Trade-off

Having briefly discussed the main benefits of originalism and precedent, we are now in a position to compare those competing benefits and to explore the trade-off between them. Under our consequentialist approach, the goal is to use the original meaning when it produces greater net benefits than precedent and to use precedent when the reverse holds true. Because rules have significant advantages in terms of judicial manageability, economy, predictability, and constraint, it is not desirable to have judges decide whether original meaning or precedent produces greater benefits on a case-by-case basis. Instead, judges should apply a comprehensive doctrine with rules that identify when either originalism or precedent produces greater net benefits.

We do not propose a comprehensive doctrine of precedent here. Instead, we take two preliminary steps toward such a doctrine. First, we recommend that judges follow precedent in two specific situations: when following precedent would avoid enormous costs and when a precedent is entrenched. These two rules represent an important step in the development of a precedent doctrine. Second, we identify several factors that make it more or less likely that precedent will be beneficial. These factors do not constitute rules that we recommend judges apply, but instead will prove useful in generating additional precedent rules. We provide an example of a rule constructed from such factors that seems plausible to us.

Ultimately, precedent doctrine should allow significant room for both original meaning and precedent. Of course, when an issue is one of first impression or has been previously decided in accord with the original meaning, there is no reason not to follow the original meaning. But when an existing precedent conflicts with the original meaning, an intermediate approach that sometimes follows original meaning and sometimes follows precedent is best. For example, as we note later in this chapter, our intermediate approach recommends that the Supreme Court follow *Griswold v. Connecticut*[6] as an entrenched precedent, but it does not protect *Roe v. Wade*[7] from being overturned.

Our consequentialist approach to originalism and precedent has been criticized by Jack Balkin.[8] Balkin argues that it faces a dilemma. On the one hand, providing limited protection to precedent would require the wholesale overruling of a vast swatch of cases, rendering our theory both impractical and radically inconsistent with Supreme Court practice.[9] On the other hand, broad protection of precedent would undermine our supermajoritarian justification for the desirability of the Constitution because much of the Constitution's meaning would be supplied by a majority of the justices rather than a strict supermajority of the nation.[10]

Balkin's criticism, however, is misplaced. First, he appears to commit the fallacy of the excluded middle because he ignores the possibility of pursuing the intermediate approach that we endorse. This intermediate approach requires neither overruling on a vast scale nor ignoring the original meaning. Rather, it pursues a middle path that attempts to gain the greatest benefits from both original meaning and precedent.

Moreover, embracing both originalism and substantial precedent is hardly incongruous. We are consequentialists and therefore must consider the interrelation of different and sometimes conflicting objectives in a complex and mature legal system. One objective of this system is to obtain the best possible rules, operating on a clean slate. Originalism furthers this goal. Other objectives include promoting clarity, predictability, constraint, and the protection of reliance. Precedent furthers these goals. These different objectives may conflict, and so we have to make the best trade-off possible.

It would be wonderful if constitutional decision makers never made any mistakes. Yet in the real world, where such mistakes are not infrequent, one must consider how to respond to them. Clearly, it is not feasible to correct all mistakes because the costs are simply too large. But while some nonoriginalist precedents must thus be accepted, we still can correct those errors that are not too costly to rectify.

Precedent Rules

Having examined the benefits and costs of following originalism and of following precedent, the next two sections recommend two specific precedent rules. These rules are determinate enough form so that they can be applied by judges. While we believe that a comprehensive precedent doctrine would include additional rules, here we fully recommend only these two.

Precedent That, if Overruled, Would Result in Enormous Costs

Precedents should be respected when overruling them would result in enormous costs. Extremely important institutions are sometimes based on judicial interpretations of the Constitution. Two obvious examples are Social Security and paper money. Although some originalists believe that the Supreme Court decisions interpreting the Constitution to allow Social Security[11] and legal tender laws for paper money[12] were wrongly decided, overruling those cases would result in enormous costs. The fear, uncertainty, and chaos that overruling these decisions would cause to the nation's public pensions and monetary system are so tremendous that they would far exceed any benefits from returning to the original meaning.

But this category of enormous costs is broader than simply these two extreme cases. Where a decision would require a large number of programs to be struck down, a strong case exists for concluding that the costs are simply too great to allow it to be overruled. For example, while there is a strong case for concluding that the original meaning of the Commerce Clause was much narrower than the New Deal interpretation,[13] returning to that original meaning would require the immediate elimination of a vast number of government programs, from securities regulation to environmental protection. The benefits of fully returning immediately to the original meaning now do not compare with these costs.

One way of giving substance to the concept of enormous costs in this context is to pose the question of whether legislatures would have to act immediately to address the problems caused by the overruled precedent. If Social Security were ruled unconstitutional because Congress lacked an enumerated power to pass it, Congress would have to legislate alternatives very expeditiously to replace a program that has become part of the US way of life. Similarly, if the Commerce Clause were cut back substantially, Congress or the states would have to immediately find ways of replacing the large regulatory regime that the Clause had made possible. The obvious political necessity of immediate action in such circumstances strongly suggests that the costs of overruling a precedent are enormous.

In contrast, many important precedents do not rise to this level, even if overruling them would render a large number of statutory provisions unconstitutional. As an example, consider *INS v. Chadha*,[14] which in effect held approximately 300 legislative veto provisions in 200 statutes to be unconstitutional. While *Chadha* did not overrule a Supreme Court precedent, that consideration is not relevant to the question of whether the decision had enormous costs. *Chadha* did not create enormous costs because the statutory provisions in most cases could continue to operate even in the absence of the legislative veto and in other cases were relatively easy to correct.[15] Congress did not feel substantial political pressure to legislate replacement schemes quickly.

There are a variety of important precedents, sometimes thought suspect on originalist grounds, whose overruling would not create enormous costs. The set of precedents from *Humphrey's Executor v. United States*[16] to *Morrison v. Olson*[17] that upheld Congress's power to insulate agency heads from presidential dismissal could be overruled without prompting immediate reaction from Congress. The work of the agencies could continue unabated, as occurred in the analogous case of *Free Enterprise Fund*,[18] in which the Court declared that a double level of insulation was unconstitutional. Indeed, the effect of a decision by the Supreme Court to restore the president's formal power to fire at will previously independent agency heads should not be overstated. Any president faces substantial political costs in firing even dependent subordinates, including disruption of programs, unfavorable publicity, and the subsequent effort needed to confirm a new agency head.[19]

Many criminal justice precedents of similarly dubious originalist provenance also would not impose enormous costs if overruled. For example, the requirement of issuing *Miranda* warnings could be eliminated without imposing such costs. If the Supreme Court overturned that holding, the law would once again require that statements made by criminal defendants be reviewed for voluntariness. While one might view such an approach as either normatively superior or inferior to the *Miranda* warnings, it would not involve huge expense. Of course, it is quite possible that, if *Miranda* were overturned, the federal government or the states might choose to enact new laws designed to regulate this area. In fact, the elimination of *Miranda* might actually serve as a catalyst for legislatures to enact alternative reforms, such as the video-recording of interrogations, which many reformers believe would be superior. But the choice of some governments to deliberate and then enact reforms is quite different from the necessity to act quickly to avert enormous costs.

This rule would also suggest that judges should partially overrule precedents if they can find clear legal rules that would avoid enormous costs and yet move constitutional interpretation closer to the original meaning. Even if the best interpretation of the New Deal Commerce Clause cases, for example, was that they bestowed plenary power on Congress to regulate behavior that had some effect on commercial activity, however remote, the Court in *United States v. Lopez* would have been correct to cut back on that precedent and hold that Congress could not regulate noncommercial activity on such an insubstantial basis. After all, *Lopez* certainly did not impose enormous costs. The significant question going forward is what additional legal rules might be found that would further cut back on the New Deal's expansive interpretation without incurring very heavy expenses.

Thus, the rule requiring that we retain precedent if overruling it would create enormous costs still offers an important space for eliminating precedents that are contrary to the original meaning. The rule is an important part of a framework for correcting constitutional error that takes an intermediate view of the relation between precedent and the original meaning—one that allows substantial opportunity for moving the Constitution toward more originalist results but that does not require judges to ignore all costs in doing so.

Entrenched Precedent

The second rule involves entrenched precedent. Entrenched precedents are judicial decisions that have the same degree of support enjoyed by constitutional amendments and therefore would likely be enacted by constitutional amendment if they were overturned by the courts. For instance, if the Supreme Court were to hold that sex discrimination was not significantly restricted by the Equal Protection Clause, it is quite likely that the nation would pass an amendment placing this protection back into the Constitution. Similar reasoning would apply if the Supreme Court were to reverse *Brown v. Board of Education*[20] based on the mistaken view that the doctrine of separate but equal reflected the Fourteenth Amendment's original meaning.

Under our approach, it is straightforward that entrenched precedent should take priority over the original meaning. For entrenched precedents, the benefits of following the original meaning are small and the benefits of following precedent are large. The benefits of following the original meaning are small because there is strong support for the constitutional rule announced in the precedent. It is the precedent rather than the original meaning that currently has consensus support and thus a presumption of beneficence. The benefits of following the precedent are large, not only because of the presumed desirability but also because it does not involve a change in the law.

Now, it might be argued that the consensus represented by the entrenched precedent is inferior to that forged by a constitutional amendment. The advantage of the amendment process is that it not only creates a consensus but also renders it visible to the polity, thus muting disagreement. Moreover, it may be difficult for the Supreme Court to determine what decisions would have attained the requisite consensus and to identify the actual underlying principles of those decisions. Consequently, one might argue that the judiciary should be required to overrule the precedent in favor of the original meaning and allow the formal amendment process to prove that a consensus indeed exists.

Such a requirement, however, would have great costs. Because this approach would require overruling all precedents that conflict with original meaning, including those that are genuinely entrenched, it would cause great harm to the nation's attachment to widely accepted opinions. These opinions have now come to be valued; overruling them would harm people's attachment to their understanding of the Constitution—an attachment that helps to unify the nation.[21] Further, a practical and rationally ignorant public is unlikely to understand or sympathize with such overrulings.[22] They might regard it as burdensome to have to pass a constitutional amendment merely to confirm what they believe everyone already knows—that the Constitution authorizes the precedent and a consensus supports that precedent. Moreover, the public might be suspicious of such overrulings, believing that the justices did not actually support the entrenched decision. This public opposition might also make it harder for the justices to reach originalist decisions on other difficult issues because the public would be more likely to doubt the Court's legitimacy. Finally, fearing the reactions of the public, the justices might be reluctant to overrule the decision and be led to engage in dishonest evasions, thus undermining the goal of making the law clear and accessible.

Consequently, it is less costly for the Court to follow genuinely entrenched precedents. While the Court may make mistakes in determining when such a consensus exists, there are factors that can discipline their inquiry. Most important, the search for consensus is factual, not ideological. The Court can assess whether the principle in the proffered precedent would now secure the consensus requisite to a constitutional amendment, not whether or not the principle is sound. Thus, as with originalist inquiries themselves, the justices are directed away from their own commitments and passions to purposes that are not their own. This focus is a source of discipline.[23]

The proper way to test whether the requisite consensus exists is to ask whether there is any significant opposition to the substance of the constitutional principle embedded in the precedent. By focusing on substance, we mean to exclude opposition that rests on disagreement with the means by which the principle was created—by judicial lawmaking rather than constitutional amendment. For the reasons already discussed, it is counterproductive to force the Court to overrule a precedent simply to ensure that the constitutional principle is enacted by the legitimate constitution-making process.

The Court should also not attempt to predict whether the amendment would be passed by taking into account matters unrelated to the public's support for the principle. For example, one might believe that the public would be unmotivated to enact constitutional amendments to reenact *Griswold v. Connecticut*[24] or even midlevel scrutiny for discrimination based on sex, on the ground that existing state and federal law does not infringe on these rights. But whether or not people would be motivated to *act* on principles and symbols is difficult to predict. It is much easier to determine whether there appears to be support for a principle.[25]

In framing this precedent rule, we also have to determine what degree of likelihood should be demanded for the passage of a constitutional amendment that would enact the precedent. Our view is that the Supreme Court should be persuaded that the amendment would more likely than not be passed. Requiring a lesser probability would permit precedent to control the interpretation of a constitutional provision, even though that interpretation would probably not command the consensus necessary for an amendment and would thus be unlikely to be beneficial. Conversely, requiring a greater probability would preserve constitutional language that would probably be replaced by an amendment and thus would also be unlikely to be beneficial.[26]

Finally, it is important to correctly describe the scope of the entrenched precedent. Such description requires analysis both of the scope of the precedent and the scope of the entrenchment because entrenched precedent must satisfy two conditions to be favored over original meaning. First, the principle must actually be necessary to a previous holding or holdings. Second, the principle necessary to a holding must enjoy a consensus that approximates the consensus enjoyed by a constitutional amendment.

In examining Commerce Clause precedent, for instance, the first step is to determine the breadth of federal power that the New Deal cases endorsed. Although some commentators believe the New Deal precedent is best read as establishing a principle of plenary power over economic as well as noneconomic matters, we believe it should be read as establishing power over, at most, all economic matters. If our reading is accurate, the *Lopez* Court was correct not to consider itself foreclosed in refusing Congress plenary power over noneconomic matters, such as carrying guns around a school. But even if the New Deal precedent were fairly read to include a plenary power over noneconomic matters, the *Lopez* Court was correct in not enforcing such a principle because there is no consensus in favor of providing the federal government with such powers, whatever the consensus about federal power over economic matters.[27]

A similar two-step process should be undertaken in evaluating the scope of entrenched precedent on sex discrimination. First, the scope of the actual holdings should be evaluated. For instance, it seems likely that the principle necessary to the sex discrimination decisions is narrower than the principle against racial discrimination. Thus, the law can recognize that society regards men and women as different in ways that the races are not. But whatever the scope of the precedent in these cases, it is clear that the second step of the analysis shows that the entrenched precedent of sex discrimination is narrower than the principle against racial discrimination. That more limited scope of the consensus around sex discrimination is shown by the opposition to unisex bathrooms or women's participation in combat—opposition that emerged during the debates over the Equal Rights Amendment. Thus, even given the previous cases on sex discrimination, the law would not have to impose new norms on issues such as unisex bathrooms and women in combat about which there was no very substantial consensus.

Our theory of entrenched precedent would not, however, encompass what has become recently known as a superprecedent—a precedent that the Court has itself reaffirmed and therefore is thought by some to be entitled to dispositive weight.[28] At the time of the confirmation hearings of Chief Justice John Roberts and Justice Samuel Alito, many senators and commentators argued that the reaffirmation of some aspects of *Roe v. Wade*[29] by *Planned Parenthood of Southeastern Pennsylvania v. Casey*[30] made *Roe* a superprecedent that could not be overruled.[31] But there is no necessary or even strong relation between a judicial reaffirmation and the consensus requisite for a constitutional amendment. The judiciary cannot create popular consensus by its own fiat, even by repeating itself.[32]

Factors Relevant to Beneficial Precedent Rules

Having proposed two specific precedent rules, we now turn to more theoretical matters. First, we explore various factors that indicate when it makes more or less sense to follow precedent. These factors are not intended as precedent rules to be applied directly by judges. Rather, they provide information about the desirability of precedent in different circumstances and are useful as a means of developing precedent rules. In the next section, we use those factors to tentatively offer one additional precedent rule.

Uncertainty in the Constitution's Original Meaning

One key factor in determining whether to follow a precedent is the clarity of the Constitution's original meaning. When the original meaning is uncertain, a far stronger argument exists for following precedent—provided that the precedent constitutes a reasonable interpretation of the original meaning—than when the precedent clearly conflicts with the original meaning. In a superb article, Caleb Nelson argues that courts in the early years of the Republic generally used an approach under which they would follow precedent if it reasonably resolved an ambiguity but not if it was demonstrably erroneous.[33]

This analysis follows from the trade-off between originalism and precedent. When the Constitution is itself unclear, the benefits of following the original meaning are not as strong. One justification for originalism is that it promotes clarity in the law. But if the original meaning is unclear, then there is less reason to follow it. Instead, a precedent that reasonably resolves the uncertainty will better promote clarity, even though a court may later believe the precedent resolved the matter incorrectly.[34] A second justification for originalism—the one we emphasize most—is that it enforces provisions with desirable consequences. But here too constitutional ambiguity militates against the original meaning because we cannot be sure exactly what meaning obtained consensus support during the enactment process. Thus, there is a diminished value in following the original meaning.[35]

Reliance Costs

Another important factor in determining whether to follow a precedent is the degree of reliance on that precedent. Reliance occurs when one takes an action one would not otherwise have taken based on the assumption that a precedent will be followed. The degree of reliance on precedent varies with the number of people who have relied on it and with the costs they would incur if the precedent were overturned. Traditionally, precedent rules were significantly influenced by reliance interests. In particular, stronger precedent rules were applied to property—and sometimes commercial interests—based on the view that reliance in this area was greater. One way to think of the reliance factor is that it is a variation on the enormous costs rule discussed earlier. The costs of overruling a precedent on which there has been substantial reliance are higher than the costs of overruling a precedent on which there has been no reliance. Not only does overturning a precedent that has been relied upon upset expectations and impose costs, it also weakens people's willingness to rely on future precedent and hence to plan for the future.

Thus, the greater the reliance costs, the stronger the argument for not overturning a precedent. Reliance costs can be especially significant in at least two situations. They will be high when the government establishes a program that people rely on to a great extent, such as Social Security. And they will be great when people make significant private investments based on assumptions about the law.

Precedent Established in Violation of the Precedent Rules

Our consequentialist approach also suggests that a precedent should be followed less, other things being equal, if it was not decided according to the rules of precedent. The important benefit from such a rule is that it creates a disciplining effect. If judges know that decisions that violate precedent rules will not be treated as authoritative, they will have better incentives to comply with the rules of precedent. Such incentives are most beneficial if the precedent rules themselves reflect the optimal trade-offs that we outline here.

The Epistemic Value of Precedent

Precedent may also have an important epistemic value. Judges, like other humans, are not infallible. That the Supreme Court previously interpreted the Constitution's original meaning in one way provides evidence for that interpretation. Precedent may thus appropriately change a judge's prior beliefs about the correct interpretation, just as the opinion of an expert appropriately changes the prior beliefs of decision makers about the conclusion to which the expert testifies.[36] When a precedent raises the probability that its interpretation of the Constitution conforms to the original meaning, the Supreme Court should give the precedent weight in its assessment.

The nature of epistemic precedent in an originalist world is limited in two important respects. First, only cases that make a good faith effort to discover the original meaning deserve epistemic weight.[37] Many cases have deserved no weight on epistemic grounds because they have not attempted to derive their results from the Constitution's original meaning. Second, the Supreme Court also has reason to discount the epistemic value of past precedent if it discovers new evidence relevant to the original meaning that the previous decision did not consider. In contrast, one might believe that early Supreme Court cases that attempted good faith discovery of the original meaning deserve additional weight on epistemic grounds because those early courts' temporal proximity to the Constitution makes them more likely to get the right answer.

Other Possible Precedent Rules

Our discussion of factors is intended to clarify the benefits and costs of precedent and ultimately to guide the creation of additional precedent rules. While we endorse only two precedent rules here, we believe that others may be justified through consideration of such factors. We suggest one such rule to illustrate the type of rule that might be adopted under our proposed theoretical framework. This rule has much to commend it, although we are not yet ready to endorse it fully.

According to this rule, a precedent should be followed when four conditions are met. First, the original meaning of a provision must be unclear. Second, the precedent itself follows a reasonable interpretation of the text. Third, the precedent established a clear rule. Finally, that rule must have been significantly relied upon. Although this precedent rule has more criteria than the two rules that we endorse, it nevertheless is embodied in a structure of specific requirements that must be met, marking it as a rule rather than an amorphous balancing test.

Such a rule would capture significant advantages of precedent by generating a clear constitutional meaning on an issue that would otherwise be ambiguous or vague and by protecting reliance interests. It also would not lose many of the advantages of following the original meaning—advantages that largely consist of the good consequences of the original meaning and the clarity that objective evidence of the original meaning can provide—because the precedent rule would apply only when the original meaning was not clear. This lack of clarity reduces the likelihood that a court attempting to follow the original meaning would either correctly discern that beneficial meaning or would be significantly constrained by it. At first glance, this precedent rule illustrates the advantages of making a careful trade-off between the advantages of precedent and original meaning.

Of course, this kind of rule would be truly advantageous only if the criteria that guide it are capable of relatively determinate and neutral judicial application. Each criterion must be analyzed to see if it meets that test. The first requirement—that the provision of the Constitution be itself unclear—requires further definition to be capable of clear application. Constitutional provisions are not either clear or unclear. Their clarity ranges over a spectrum, and thus the precedent rule would have to provide a sense of the the lack of clarity that would trigger it. In our view, the best rule would require a substantial lack of clarity in the sense that no interpretation was substantially better than its competitors. A lower threshold would allow precedent to trump original meaning, even when a better interpretation was relatively obvious. A higher threshold would mean that precedent could not resolve questions about which many reasonable people could disagree.

The second requirement—that the interpretation be reasonable—flows naturally from the first. Even if a provision is unclear, only reasonable interpretations of the original meaning should be binding. Although reasonable interpretations of the original meaning might possibly be the actual original meaning and at worst are a plausible take on that meaning, unreasonable interpretations are clearly not the original meaning. Thus, reasonable interpretations are much more likely to have the desirable characteristics of the original meaning than unreasonable ones.

The third requirement—that the precedent establish a clear rule—has an obvious rationale. An unclear rule does not provide the certainty that can justify dispensing with the original meaning in favor of precedent. Like the criterion that inquires whether the original meaning is clear, this criterion of asking whether the precedent establishes a clear rule is not dichotomous: Precedents, like provisions, range over a spectrum of clarity. For much the same reasons we outlined in the context of measuring the clarity of provisions, this criterion would have to be understood as requiring substantial clarity.

Reliance, the fourth requirement, is the most well known of the criteria for this precedent rule. It too demands the qualification that the reliance be substantial.[38] Insubstantial reliance should not terminate the search for original meaning because there are few costs to continuing this search.[39] Assuming that a precedent meets all four criteria, we believe there is a strong case that it should be controlling because such precedents have substantial benefits that outweigh those attending a renewed search for the original meaning.

The Contrast with Other Approaches to Precedent

The Contrast with the Supreme Court's Approach in *Casey*

The Supreme Court's most famous and extended recent discussion of precedent is in *Planned Parenthood of Southeastern Pennsylvania v. Casey*.[40] In that case, the Court's plurality listed several factors that bear on its willingness to decline to follow precedent. Here, we critique the Court's approach, both to show its weakness from a consequentialist perspective and to highlight its differences from our own approach.[41]

Our approach contrasts with the *Casey* approach in two general ways. In *Casey*, the plurality appears to adopt a presumption in favor of following precedent. We reject this presumption because the strong reasons for following the original meaning generally preclude a presumption in favor of precedent. Further, the *Casey* opinion does not articulate specific rules, but rather mentions a variety of factors that must be weighed in determining whether precedent should be disturbed. In contrast, we believe that questions of precedent should be settled by rules, not by open-ended balancing tests, because of the advantages in terms of predictability and constraint that rules confer.[42]

Even if we accepted a precedent doctrine based on a general balancing test rather than rules, we would disagree with how the plurality employs some of the factors in *Casey*. First, the *Casey* plurality suggests that it is less likely to follow a precedent that is "unworkable" in practice.[43] We agree that a precedent that is unworkable (either because the rule it furnishes is unclear or because it leads to inconsistent results) is a precedent without significant value. Far from offering good consequences that may counterbalance the bad consequences of departing from the original meaning, precedent that is unworkable itself wreaks a kind of legal havoc.

Our analysis, however, does not embrace the converse proposition that a precedent should be retained because it is workable. Many legal rules may be workable, but may still be unsound. The advantage of following the original meaning is that it is likely not only to be workable but also to lead to better consequences than other rules. Thus, unworkability undermines the force of precedent, while workability does little to generate that force.

We have a similar skepticism about another *Casey* factor: "[W]hether related principles of law have so far developed as to have left the old rule no more than a remnant of abandoned doctrine."[44] If a precedent is a "remnant" and is inconsistent with other related rules, the precedent is likely contributing to legal incoherence.[45] Legal incoherence in jurisprudence means that individuals have more trouble complying with a set of rules that are incoherent and hard to understand. Such incoherence does militate against retaining precedent.

But the coherence of a precedent with the rest of law is, by itself, not a reason for retaining a precedent. That a precedent coheres with the rest of the law does not mean that a case overruling it may not also be coherent. Many different plausible rationales can serve to make a set of cases coherent, just as many plausible shapes can connect a set of dots. Moreover, coherence with other precedents counts as a reason for preserving the precedent at issue only if those other precedents should themselves be preserved. Thus, a proper analysis would require an assessment of whether these other precedents are themselves protected by appropriate rules, such as whether overruling them would create enormous costs.

Another factor discussed by the *Casey* plurality is "whether facts have so changed, or come to be seen so differently, as to have robbed the old rule of significant application or justification."[46] Once again it is relatively clear how changed facts can undermine a precedent if they rob it of "legal significance." If a precedent depends on a set of facts that no longer holds, it is manifestly subject to revision. But again, the converse is not true. Unchanging facts underlying a precedent do not justify its retention. The Constitution's original meaning should lead to a better result even if the facts have not changed from the time the precedent was decided. A precedent should be followed rather than the original meaning only if it fits within a precedent rule that ensures important beneficial consequences.

In short, the *Casey* plurality tried to establish a presumption in favor of following precedent. The plurality suggests that precedent should be followed unless there are particular factors that undermine its utility. Our analysis of the trade-off between precedent and original meaning does not support such a presumption. Instead, the original meaning should be followed unless a justified precedent rule indicates otherwise. Moreover, the rule-oriented analysis we have advocated provides a more disciplined framework than *Casey*'s multiple factor analysis.

The Contrast with Other Scholars

We previously expressed our disagreement with scholars who argue that nonoriginalist precedent should have no role in constitutional adjudication because it is necessarily unconstitutional. In contrast, we suggest that precedent should be followed in cases where following a precedent rule will have better consequences than adhering to the original meaning. Depriving constitutional law of all reliance on precedent would create substantial instability because it would require the Court to overrule cases that enjoy consensus support among the people or would cause enormous costs. Examples of these cases include those that give Congress more power under the Commerce Clause than does the original meaning,[47] as well as widely accepted results such as *Griswold v. Connecticut*.[48] We cannot help but note that opposition to all precedent is also tactically hopeless: No Supreme Court, now or in the foreseeable future, is going to reconsider decisions that would have enormous costs or that are widely accepted. As a result, a no-precedent position is not likely to be followed.

We also disagree with Professor Randy Barnett's more nuanced rejection of precedent.[49] Like Lawson and Paulsen, Barnett argues that precedent should never insulate from reversal a decision that is contrary to the original meaning.[50] But he also argues that, in many cases, the Constitution is so ambiguous or vague that many different interpretations are compatible with the original meaning.[51] In such cases involving "constitutional construction," Barnett argues that originalism does not preclude a precedent from being respected even if other decisions might also have been consistent with the original meaning.[52] We have already noted our disagreement with Barnett's theory of constitutional construction in Chapter 8. But even if one accepts the theory, it still does not prevent Barnett's precedent theory from having many of the same practical difficulties as those of Lawson and Paulsen. Some important precedents are incompatible with the original meaning, and yet they reflect a current consensus or they cannot be overturned without enormous social costs. Consequently, his theory has many of the same defects as the theories that deny any substantial weight to prior cases.

Our intermediate position also differs from those who argue that precedent should be routinely and presumptively followed. A leading modern exponent of this view is Tom Merrill.[53] Like ours, Merrill's normative theory is consequentialist. But unlike our approach, Merrill's article focuses only on advancing the objective of judicial constraint.[54] He thus overlooks a crucial comparison—whether adherence to original meaning or to precedent is more likely to generate good rules and preserve the amendment process.

Even the question of whether the original meaning or precedent better constrains judges seems to us far closer than Merrill allows. First, when the original meaning yields a clear rule, it may well be more constraining than precedent. Merrill appears to suggest that precedents create thicker norms and thereby inherently tend to be more constraining than the original meaning.[55] But given that precedents span many eras and emerge from conflicting majorities,[56] they may be less coherent and more subject to manipulation than the more uniform original design. Thus, precedent may be ultimately less constraining than the original meaning. Moreover, stare decisis in the US system is not absolute, and the possibility that precedent can be overruled creates additional uncertainty not present in adherence to original meaning.

In addition, our version of originalism—original methods originalism— thickens originalism's norms, to use Merrill's own term. The original methods approach directs interpreters to follow the enactors' interpretive rules.[57] It thus provides jurists with additional methods to resolve ambiguities and vagueness. Accordingly, it potentially offers more constraint than other originalist theories.

Our approach to precedent canvasses the full range of relevant considerations for a consequentialist theory and appropriately confines precedent to circumstances in which it is likely to have better consequences than the original meaning. Such a framework preserves the beneficial original meaning through the ages better than does Merrill's. In particular, it leaves open to challenge precedents that the Court has reaffirmed but that are incompatible with original meaning, and whose overruling would not offend the kind of consequentialist precedent rules that we have described.

Applying the Approach to Previous Supreme Court Overruling Decisions

Here we illustrate the reach of our precedent rules by considering important Supreme Court decisions that overrule precedents from *Brown v. Board of Education* onward. Our purpose here is illustrative only, and we are not attempting to provide a comprehensive picture of the Court's decisions whether to overrule precedent. To focus on the question of whether the Court should overrule precedents to pursue the original meaning, we generally assume that the overrulings would move constitutional jurisprudence closer to the original meaning. In some of the cases, we believe that the Court acted correctly, but in one important case—*Planned Parenthood v. Casey*—we think the Court's use of precedent to protect the constitutional right to abortion was misplaced.

In *Brown*, the Supreme Court did not follow *Plessy v. Ferguson's*[58] holding that separate but equal accommodation of the races complied with the Fourteenth Amendment.[59] Under our doctrine of precedent, *Plessy* should not have been retained. Its holding was not supported by a substantial consensus, and its overruling did not create enormous costs. Separate but equal did not command the kind of national consensus needed to reach a constitutional amendment in 1954. A more superficially plausible argument in favor of retaining *Plessy* is that overturning it would lead to enormous costs in the form of social disruption. But this social disruption is very different from the kind that might stay the Court's hand in overruling entirely the New Deal cases that authorized Congress to engage in economic regulation of manufacturing and labor. The disruption from overruling *Plessy* occurred because of the threat of violence from a number of people—particularly Southern whites—who refused to comply peacefully with the decision. This kind of disruption is not one the Court should be quick to take into account because it amounts to the legal equivalent of a heckler's veto. Declining to overrule a case simply because of fear of opposition, even of a violent kind, would encourage others to threaten disruption should other decisions be overruled. Thus, this kind of defense of precedent could lead to unfortunate consequences for social peace and thoughtful public deliberation about constitutional issues.

Moreover, in this particular case, another group—African Americans— would have been harmed and offended if the doctrine of separate but equal had been reaffirmed. And if, as we believe, the oppression that led to their distress directly contravened the Constitution, it would seem especially problematic to allow the feelings of their oppressors to block the vindication of their long-denied constitutional rights.

In *Gregg v. Georgia*,[60] the Supreme Court essentially overruled its previous decision in *Furman v. Georgia*[61] that the death penalty was unconstitutional. The Court was correct not to follow *Furman*. Once again, the precedent did not represent the consensus of the country and was not overruled at great cost. Far from being an entrenched precedent that was supported by a national consensus, *Furman* triggered an adverse public reaction and prompted states to reenact their death penalty statutes.[62] Nor did permitting the states to impose the death penalty undermine specific forms of reliance or create social disruption.[63]

The Court's decision in *United States v. Lopez*[64] was also justified. Although the Court did not explicitly say that it was overruling prior precedent, many commentators thought that earlier New Deal cases have given Congress plenary regulatory power under the Commerce Clause and that *Lopez* had cut back on those cases.[65] We do not read those cases so broadly. But even if one read some of the New Deal cases as covering noneconomic matters, *Lopez* was correct, under our approach, to depart from these precedents.

Lopez did not disturb the precedent that gave Congress plenary power over core economic matters, such as regulation of manufacturing, labor, and production.[66] Strong arguments have been made that overruling significant portions of such congressional authority would lead to very substantial disruption.[67] Moreover, there seems to be a consensus that the federal government should have at least some powers over economic matters that an originalist reading of the Commerce Clause might well deny.

Instead, the Court merely denied Congress the authority to regulate matters that were not commercial. While there may be a consensus to give the federal government regulatory power over some economic matters, there is no similar consensus to allow the federal government control over noncommercial matters, such as the restriction on possession of guns in school zones at issue in *Lopez*. Similarly, overruling the New Deal precedent over noncommercial matters is unlikely to cause substantial disruption because Congress has not substantially regulated noncommercial matters.

Assuming that *National League of Cities v. Usery*[68] accorded with the original meaning, the Court was similarly correct to overrule *Maryland v. Wirtz*[69] and hold that Congress lacked power to regulate certain state operations.[70] Overruling *Wirtz* did not cause substantial disruption. Also, the notion that the federal government could regulate the operations of states certainly did not command consensus support.

In our view, the plurality opinion in *Planned Parenthood v. Casey*[71] was wrong to rely on the precedential effect of *Roe v. Wade*.[72] Here, we contrast *Roe* with *Griswold v. Connecticut*.[73] Under our analysis, *Griswold* is an entrenched precedent that enjoys the kind of consensus support equivalent to a constitutional amendment.[74] In other words, while some constitutional commentators still argue that *Griswold* was wrong as an original matter,[75] almost no one argues, as a policy matter, that contraception should be illegal or even that it would be desirable for the states to retain the authority to prohibit contraception. In contrast, *Roe* is not an entrenched precedent and overruling it would not create enormous costs.

It is obvious that *Roe* does not command the kind of consensus that would be needed to pass a constitutional amendment. In addition, the costs of overruling *Roe* would not be enormous. To be clear, we are not addressing the costs of prohibiting all abortions. We focus only on the costs of the transition to a regime in which it is legal for states to prohibit abortion. Overruling *Roe v. Wade* will not make abortion illegal, and most states will probably maintain relatively permissive abortion laws. Thus, the transition costs may be relatively small because the effective legal norms are not likely to change very substantially in most places.

Precedent is often seen as an embarrassment for originalists. We have argued, to the contrary, that precedent is a legitimate and coherent doctrine within originalism. It is legitimate because the Constitution itself authorizes a common law of precedent that is revisable by statute. It is coherent because the values relevant to precedent, like stability and reliance, can be balanced against the values of originalism, such as the beneficence of rules from a desirable constitution-making process. This balance can result in precedential doctrines that are workable and attractive.

We have also shown how our theory generates justifications for two important kinds of precedent—entrenched precedent and precedent that would result in enormous costs if overruled. This justification provides a sound basis for following cases like *Brown v. Board of Education* and *Frontiero v. Richardson*, even if one does not believe these cases were decided correctly as an original matter. Thus, our theory deprives originalism's opponents of their familiar complaint that to embrace originalism is to abandon cases that have become fundamental to our constitutional order. Yet it continues to permit the original meaning of provisions to have generative force across a wide range of constitutional law.

11

IMAGINING AN ORIGINALIST FUTURE

We end our defense of originalism by imagining a world where originalism is the dominant view of constitutional jurisprudence. Such a world would improve our polity, creating both better judicial decisions and a more vigorous constitutional politics. It is a world where constitutional decisions would have good consequences and constitution making would become both popular and future-oriented. It bears no resemblance to the world that critics of originalism fear—where the dead hand of the past traps the living into a dead end of anachronistic principles. Only through a systematically originalist jurisprudence can constitutional law become what it must be if it is to act as the true rudder of the nation—simultaneously law that is enduring and objective, law that is of high quality, and law that is subject to revision by the people of each generation.

A Culture of Originalism

We have already shown why originalism leads to constitutional interpretations that are likely to generate good consequences for today. The supermajoritarian constitution-making process leads to the entrenchment of good norms. It is in the nature of good entrenched provisions that they are good not only at the time that they are enacted but for the future as well. And because constitutional provisions are good by virtue of the consensus support they received, their continued beneficence depends on giving them the meaning that gained the consensus.

Here we focus on the additional benefits that flow from the growth of a distinctive culture of originalism, and in particular a culture of original methods originalism. The practical success of a legal theory depends on support from the legal culture of its time. For years, academics and the broader legal culture have been hostile to originalism. As a result, scholars have not developed the cumulative knowledge of the historical meaning of both particular provisions and the original methods that would support the Supreme Court in a comprehensively originalist application of constitutional law. Nor have justices who consistently write originalist opinions received widespread praise for their behavior.

But in a world dominated by originalism, academics would work to create the knowledge that would improve the performance of originalist judges and reinforce their inclination to be consistently originalist. Indeed, if the contemporary world were to become predominantly originalist, this new culture could help usher in a golden age of originalism because the modern world has characteristics particularly conducive to a theory of constitutional interpretation that rests on knowledge of the past.

First, law professors today have more specialized knowledge and, as a result, generate more comprehensive and accurate information within their specialized fields. In the area of originalism, we are already witnessing the fruits of substantial specialization. Some originalist professors largely concentrate on questions of methodology.[1] Others focus on a deeper understanding of the original meaning of particular constitutional provisions.[2] Because historical knowledge of particular eras helps provide the context to clarify original meaning, some originalists specialize in particular periods of US history, like the Founding era, in which the original Constitution was framed, or the Reconstruction period, in which the Thirteenth, Fourteenth, and Fifteenth Amendments were enacted. Still others specialize in certain subject matter areas of the Constitution, like the provisions that divide the foreign affairs powers among the branches of the federal government.[3] Despite such specialization, the modern academy circulates information ever more rapidly through conferences, online commentary, and blog posts, thus ensuring that the various areas of knowledge do not remain hermetically sealed.

Yet another advantage for originalism is the variety of political ideologies to which originalists now adhere. The more heterogeneous are the ideological priors of originalists, the richer originalist inquiry becomes. Bias must be made to counteract bias. Less ideologically committed scholars then can judge which side has the better assessment.

Already originalism has been greatly enriched as professors with different ideological perspectives have embraced it. The renaissance of originalism in the modern era began with a particular ideological valence—the conservative critique of the Warren Court. This critique, exemplified by the writings of Robert Bork, had a strong majoritarian flavor.[4] As a result, the initial inclination of the originalist movement was to find an original meaning that gave space to the political branches, at the state and federal levels, to enforce the contemporary social norms they chose.

But this perspective may well have reflected as much the views of the Progressive Era and the New Deal as that of the Constitution's original meaning. Subsequently, more libertarian scholars focused on the original meaning of provisions that protect individual liberty and limit the reach of the states, the federal government, or both.[5] Even more recently, some liberal law professors have become originalists.[6] They have found in the original meaning of the guarantees of equality in the Fourteenth Amendment politically liberal results.

To be sure, not every scholar can be equally correct. Ideology itself prompts false starts and wrong turns. Sometimes originalist inquiry into original meaning is distorted by bias. We have ourselves criticized some new forms of originalism in this book. Nevertheless, many originalists of varying ideology are engaged in a good-faith inquiry to discern objective truths rooted in historical fact. Over time, new scholars will enter these debates, sift through the various claims, and help the profession reach a better consensus.

The technology of our age also facilitates originalism. As more and more historical documents appear online, the past becomes more accessible to all. As more sophisticated techniques of search and categorization are honed, we can better evaluate the nuance and context of the Constitution's text. Modern information technology brings the past closer to the present than ever before.

Our own distinctive contribution to originalist methodology—a focus on original methods—benefits from these same phenomena. The interpretive methods originally applied to the text, no less than the meaning of the words of the text, are objects of historical inquiry that can be advanced by the diversity of originalist scholars and the growing amount and accessibility of data. As the original methods are fleshed out, these methods can help resolve ambiguity and vagueness in the text of constitutional provisions.

The final step in an originalist world would be reconciling the originalist future with the often nonoriginalist past of Supreme Court decisions. It is not surprising that originalists have, for the most part, not yet seriously confronted the challenge of integrating originalism with precedent. This task did not seem fruitful until originalism gained enough power to potentially serve again as the warp and woof of the law. We hope that the work on precedent in this book will be part of a greater movement undertaking this task.

A world where originalism is dominant is not simply a dream. There are signs it is becoming a reality. In the last twenty years, an extraordinary outpouring of Second Amendment scholarship has occurred, all focused on fixing the meaning of its text: "A well regulated Militia, being necessary to the security of a free State, the right of the people to keep and bear Arms shall not be infringed."[7] Legal scholars of conservative, libertarian, and liberal bent have joined in the debate over the provision's original meaning. All were aided by the increasing accessibility of historical materials.

A widespread view that emerged across the political spectrum favored interpreting the Second Amendment as a right that could be exercised by individuals without regard to their membership in a militia.[8] To be sure, some scholars continue to dissent from that conclusion, but a consensus spanning professors of differing ideologies provided greater confidence that the view embraced was likely correct. This consensus in turn influenced the Court to interpret the amendment as an individual right that protected gun possession in the home. Such a result would have been unimaginable a generation ago, when even the conservative Chief Justice Warren Burger denigrated without substantial historical support the individual rights interpretation of the Second Amendment.[9] Another measure of the increasing prevalence of originalism was that Justice Stevens's dissent was also originalist, disagreeing on the history but generally accepting the methodology.

These developments illustrate the virtuous circle that can continue the renaissance of originalism. In the last two decades, originalism in the academy was motivated in part by having two originalist justices on the Court—Antonin Scalia and Clarence Thomas. This originalist scholarship, like that on the Second Amendment, then provided support for Supreme Court majority opinions that were systematically originalist. We can expect that development in turn to encourage yet more originalist scholarship. The virtuous circle can continue yet again as such scholarship further reinforces originalism in the judiciary.

Of course, the Court will not follow every twist and turn of originalism arising in the legal academy. There is a necessary division of labor between the high theory of law professors and the quotidian practice of the courts. But that division does not mean that the turn to originalism in legal academy does not have an effect on the wider world. The Chicago school of antitrust economics has transformed antitrust law, although the Courts have not written all the nuances of the theory of industrial organization into competition law.

A virtuous circle of originalism has yet another important consequence. It encourages greater attention to and resort to the amendment process. We now turn to this important aspect of an originalist renaissance.

Originalism and the Reinvigoration of the Amendment Process

A renaissance of originalism will also directly lead to a revival of the constitutional amendment process. When citizens recognize that they can no longer change the Constitution by getting the Supreme Court to update it according to their preferences, they will naturally focus on changing it through the only avenue left to them—the amendment process. A renewed focus on the constitutional amendment process can transform the constitutional identity of the citizenry. In an originalist world, a generation naturally sees itself not simply as subjects of the Constitution but also as its potential framers. Each generation then can contribute to our fundamental law no less than previous generations, including those of the Founding, Reconstruction, and Progressive eras.

That the revival of originalism will breathe life again into the amendment process is not surprising because originalism and the amendment process are inextricably bound together. There can be no normatively attractive originalism without the amendment process. As we have shown, the case for originalism depends on a beneficial process, like Article V, that permits each generation to change the Constitution. But there also can be no effective amendment process without originalism. Without originalism, constitutional change can occur through other means, allowing groups to change the Constitution without amending it and leaving the amendment process a dead letter. Proper constitutional interpretation and a vigorous constitutional politics march under a single banner: no originalism without the amendment process and no amendment process without originalism.

The revival of originalism would thus restore Article V to its central place in the constitutional order—a place it had from the early Republic through the early twentieth century—when transformative constitutional amendments could be passed. This past dynamism contrasts with the disuse of the constitutional amendment process today. We have already detailed how judicial nonoriginalism derailed the Equal Rights Amendment (ERA) and amendments that would have expanded federal power during the New Deal. Indeed, it is impossible to count all the amendments that have not been born because of nonoriginalism. Part of the tragedy of nonoriginalism is the Lost Amendments—amendments that would have represented a generation's contribution to high-quality fundamental law. An indication of the desuetude of our process for making fundamental law is the remarkably small part that drives for federal constitutional amendments play in recent political and social movements. To be sure, some proposed constitutional amendments, like the flag-burning amendment, have gained momentum at times, but they are generally not the kind of transformative provisions around which a movement can crystallize.

Originalism's renewal of the constitutional amendment process would have substantial benefits for our politics. First, because political and social movements could not depend on the courts to change the Constitution, they would then have to focus on persuasion in the high politics of the constitutional amendment process. This dynamic encourages more political compromise, harnessing the energy of social movements to move the nation forward while tamping down on their tendency to polarize the polity. Constitutional compromise was at the heart of the nation's Founding. But as political and social movements came to believe they could get their wish list by engaging the courts rather than their fellow citizens, that art of compromise was lost. That loss reflects yet another aspect of the tragedy of nonoriginalism.

Second, the amendment process delivers constitution making back into the hands of the people. Rather than leaving fundamental decisions about new societal norms to the judicial elites, the reinvigorated constitutional amendment process would tap into the dispersed judgments and diverse attachments of people across the nation. While there has been much discussion of the virtues of popular constitutionalism, a real popular constitutionalism—one that is likely to lead to good results—is possible only through a vigorous amendment process. Only an uninhibited Article V that fully engages the whole people can ensure that changes in our fundamental law reflect the crystallized consensus of their views.

Adherence to the original meaning of the Constitution's substantive provisions also increases the information available and thus improves constitutional decision making. Constitutional federalism, for instance, offers the nation the capacity to conduct experiments on the effects of novel constitutional rights or structures. Insofar as the experiments yield beneficial results, they may then serve as templates for national amendments to achieve similar objectives. For example, if the Supreme Court does not update the Constitution to include a right to same-sex marriage, we will be able to observe the effects in states that decide to provide such a right. As a result, the people will be better informed when it comes to deliberations over whether such a right should be placed in the federal constitution.

Similarly, within the scope of its power, the federal government can experiment with expanding rights through statutes. For instance, even if it turns out that some novel forms of surveillance, such as global-positioning system tracking that does not involve a trespass, are not searches or seizures within the original meaning of the Fourth Amendment, Congress could choose to regulate the federal government's use of these devices. Such regulation can serve as a test for determining whether these protections should be entrenched as constitutional provisions. Originalism not only promises to revive Article V, but also to improve its decision-making process.

The Constitution as Formal Law, Higher Law, and Our Law

In his recent book on originalism, Jack Balkin has suggested that, for the Constitution to be normatively attractive, it must function simultaneously as basic law, higher law, and our law.[10] For Balkin, basic law provides the foundational legal framework for a society by "promot[ing] political stability and allocat[ing] rights, duties, powers and responsibilities."[11] Higher law serves as critique of current injustices, including those in the Constitution itself.[12] Our law demands that each generation be able to make the Constitution its own.[13]

We agree with Balkin that three such qualities are essential to a normatively attractive Constitution. But we would reinterpret them to connect with the true foundations of constitutionalism. We agree that the Constitution must create a framework for political stability and rights, but the better term for such a quality is *formal law*, not *basic law*. Formal law has a meaning that cannot be changed by ordinary government actors and is objective in the sense of being rooted in verifiable facts. The Constitution must be formal law if it is to provide the foundation for social stability and the protection of individual rights that constitutions can furnish. We also agree that the Constitution must function as higher law. It must have higher quality than ordinary law, not least because judicial review contemplates that ordinary law will be invalidated when constitutional and ordinary law conflict. It must also be our law: Each generation must have the capacity to change the Constitution to reflect its values.

Originalism, as we have understood and justified it, provides the only theory that reconciles these three normatively attractive features of a constitution. Originalism provides a binding, determinable meaning, making the Constitution formal law like other written law. The supermajoritarian process that generates the Constitution and its amendments provides substantial assurance of its good quality. Finally, the amendment process that originalism protects permits each generation to make the Constitution its own, by deciding whether to place its additional provisions in the Constitution on much the same terms as previous generations did.

First, originalism makes the Constitution formal law. Originalism's essential claim is that the meaning of law is fixed at the time of its enactment, permitting citizens to rely on it into the indefinite future. Our own version of originalism helps resolve ambiguities and vagueness by reference to other materials fixed by history—original interpretive methods. It thus reinforces the objective and formal nature of constitutional law, promoting additional stability and reliance.

In contrast, living constitutionalism undermines the objectivity of law. By its very nature, it seeks to root constitutional decisions in something other than the original meaning of the written text. What constitutes that secret sauce of constitutional decision making is something about which living constitutionalists themselves disagree. But the additional element, whether evolving moral principles or the current majority's view of good constitutional norms, is guaranteed to fluctuate, undermining the stability and reliance on rights that the Constitution's original meaning provides.

Jack Balkin's theory of living originalism suffers from defects similar to living constitutionalism. He argues that the Constitution has an open-ended texture where successive generations, spurred on by social movements of the time, can construe its principles in radically different ways. But his extremely flexible and mutable conception of constitutional law gravely undermines the stabilizing function he himself recognizes as essential to the concept of basic law, not to mention the function of protecting rights. The difficulty with Balkin's theory is shared more generally by constructionist originalists because the parts of constitutional law that are subject to construction depend on contestable choices external to the Constitution and are thus unconstrained by formal law.

Second, under our approach to originalism, the Constitution is higher law because it is of higher quality than the ordinary legislation that it displaces when the two conflict. The appropriate supermajority rules used to enact the Constitution's provisions are likely to produce such higher quality entrenchments. The desirability of these provisions justifies judges in displacing ordinary law with higher law. Moreover, our argument creates an identity between formal law and higher law. Because the Constitution is higher law by virtue of the consensus that gave rise to it, we have shown that it should be interpreted according to the interpretive rules the Framers' generation would have deemed applicable to it— interpretive rules that reflect originalism as conventionally understood.

Living constitutionalism, in contrast, has no plausible theory of why its process of constitutional interpretation likely leads to good results. As we have shown, updating the Constitution through judicial interpretation has none of the virtues of the consensus-producing procedures that are at the heart of a good process for constitution making. Constructionist originalism has similar problems whenever it resorts to construction. The principles chosen for construction do not have to reflect majoritarian support, let alone consensus. They do not relate to a process that is likely to render constitutional decisions beneficent.

Bruce Ackerman does have a theory of the Constitution that lays claim to its being genuinely higher law. He argues that constitutional moments can occur when a popular consensus of "breadth, depth and decisiveness" is reached.[14] For instance, Ackerman claims that Congress legitimately gained essentially plenary constitutional powers over economic matters because, as part of the New Deal, the president and Congress used such powers through successive elections, and the Court acceded to them.[15] But the defect of Ackerman's theory is that his higher law is decidedly not formal law. This lack of formality in turn creates uncertainty about its status and content that makes it impossible to function as higher law.

For instance, plausible but easily contestable claims have been made that Ackerman's criteria for a constitutional moment were satisfied in numerous episodes, including the emergence of Jacksonian democracy, the end of Reconstruction, the establishment of US imperialism, and the civil rights movement.[16] But even if a constitutional moment had clearly occurred, tremendous uncertainty remains about what the moment established. To take just one example, it is not clear whether the alleged constitutional moment during the New Deal was restricted to the expansion of the Commerce Clause or also included the elimination of economic due process. These two types of uncertainty—about when a constitutional moment occurs and what is its content—deprive constitutional norms of the deliberativeness, seriousness, and consciousness of purpose that Ackerman himself believes are required to amend the Constitution intelligently.

Third, under our view, the Constitution is also our law. It is ours by virtue of the fact that each generation can amend the Constitution under the same rules as previous generations could amend and under rules similar to those employed by the Founding generation. The democratic and deliberative process of constitutional amendments ensures that all voters have a chance to participate. It is manifestly a structure where "We the People" remain the pivotal decision makers.

But a vibrant amendment process and vigorous constitutional politics that draw in the citizenry at large are possible only through originalism. It is originalism that sustains the amendment process because it forces those who want to change the Constitution to use that process rather than persuade the Court to transform the Constitution without requiring a consensus of the American people.

The judicial updating inherent in living constitutionalism is necessarily in tension with a constitution belonging to the whole people. Supreme Court decisions may sometimes reflect popular social movements, but social movements are various and conflicting. The Tea Party does not agree with Occupy Wall Street. Secularists fight with those who want a politics animated by Christian values. It is justices who choose which movement to embody in their decisions. Their decisive role ensures that, under living constitutionalism, "We the Elite Lawyers" rather than "We the People" rule.

To be clear, we are not making an ideological point. Elites sometimes favor interests on the right and sometimes interests on the left. But the social movements that the Supreme Court chooses to heed almost always have elite support.

Our conception of "our law" also has the great advantage of making its content coextensive with formal law and higher law. Some of the formal law was enacted by the original Constitution, and the rest was enacted by the similarly stringent process of constitutional amendment. Thus, all constitutional law derives from a similar process of intense public deliberation.

The union of our law, higher law, and formal law is a great achievement of originalism—a correspondence of elegance and beauty that helps sustain the Republic. The final aspect of the tragedy of nonoriginalism is that years of nonoriginalist jurisprudence have obscured the powerful identity among these avatars of law, which is a large part of the genius of the system of government we have inherited.

Our understanding of the making of the Constitution and its proper interpretation links the generations together in a continuing enterprise of self-government. Each generation can participate on equal terms in adding to our fundamental document. Each generation also reaps the advantages of the work done by previous generations. Each generation can be assured that its work will be respected by the next, just as it respects the work of its predecessors. Edmund Burke famously said that a good society was a compact among the dead, the living, and the unborn as traditions of a past age become refined in the present with a view to additional developments in the future.[17] The Constitution, as generated through successive supermajoritarian processes and as interpreted according to its original meaning, translates Burke's great insight into the most effective legal mechanism for the enduring governance of a flourishing society.

NOTES

1. Originalism

1. Letter from James Madison to Henry Lee (June 25, 1824), in *The Writings of James Madison*, vol. 9: 1819–1836, ed. Galliard Hunt (Whitefish, Montana: Kessinger Publishing, 2010) (1910), 192.
2. See Randy E. Barnett, *Restoring the Lost Constitution: The Presumption of Liberty* (Princeton, NJ: Princeton University Press, 2005); Jack Balkin, *Living Originalism* (Cambridge, MA: Belknap Press of Harvard University Press, 2011).
3. U.S. Const. art. II, sec. 2; art. I, sec. 5.
4. For the argument that originalism advances democracy, see Robert H. Bork, *The Tempting of America* (New York: Touchstone, 1991), 143–153 ("In truth, only the approach of original understanding meets the criteria that any theory of constitutional adjudication must meet in order to possess democratic legitimacy.").
5. See generally Antonin Scalia, "Originalism: The Lesser Evil," *University of Cincinnati Law Review* 57 (1989): 849, 863–864.
6. The constraint rationale for originalism may animate *Employment Division v. Smith*, 494 U.S. 872, 872–90 (1992), in which Justice Antonin Scalia, a noted originalist, spends little time investigating the original meaning of the Free Exercise Clause but emphasizes that his result will provide a clearer rule than other constructions.
7. See generally Barnett, *Restoring the Lost Constitution*, 1–131.
8. Keith E. Whittington, *Constitutional Interpretation: Textual Meaning, Original Intent & Judicial Review* (Lawrence: University Press of Kanas, 1999), 137.
9. Ibid. at 142 ("I adopt the metaphorical label. . . . [P]opular sovereignty is a metaphor for our constitutional order. Our Constitution is like self government, but it is not actually self government.")
10. See Akhil Reed Amar, "The Central Meaning of Republican Government: Popular Sovereignty, Majority Rule, and the Denominator Problem," *University of Colorado Law Review* 65 (1994): 749.

11. *Cf.* James M. Buchanan and Gordon Tullock, *The Calculus of Consent: Logical Foundations of Constitutional Democracy* (Ann Arbor: University of Michigan Press, 1962), 15.
12. See Akhil Reed Amar, "Foreword: The Document and the Doctrine," *Harvard Law Review* 114 (2000): 26.
13. See Paul Brest, "The Misconceived Quest for the Original Understanding," *Boston University Law Review* 60 (1980): 204.
14. Lawrence B. Solum, "*District of Columbia v. Heller and Originalism*," *Northwestern University Law Review* 103 (2010): 923, 951–952.
15. See Barnett, *Restoring the Lost Constitution*, 118–125; Whittington, *Constitutional Interpretation*, 7–15.
16. See, e.g., Peter J. Smith, "How Different Are Originalism and Non-Originalism?" *Hastings Law Journal* 62 (2011): 707, 721–722.
17. See Michael W. McConnell, "Textualism and the Dead Hand of the Past," *George Washington Law Review* 66 (1998): 1127, 1127–1128.
18. See David E. Bernstein, "Philip Sober Controlling Philip Drunk: *Buchanan v. Warley* in Historical Perspective," *Vanderbilt Law Review* 51 (1998): 797, 815 (discussing this Progressive attack).
19. See Richard A. Primus, "When Should Original Meanings Matter?" *Michigan Law Review* 107 (2008): 165, 193–195.
20. See, e.g., Thurgood Marshall, Commentary, "Reflections on the Bicentennial of the United States Constitution," *Harvard Law Review* 101 (1987): 1, 2.
21. See *Brown v. Board of Education*, 347 U.S. 483 (1954).
22. See Alexander M. Bickel, "The Original Understanding and the Segregation Decision," *Harvard Law Review* 69 (1955): 1; Alfred Avins, "De Facto and De Jure School Segregation: Some Reflected Light on the Fourteenth Amendment from the Civil Rights Act of 1875," *Mississippi Law Journal* 38 (1967): 179; Michael Klarman, "An Interpretive History of Modern Equal Protection," *Michigan Law Review* 90 (1991): 213.
23. See Michael W. McConnell, "Originalism and the Segregation Decisions," *Virginia Law Review* 81 (1995): 947.
24. Randy E. Barnett, "Scalia's Infidelity: A Critique of 'Faint-Hearted' Originalism," *University of Cincinnati Law Review* 75 (2006): 7, 12.
25. See William Michael Treanor, "The Original Understanding of the Takings Clause and the Political Process," *Columbia Law Review* 95 (1995): 782, 856 (arguing that originalism is animated by the belief that "the rule of law requires judges to follow externally imposed rules").
26. To be more exact, statutes are passed, not under simple majority rule, but under a tricameral process that creates the equivalent of a mild supermajority rule. See John O. McGinnis and Michael B. Rappaport, "Our Supermajoritarian Constitution," *Texas Law Review* 80 (2002): 703, 769–774. But this

process is not nearly as stringent as the supermajoritarian process for enacting and amending the Constitution and is not stringent enough to correct for the serious defects in majoritarian entrenchment.

27. The reasons for the view that majority rule is beneficial are complex, but they include both preference and epistemic arguments. See Frank I. Michelman, "Why Voting," *Loyola of Los Angeles Law Review* 34 (2001): 985, 996. One important exception to the presumed beneficence of majority rule occurs if citizens have preferences of different intensity about an issue. In that case, a majority that enjoys modest benefits can get a law enacted, even if the minority suffers much greater costs. In chapter 3 we suggest that supermajoritarian entrenchment actually tempers this problem as well.

28. *Cf.* Robert A. Schapiro, "Identity and Interpretation in State Constitutional Law," *Virginia Law Review* 84 (1998): 389, 394 (stating that state constitutionalism helps transcend communal identities).

29. On the veil of ignorance, see Michael A. Fitts, "Can Ignorance Be Bliss? Imperfect Information as a Positive Influence in Political Institutions," *Michigan Law Review* 88 (1990): 917, 922–923.

30. Again, the one glaring defect in those supermajority rules was their exclusion of African Americans and women from the franchise, which we discuss below.

31. U.S. Const. art. V.

32. U.S. Const. art. VII.

33. See Catherine Drinker Bowen, *Miracle at Philadelphia: The Story of the Constitutional Convention, May to September 1787* (Boston: Little, Brown and Company, 1966), 225–228.

34. See Michael B. Rappaport, "The Original Meaning of the Recess Appointments Clause," *UCLA Law Review* 52 (2005): 1487, 1494–1495 n. 21.

35. See John O. McGinnis, "Justice Without Justices," *Constitutional Commentary* 16 (1999): 541, 542–543 (discussing factors that make Supreme Court justices remote).

36. For similar but distinct arguments about why the Constitution and its amendments should take priority over judicial doctrine, see Amar, "Foreword," 34–48.

37. The third alternative of departing from some of the provisions of an imperfect constitution can take several different forms, depending on which institution does the departing. Here we focus on departures by the judiciary because it is the most commonly proposed alternative.

2. The Nature of the Argument

1. We should also note that we are discussing here a good constitution for liberal democracies. Just as John Rawls limits the extension of his theory of justice to

liberal democracies, our prescriptions here are limited to a society with the characteristics, material and cultural, that can sustain such democracies.

2. See Sotirios A. Barber, "Professor Eisgruber, the Constitution and the Good Society," *Fordham Law Review* 69 (2001): 2151, 2151–2152; Steven P. Croley, "The Majoritarian Difficulty: Elective Judiciaries and the Rule of Law," *University of Chicago Law Review* 62 (1995): 689, 694–697.

3. Barry Friedman and Scott B. Smith, "The Sedimentary Constitution," *University of Pennsylvania Law Review* 147 (1998): 1, 87.

4. See Hannah Arendt, *Crises of the Republic* (New York: Harcourt Brace & Company, 1972), 76.

5. While we say that constitutions should be assessed based on their consequences for "the welfare of the people of the nation," we do not mean to imply that foreigners do not count, but merely to put to the side the complicated issue of the correct weighing of foreigners in this context.

6. *See* Richard Mervyn Hare, *Moral Thinking: Its Levels, Methods, and Point* (New York: Oxford University Press, 1982); see also John Gray, "Indirect Utility and Fundamental Rights," J. Soc. Phil & Pol p 1 (Spring 1984). For a general discussion for the nonspecialist of the arguments for and against such an approach, see William H. Shaw, *Contemporary Ethics: Taking Account of Utilitarianism* (Malden, MA: Blackwell Publishers Inc., 1999).

7. Our consequentialism is also welfare-oriented in the sense that we believe that the primary value that should be maximized is human welfare. We are aware that there is significant controversy about what constitutes a person's welfare. Different views argue that it involves either the satisfaction of a person's preferences or the attainment of a list of objectively desirable characteristics. We do not believe it is necessary to address or select between these rival views here. In our judgment, the correct approach to determining a person's welfare includes a significant degree of satisfying his or her preferences, but takes into account that those preferences can be based on false beliefs, failures of rationality, or other problems. Therefore, an account of a person's welfare needs to revise or ignore some of those preferences. In our view, the exact resolution of this dispute between properly sanitized preferences and the attainment of a list of objective characteristics is unlikely to have a significant effect on the character of the good constitution or the argument for originalism.

8. In judging the combination of the Articles of Confederation and the state constitutions to fall into the category of a fair constitution, we are excluding from our evaluation those constitutions' allowance of slavery and other exclusions. The approval of slavery would make those constitutions significantly inferior to a fair constitution.

9. It is true that we argue in this book that a supermajoritarian process has a

strong tendency to rely on accurate factual views. But this effect is limited and depends on a variety of assumptions that may not hold in all circumstances. As a result, someone with a belief in the strong grounds for his or her factual views might be justified, from this perspective, in rejecting the results of the supermajoritarian process on the grounds that they were based on factually inaccurate premises.

10. We qualify our arguments here as addressed to reasonable people because we readily admit that fanatics may not accept them. By fanatics, we mean people who think it is better to take any chance, however small, to get their vision of society instantiated, whatever the competing considerations and whatever the costs.

11. Our view of the US Constitution thus parallels Paul Bator's view of the criminal trial. No human institutions can be certain of being transcendentally correct. The results obtained by the best procedures on offer have a claim to finality. See Paul M. Bator, "Finality in Criminal Law and Federal Habeas Corpus for State Prisoners," *Harvard Law Review* 76 (1963): 441, 447–448.

3. The Supermajoritarian Theory of Constitutionalism

1. By democratic representatives, we include anyone elected to make decisions about legal enactments, including both legislators and members of conventions elected to decide on constitutional provisions.

2. The preference perspective is discussed in greater depth in John O. McGinnis and Michael B. Rappaport, "Majority and Supermajority Rules: Three Views of the Capitol," *Texas Law Review* 85 (2007): 1115, 1152.

3. The accuracy perspective is discussed in greater depth in John O. McGinnis and Michael Rappaport, "The Condorcet Case for Supermajority Rules," *Supreme Court Economic Review* 16 (2008): 67, 73.

4. See generally McGinnis and Rappaport, "Majority and Supermajority Rules" (offering a preference model to explain the operation of supermajority rules); McGinnis and Rappaport, "The Condorcet Case for Supermajority Rules" (offering an accuracy model to explain the operation of supermajority rules).

5. The reason is that only laws that secure fifty-one votes or more produce net benefits, and only such laws pass.

6. In some instances, we believe that supermajority rule is better than majority rule even for ordinary legislation. But the optimal supermajority rule in that context is generally much less stringent than the optimal rule for entrenchment. For a more complete discussion of voting rules for ordinary legislation, see John O. McGinnis and Michael B. Rappaport, "Our Supermajoritarian Constitution," *Texas Law Review* 80 (2002): 703; McGinnis and Rappaport, "Majority and Supermajority Rules."

7. In other writings, we have suggested that to complete the analysis of the difference between majority and supermajority rule, we must consider redrafted as well as marginal legislation. See McGinnis and Rappaport, "Our Supermajoritarian Constitution," 734 n. 136. Redrafted enactments are those enactments blocked by majority rule that are redrafted to get additional support under majority rule. In the context of entrenchment, we think this additional concept simply underscores the advantages of supermajority rule. To gain supermajority support, constitutional provisions that could not succeed under majority rule would have to be redrafted to get consensus and more bipartisan support. Thus, almost by definition, redrafted legislation would represent an improvement, making supermajority rule better than majority rule for entrenchments by an even larger margin.

8. See, for example, Rick A. Swanson and Albert P. Melone, "The Partisan Factor and Judicial Behavior in the Illinois Supreme Court," *Southern Illinois University Law Journal* 19 (1995): 303, 305 (arguing that partisan identification helps voters cast more informed votes).

9. Legislators will have the support of citizens if citizens favor the partisan measures for strategic reasons. Legislators will lack the support of citizens if citizens do not favor the entrenchments for strategic reasons, but legislators can exploit agency costs to pursue a measure that citizens do not favor.

10. The problem of partisanship entrenchment has been recognized in the legal literature largely in the context of stacking the Supreme Court with partisans of one party. See, for example, Michael J. Gerhardt, "The Constitution Outside the Courts," *Drake Law Review* 51 (2003): 775, 789. But majoritarian entrenchment by the legislature presents a more extreme version of the same problem because it is easier for legislators to coordinate on a present entrenchment than for the president and his or her party to ensure that judges they appoint will do so in the future.

11. It might be argued that parties could avoid the prisoner's dilemma created by majoritarian entrenchment simply by entrenching a prohibition on matters that the other party would entrench when it came to power. One difficulty with this strategy is that a party cannot necessarily predict the full range of measures the other party will want to entrench and thus faces far more uncertainty in determining what entrenchments to prohibit than in determining what entrenchments to make. For instance, one party may seem to be interested in entrenching healthcare entitlements. Although that entrenchment could be prohibited, a party coming to power might also desire to make a different entrenchment. Moreover, it is often harder to motivate people to prohibit potential entrenchments of another party. Because the other party is not in power, their potential entrenchments are actions to be taken in the future, making them appear less salient in the politics of the present.

12. We discuss below how vote trading can help with problem of minority prefer-
    ences, but we also show that supermajority rule remains superior to majority
    rule even with vote trading.

13. See Michael A. Fitts, "Can Ignorance Be Bliss? Imperfect Information as a
    Positive Influence in Political Institutions," *Michigan Law Review* 88 (1990):
    917, 922–923.

14. It might be argued that a majority entrenchment rule would also establish a lim-
    ited veil of ignorance because entrenched provisions passed by a majority would
    still require a supermajority to amend. Although a majority entrenchment rule
    would also help to establish a veil of ignorance, it would not function as well as
    supermajority rule because it would not address the problem of majoritarian
    threats. A supermajority entrenchment rule would be superior because the
    majority entrenchment rule would produce the undesirable consequence of
    allowing a majority to threaten to pass problematic entrenchments in order to
    secure the repeal of an existing entrenchment that it disliked. To illustrate this
    problem, assume that a majority lacks the supermajority of votes needed to
    repeal an existing constitutional provision. That majority, however, does have
    the power to pass a new entrenchment. To secure the additional votes necessary
    to repeal the constitutional provision from those who are opposed to its repeal,
    the majority could threaten to entrench another measure that is disliked by the
    minority even more than the repeal of the existing entrenchment. If this threat
    succeeded, it would reduce the extent to which constitutional provisions are
    entrenched. But even if it did not always succeed, it would create a situation
    where the possible passage of constitutional amendments could be used as bar-
    gaining chips in an effort to secure repeal of existing amendments. Such polit-
    ical games can only undermine the public's allegiance to the constitution.

15. See Adrian Vermeule, "Veil of Ignorance Rules in Constitutional Law," *Yale
    Law Journal* 111 (2001): 399, 417. A high discount rate suggests that future con-
    cerns are given substantially less weight than present concerns in decision
    making.

16. Ibid., 418.

17. Although a ruling coalition could not easily pass constitutional amendments
    when existing constitutional provisions no longer serve its interests, it is pos-
    sible that judges could depart from the original meaning of those provisions
    when desired by the ruling coalition. We discuss ways for inducing judges to
    follow the original meaning below, arguing that the best method involves
    developing a legal culture that values originalism. But even if one ignores this
    cultural effect and assumes that judges may sometimes not follow the original
    meaning, that would not allow a ruling coalition to dictate constitutional
    results because the Supreme Court's behavior is neither predictable nor easily
    controlled.

18. Vermeule, "Veil of Ignorance Rules in Constitutional Law," 418.

19. It is also worthwhile drawing a distinction among the three types of preferences for consensus, bipartisanship, and protecting minority rights. Consensus and bipartisanship are preferences that people have that are unlikely to be realized under majority rule due to the prisoner's dilemma discussed in the text. By contrast, the preference for protecting minority rights may be a preference that the majority holds, but it may not be. Instead, protecting minority rights may be justified by the fact that a constitution that does so is likely to result in a greater satisfaction of preferences because the gains to minorities from protecting their vital interests may exceed the harm to majorities from preventing them from passing laws that they mildly favor. At the time of a constitution's enactment, people may happen to hold these preferences, but they are much more likely to do so if the entrenchments are difficult to eliminate and therefore establish a limited veil of ignorance.

20. As we noted in the model that assumes preferences of equal intensity, both supermajority rule and majority rule create a limited veil of ignorance. But, as we discussed above, supermajority rule creates a veil that is more effective and produces fewer side effects than does majority rule.

21. We also believe that a supermajority entrenchment rule is superior to a majority entrenchment rule under an assumption of unequal intensities and no vote trading. A supermajority rule is superior to majority rule at promoting consensus entrenchments. It is true that the rule may not work as well as it does under an equal intensity model because there could be intense opponents of the entrenchment. But supermajority rule is still superior because the number of intense opponents is considerably smaller under supermajority rule. A supermajority rule is superior at promoting bipartisanship for much the same reasons. While there can be intense opposition from one party, there can be a much larger intense opposition under majority rule. Supermajority rule also does a better job of protecting minority rights. As we discussed in the case of equal intensity, supermajority rule creates a more effective and more smoothly functioning veil of ignorance. While majority rule is likely to be superior in regard to narrow preferences, supermajority rule is very likely to be superior overall for much the same reasons that it was in the vote-trading case: The marginal entrenchments are the least desirable of the beneficial entrenchments that are passed, and the benefits of these entrenchments are likely to be outweighed by the significant benefits of the other three values.

22. See Thomas Stratmann, "Logrolling," *Perspectives on Public Choice: A Handbook*, ed. Dennis C. Mueller (New York: Cambridge University Press, 1997), 328–332.

23. Cycling occurs when there is no majority victor—when no single proposal can defeat others in pairwise contests. Consequently, proposal A may defeat B, B

may defeat C, and C may defeat A. As a result, there may be no majority victor. See Saul Levmore, "Voting Paradoxes and Interest Groups," *Journal of Legal Studies* 28 (1999): 259, 261–263.

24. See David Luban, "Social Choice Theory as Jurisprudence," *Southern California Law Review* 69 (1996): 521, 536.

25. Another argument sometimes made against supermajority rule in a vote-trading context is that the strategic interactions of legislators under supermajority rule leads to unattractive package deals, where a consensus is obtained in favor of a package, although the individual provisions are unpopular. But neither the theory of supermajority nor the results of our own Constitution suggests that supermajority rules lead to unattractive package deals, certainly not any more than majority rule. First, supermajority rules make it harder to get unpopular provisions into the Constitution. An unpopular provision has a cost to each member of the coalition who agrees to its inclusion in the package while disagreeing with its substance. By requiring more members of the coalition, a supermajority raises these costs. Second, we do not observe packages made up of a panoply of special-interest provisions in proposals for constitutional amendments. Most constitutional amendments focus on single subjects. Of course, the original US Constitution necessarily covered more than one subject. But even here it would not be fair to characterize it as an unattractive package deal. There were two grand compromises—one between small states and large states and one on the subject of slavery—but these deals were necessary to forge the union of the thirteen states. Majority rule could not have dispensed with them and still created an effective system of governance that contained both small and large states, and free and slave states.

26. See Dennis C. Mueller, *Constitutional Democracy* (New York: Oxford University Press, 1996), 109.

27. If one does try to predict a distributional divergence between the two voting rules, the most likely divergence actually seems to suggest the superiority of supermajority rules. One major concern is that the wealthy might attempt to enact entrenched provisions that would provide benefits to the rich of the future. But, as we discussed earlier in this chapter, supermajority rule creates a veil of ignorance superior to that created by majority rule. The wealthy are unlikely to support such provisions if they cannot predict that their children and/or grandchildren will also be wealthy and beneficiaries of these provisions. Thus, supermajority rule may better deter than majority rule the wealthy from enacting class-based entrenchments.

28. See Daniel A. Farber and Philip P. Frickey, *Law and Public Choice: A Critical Introduction* (Chicago: University of Chicago Press, 1991), 31 (describing evidence that "one factor in determining how a legislator votes is simply that legislator's view of the public interest").

29. For a more technical defense of the Condorcet Jury Theorem's application to legislative voting, see generally McGinnis and Rappaport, "The Condorcet Case for Supermajority Rules."

30. Prominent among legal theorists supporting this view are Jeremy Waldon and Frank Michelman. See, for example, David M. Estlund, Jeremy Waldron, Bernard Grofman, and Scott L. Feld, "Democratic Theory and the Public Interest: Condorcet and Rousseau Revisited," *American Political Science Review* 83 (1989): 1317, 1317–1318 (applying the Condorcet Jury Theorem to Rousseau's theory of the general will to justify majority rule); Frank I. Michelman, "Why Voting?" *Loyola Los Angeles Law Review* 34 (2001): 985, 996 (stating that, in an epistemic theory of justice, the Condorcet Jury Theorem serves as justification for majority rule).

31. See, for example, Dennis C. Mueller, *Public Choice III* (New York: Cambridge University Press, 2003), 129–133 (describing the Condorcet Jury Theorem).

32. The Condorcet Jury Theorem has been generalized to analyze more than two alternatives. See Christian List and Robert E. Goodin, "Epistemic Democracy: Generalizing the Condorcet Jury Theorem," *Journal of Political Philosophy* 9 (2001): 277, 285 (extending the Condorcet Jury Theorem to a case with k options). We look at two alternatives in this section to simplify the analysis.

33. Ibid., 285.

34. One might think that legislators do evaluate factual states of the world as part of their assessment of legislation. In that case, the Condorcet Jury Theorem may apply more directly.

35. We are not arguing and do not believe that legislators consider only the welfare of the people in deciding whether to vote for an entrenchment. But we do believe that considerations of the welfare of the people are an aspect of almost any representative's vote. Thus, we are deploying an accuracy model to consider only an aspect of legislative voting. Of course, it may well be that the representatives have some other metric by which all evaluate legislation. Given any agreed-upon criterion that can be measured objectively, the Condorcet framework can be used to assess the accuracy rates of legislators in determining whether legislation meets this criterion.

36. We use the term "Condorcet approach" to refer to our modification of the assumptions of the Condorcet Jury Theorem. While our model still employs the basic framework of the Jury Theorem, it modifies enough of the assumptions to warrant a slightly different name.

37. See McGinnis and Rappaport, "The Condorcet Case for Supermajority Rules," 73–101.

38. This point is explicit in our discussion of the Condorcet Jury Theorem, but it has also been specifically made in the law review literature. See Lewis A. Kornhauser, "Adjudication by a Resource-Constrained Team: Hierarchy and

Precedent in a Judicial System," *Southern California Law Review* 68 (1995): 1605, 1626 n. 43 (arguing this point in the context of judicial decision making).

39. The representativeness heuristic tends to make people extrapolate overconfidently about predicted characteristics of a class based on a small sample size of which they happen to be aware. See Amos Tversky and Daniel Kahneman, "Belief in the Law of Small Numbers," *Judgment Under Uncertainty: Heuristics and Biases,* ed. Daniel Kahneman et al. (New York: Cambridge University Press, 1982), 23, 24–25. If the sample consists of events rather than objects, the heuristic should tend to make people extrapolate in a similarly irrational manner from events of which they are aware to uncertain future events. Thus, individuals tend to think that future events will resemble past events more than probability warrants. For an important present-day application to people's mistaken attitudes about the stock market, see Robert J. Shiller, *Irrational Exuberance* (Princeton, NJ: Princeton University Press, 2000), 144.

40. Ibid., 142–138.

41. See also, U.S. Const. art. I, sec. 10, cl. 1 (providing an example of a constitutional provision that might restrain such legislation by prohibiting states from "impairing the obligation of contracts").

42. The veil of ignorance guards against biases based on partiality (as opposed to cognitive failures, such as the heuristic of assuming that the future will be like the present). In particular, it guards against a bias that afflicts all decision makers—favoring the interests of oneself, one's family, friends, and socioeconomic class.

43. One might think that Article V's double supermajoritarian rule both in the Congress and in state legislatures increases the power of this effect. See U.S. Const. art. V. Very few constitutional amendments are proposed by Congress and sent to the states for ratification. *Congressional Quarterly's Guide to Congress* 1 (Washington: Congressional Quarterly, Inc., 2000), 360 ("[o]nly thirty-three proposals have been approved [by Congress] and sent to the states for ratification.") This restricted agenda ensures substantial scrutiny of the proposals and a rich stream of information about their merits, raising the accuracy rate of the state legislators who are to consider them.

44. See McGinnis and Rappaport, "The Condorcet Case for Supermajority Rules," 100–103.

45. See McGinnis and Rappaport, "Majority and Supermajority Rules," 1167.

46. Supermajority rule may also improve the quality of entrenchment proposals under this analysis. Because of the high hurdle that entrenchment proposals face, members of the legislature are less likely to advance weak ones.

47. Risk-averse people would rather face a certain smaller loss than risk the possibility of a greater loss, even though the probability of that loss times its value is

equal to the certain loss. That is the reason individuals purchase insurance. See Richard A. Posner, *Economic Analysis of Law* (Boston, MA: Little, Brown & Co., 1976), 75–76.

48. We have demonstrated this fact elsewhere with numerical examples. See McGinnis and Rappaport, "Majority and Supermajority Rules," 1169–1170.

49. The strongest argument against our claim that constitutional provisions accords with the preferences of the people is that the supermajority rule might appear to block good marginal provisions. If the marginal provisions are desirable, then supermajority rules prevent those from being enacted and that deprives the nation of those desirable provisions. This objection fails, however, for two basic reasons. First, even if a supermajority rule were to block good marginal entrenchments, this obstruction would not mean that the entrenchments passed under the supermajority rule would not be good ones. The desirability of marginal entrenchments is the test for whether supermajority rule is superior to marginal rule. The desirability of marginal entrenchments does not indicate whether the entrenchments passed under the supermajority rule are desirable. Second, even assuming that marginal entrenchments are directly relevant to the desirability of the entrenchments passed under a supermajority rule, we have already shown that such marginal entrenchments are very likely to be undesirable. Above, we argued that even if marginal entrenchments are desirable based on the narrow preferences of the people, they are the least desirable of those entrenchments because they are passed by a mere majority. Those small benefits in terms of narrow preferences are likely to be far outweighed by the significant costs in terms of consensus, partisanship, and minority rights that marginal entrenchments incur.

50. One reason why one might question whether supermajority rules produce good entrenchments under the preference model is the existence of special interests. Special interests, which have disproportionate influence in the political process because of their organizational advantages, might use their power to promote bad entrenchments or block good ones. While special interests certainly are important in regard to legislation, they are considerably less influential in the entrenchment context. Special interests wield less influence in the entrenchment context because they possess less of an information advantage. The ordinary public knows much more about proposed constitutional enactments than it does about the average piece of legislation for a variety of reasons: There are relatively few proposed constitutional enactments that are seriously considered; they are more important than the average piece of legislation, which can be repealed more easily; and they are considered to be a more interesting, politically salient topic.

51. McGinnis and Rappaport, "The Condorcet Case for Supermajority Rules," 113.

4. The Compliance of the US Constitution with Desirable Supermajority Rules

1. See U.S. Const. art. V.

2. Ibid.

3. See Akhil Reed Amar, "The Central Meaning of Republican Government: Popular Sovereignty, Majority Rule, and the Denominator Problem," *University of Colorado Law Review* 65 (1994): 749, 774.

4. Five states demanded a bill of rights as part of the ratification process. See, for example, James W. Ely, Jr., *The Guardian of Every Other Right: A Constitutional History of Property Rights* (Oxford: Oxford University Press, 1998), 52. If majority rule had been in place, it would have been easier to ignore these states, but under the Constitution's requirement of the approval of nine of thirteen states for ratification of the Constitution, support from these states was necessary.

5. It is well established that the doctrine of federalism emerged as a compromise between nationalist and more states-oriented forces. Gordon Wood, *The Creation of the American Republic, 1776–1787* (Chapel Hill: University of North Carolina Press, 1969), 525–526. At the convention, the nationalists introduced the Virginia Plan; in response, the small states proposed the more states-oriented New Jersey Plan. See Richard Beeman, *Plain Honest Men: The Making of the American Constitution* (New York: Random House, 2009), 88. Subsequently, it was unclear which side, given the shifting attendance of delegates, had a majority (ibid., 172–173), and a committee was appointed to find a compromise that formed the basis of the eventual Constitution (ibid., 189). While it was possible that either the nationalists or their opponents might have gained a majority for their plan in the convention or among the ratifying states, the need to secure a consensus of the ratifying states (whatever the precise consensus requirement turned out to be) would have made such a strategy extremely risky. Instead, the Connecticut Compromise allowed the Constitution to secure the unanimous support of the twelve states at the convention and to move forward to the ratification process with significant momentum.

6. Michael Kammen, *A Machine That Would Go of Itself: The Constitution in American Culture* (New York: Knopf, 1986), 162 (quoting William Gladstone).

7. As James Madison himself stated, Article V "guards equally against that extreme facility, which would render the Constitution too mutable; and that extreme difficulty, which might perpetuate its discovered faults." See Alexander Hamilton, James Madison, and Jon Jay, *The Federalist*, No. 43, ed. Clinton Rossiter (New York: New American Library, 1961).

8. Ibid.

9. See, for example, Hamilton, Madison, and Jay, *The Federalist*, No. 40, 251 (noting "the absurdity of subjecting the fate of twelve States to the perverseness or corruption of a thirteenth [i.e., Rhode Island]").

10. Our focus here is not to decide absolutely whether particular amendments are bad or good but rather to assess how Article V has performed overall in history. Our criteria for evaluating whether amendments are good or bad consist of two components, one abstract and one more specific. First, we consider whether the amendment comports with the outline of the liberal constitution set forth in Chapter 2. Second, because an amendment must be consistent with the long-term preferences of society, we evaluate the amendment in light of the popular preferences of its time as well as subsequent developments. Thus, we do not assess a provision by reference to some set of narrow political principles like socialism or libertarianism. Moreover, it generally becomes easier to evaluate amendments with the passage of time and with a perspective outside the controversies that gave rise to these proposals than it would be to make a similar judgment on contested contemporary issues of constitutional law.

    We have offered strong theoretical reasons to believe that relatively stringent supermajority rule is a good way of generating a constitution and superior to other methods. But we would be foolish to refuse to consider the results of this process in our evaluation of the method. Architecture progresses by attention to the laws of physics and the heuristics of engineering, but in evaluating building processes, we must consider how buildings constructed by these processes have stood the test of time.

11. See 1 Pub. Res. 3, at 97 (1789).

12. See Akhil Reed Amar, *The Bill of Rights: Creation and Construction* (New Haven, CT: Yale University Press, 1998), 15–16.

13. Ibid., 16–17. There does not seem any reason to believe that Congress is more likely to abuse discretion in setting the number of its members than in using its other powers.

14. See J. Res. No. 11–2, at 613 (1810).

15. See H.R.J. Res. No. 36–13, at 251 (1861).

16. See H.R.J. Res. No. 68–184, at 670 (1924).

17. See H.R.J. Res. No. 92–208, at 1523 (1972).

18. See H.R.J. Res. No. 95–554, at 3795 (1978).

19. As has been proposed by the District of Columbia–Maryland Reunion Act, H.R. 1858, 110th Congress (2007).

20. We could continue our assessment by discussing amendments that did not come quite as close to passage as these six, such as those that passed one house but foundered in the other. We believe, however, that the arguments above are sufficient. It is worth noting, though, that the proposed flag-burning amendment would have been proposed by the Congress had it received one more vote

in the Senate. See H.R.J. Res. No. 109–10 (2006) (passed by House); S.J. Res. No. 109–12 (2006) (rejected in Senate by one vote). A slightly less stringent amendment process might have permitted this amendment to pass, despite the fact that it appears to be a largely symbolic piece of legislation rather than an attempt to solve a real social problem.

21. See U.S. Const. amend. XVII. See George H. Haynes, *The Senate of the United States: Its History and Practice* (Boston, MA: Houghton Mifflin Company, 1938), 104.

22. See U.S. Const. amend. XIX.

23. See, for example, Bruce Ackerman, *We the People*, vol. 1: *Foundations* (Cambridge, MA: Belknap Press of Harvard University Press, 1991); David A. Richards, *Conscience and the Constitution: History, Theory, and Law of the Reconstruction Amendments* (Princeton, NJ: Princeton University Press, 1993).

24. See Bruce Ackerman, *We the People*, vol. 2: *Transformations* (Cambridge, MA: Belknap Press of Harvard University Press, 1998).

25. Ibid., 99–119, 207–34.

26. Akhil Reed Amar, *America's Constitution: A Biography* (New York: Random House, 2005), 366–368.

27. Moreover, since the Confederate state ratifications would not be necessary for the ratification of the amendment, any possible coercion of those states would not need to be justified as constitutional.

28. Indeed, if African Americans had been permitted to participate in ratification, their numbers are such that ratification might have been obtained even with the inclusion of southern states. Ratification would have been even more likely if those who had taken up arms against the union had been excluded from voting.

29. John Harrison, "The Lawfulness of the Reconstruction Amendments," *University of Chicago Law Review* 68 (2001): 375, 451–452.

30. The existing literature on the 14th Amendment does not exhaust all of the plausible theories. One set of promising theories—reduced denominator theories—is based on the idea that the purported secession of the former Confederate States operated to deprive them of their full status as states, either because the secession had destroyed the state governments or because they had become territories (with perhaps a moral obligation on the Union to readmit them as states when appropriate). See generally, Harrison, "The Lawfulness of the Reconstruction Amendments," 391–393, 410–414. These theories would eliminate the former Confederate States from the denominator, which would render the Amendment validly enacted, but would not understand the former Confederate States as fully seceding from the Union.

31. Even if one did conclude that the Civil War Amendments lacked the usual supermajoritarian consensus, we believe that following these Amendments

today would still be justifiable for two reasons. First, under our theory of correction of supermajoritarian failure that we outline in Chapter 6, we acknowledge that the original consensus of the Constitution is somewhat defective in part because of the restrictions on voting by African Americans. Because of this defect, some provisions may be absent from the original Constitution that would have been included, particularly provisions that protect against discrimination that would have been a priority for such a minority. As a result, we suggest that judicial correction to ameliorate such defects is more plausible than judicial updating.

We nevertheless conclude that the case for judicial correction today is still not strong enough. One important reason is that the Civil War Amendments provided the essential antidiscrimination that African Americans would have most likely demanded. But if these provisions had not been enacted, the case for judicial correction imposing similar provisions would be much stronger. Thus, even if no Fourteenth Amendment had been enacted, there would be a relatively strong case for following the antidiscrimination provisions of that Amendment.

Moreover, the case for following the full text of the Amendment is strengthened by our other principal reason for resisting judicial correction, namely that the judges would have a difficult time figuring out what corrections would be made and that this inquiry would be fraught with ideological divisiveness as judges disagreed about what provisions should be added to make the necessary corrections—an inquiry without any clear legal standard. These problems are much ameliorated if judges follow a plausible correction that was made through the amendment process even if that process fell a little short of the requisite consensus. Judges would then not have to determine what correction to apply: they would just have to follow the meaning of a textual provision that had been recognized as law for over a hundred years.

Second, in chapter 10 we argue that judges should follow precedent under certain conditions. One of these conditions occurs when failing to follow precedent causes enormous costs. Another occurs when the precedent would be endorsed by a consensus akin to that required to pass a constitutional amendment. Following the Civil War Amendments is independently justified as precedent under the first condition and quite possibly under the second. It would be enormously costly if the Supreme Court declared that these Amendments were not law. Settled constraints on discrimination by the government would be thrown into doubt and the diffuse sense of constitutional legitimacy would be gravely undermined if part of the text of the Constitution were to disappear by judicial decree. Moreover, it also seems likely that the Civil War Amendments command a consensus in society today.

32. U.S. Const. amend. XXVI ("The right of citizens of the United States, who are

eighteen years of age or older, to vote shall not be denied or abridged by the United States or any State on account of age").

33. *Oregon v. Mitchell*, 400 U.S. 112 (1970).

34. Robert Levy, "Suffrage-Age," *The Heritage Guide to the Constitution* (Washington, DC: Regnery, 2005): 432.

35. Nor does the passage of a single amendment that is now widely thought to be a mistake discredit the supermajoritarian process. Our point is not that the process is perfect, merely that it is good overall and superior to other processes. Moreover, the Eighteenth Amendment provides another example of the ability of the amendment process to overcome vested interests. Women were not yet fully represented in the polity, and yet Prohibition was widely seen as a response to women's concerns about the effects of excessive drinking, particularly the costs imposed on women through alcohol's fostering of spousal violence and its dissipation of male earnings that would otherwise support the family. See William N. Eskridge Jr., "Some Effects of Identity-Based Social Movements on Constitutional Law in the Twentieth Century," *Michigan Law Review* 100 (2002): 2062, 2113.

36. See U.S. Const. Amends. XX, XXV.

37. See Donald S. Lutz, "Toward a Theory of Constitutional Amendment," in *Responding to Imperfection: The Theory and Practice of Constitutional Amendment*, ed. Sanford Levinson (Princeton, NJ: Princeton University Press, 1995), 273.

38. Others have noted that lenient amendment processes are also used as a justification for judicial activism because the less strict process allows citizens to respond to judicial activism. See A. E. Dick Howard, "State Courts and Constitutional Rights in the Day of the Burger Court," *Virginia Law Review* 62 (1976): 873, 939.

39. See Sanford Levinson, "How the United States Constitution Contributes to the Democratic Deficit in America," *Drake Law Review* 55 (2008): 859, 872–873.

40. See Lutz, "Toward a Theory," in *Responding to Imperfection*, 261. The Yugoslavian constitution was more difficult to amend, but Yugoslavia has ceased to exist.

41. Ibid.

42. For a discussion of how the political culture influences the amendment process in the United States and France, see Landon Wade Magnusson, "Article V Versus Article 89: Why the U.S. Does Not Overturn Supreme Court Rulings Through Amendment," *Syracuse Law Review* 62 (212): 75.

43. Lutz, "Toward a Theory," in *Responding to Imperfection*, 258.

44. As an absolute matter, it is not very difficult to get a two-thirds vote of both houses of Congress. It takes a two-thirds vote of both houses to override a presidential veto, Magnusson "Article V Versus Article 89" at 92, and yet an override

has occurred 110 times in US history. Ibid. Moreover, votes in favor of an override are likely more difficult than those in favor of an amendment because the president is generally calling in political chits to swell the opposition.

45. Lutz, "Toward a Theory," in *Responding to Imperfection*, 258.

46. As we discussed above, six amendments passed Congress but were not ratified. Twenty-seven amendments have been ratified.

47. Germany has a variety of important provisions and principles that cannot be amended. German Const. Art LXXIX § 3. These include amendments affecting the division of the federation into states (Länder), the participation on principle of the states (Länder) in legislation, or the basic principles laid down in Articles 1 ("Human Dignity") and 20 ("Basic Principles of State, Resistance"). Ibid. See Axel Tschentscher, "The Basic Law (Grundgesetz): The Constitution of the Federal Republic of Germany" (November 12, 2009). Available at http://ssrn .com/abstract=1501131. Portugal also makes some of its constitution unamendable. Portuguese Const. art. CCLXXXVIII. Available at http://app.parlamento .pt/site_antigo/ingles/cons_leg/Constitution_VII_revisao_definitive.pdf. Switzerland prohibits amendments that violate mandatory international law. Swiss Const. art. CLXXXXIII, Section 4, art. CLXXXXIV, Sections 2–3. Available at http://www.admin.ch/ch/e/rs/1/101.en.pdf (Articles 193 & 194).

48. See David S. Law, "Generic Constitutional Law," *Minnesota Law Review* 89 (2005): 652, 684, n. 125.

49. See Daniel B. Rodriguez, "State Constitutional Failure," *University of Illinois Law Review* 2011 (2011): 1243, 1272–1273.

50. *Compare* Akhil Reed Amar, "The Consent of the Governed: Constitutional Amendment Outside Article V," *Columbia Law Review* 94 (1994): 457, 461 (positing that Article V's unanimity requirement could potentially be bypassed through a series of two amendments), with Stephen M. Griffin, "The Nominee Is . . . Article V," *Constitutional Commentary* 12 (1995): 171, 173.

51. When the Constitution was enacted, the people of the nation placed far more importance on their state citizenship and under such circumstances, some form of equal state representation makes more sense. As time has passed, however, people have become far less associated with particular states; consequently, equal state representation seems much less justifiable.

52. The Balanced Budget Amendment is an example of an amendment that probably failed on account of this feature of the Constitution because that amendment would have restricted the power of Congress to run deficits and run up debt, a considerable power and one that aids members of Congress in rewarding interest groups, thereby advancing electoral prospects.

53. See Michael B. Rappaport, "Reforming Article V: The Problems Created by the National Convention Amendment Method and How to Fix Them," *Virginia Law Review* 96 (2010): 1509. There is an argument that much of the

fear of a runaway convention is not rational because the proposals of any convention would still have to surmount the hurdle of three-fourths of state legislatures to be enacted. See Ronald D. Rotunda and Stephen J. Safranek, "An Essay on Term Limits and a Call for a Constitutional Convention," *Marquette Law Review* 80 (1996): 227, 239. But an amendment not favored by state legislatures could pass in several different ways, including because the proposed amendment developed momentum; changed circumstances made the amendment more popular; Congress chose to have the ratification decision made by state conventions rather than state legislatures; or the runaway convention chose to employ a less than the three-fourths ratification rule and this decision was accepted by the nation.

54. See Michael B. Rappaport, "The Constitutionality of a Limited Convention: An Originalist Analysis," *Constitutional Commentary* 81 (2012): 53.

55. Notable recent examples of constitutional amendments that would have constrained Congress but were not passed were term limits, the line-item veto, and a balanced budget amendment. See Rappaport, "Reforming Article V," 1509.

56. It has been said that more delegates were elected on a platform of opposition to the Constitution than those elected on a platform of support. But what *is* decisive under the procedures in a representative democracy are the votes of representatives, not their campaign platforms. Indeed, a consensus is likely to prove better and more enduring if it occurs after deliberation—both among people electing representatives and among the representatives themselves. Deliberation necessarily involves the possibility of changing minds. Significantly, the decision of many ratification conventions to approve the Constitution was a different one than the voters made when selecting delegates to those conventions. As we stated above, in five conventions, the Federalists promised to add a bill of rights to the Constitution if it were approved. We simply do not know how many of the voters who supported delegates opposed to the Constitution would have changed their position if they were voting on that Constitution accompanied by a pledge of a bill of rights.

57. See *Journals of the Continental Congress, 1774–1789*, ed. Worthington Chauncey Ford et al. (Washington DC: Library of Congress, 1904–1937), 71–72, available at http://memory.loc.gov/cgi-bin/query/r?ammem/hlaw:@field(DOCID+@lit(jc03225)) (noting approval of the Congress's recommendation for a convention). It is unclear exactly how many states were present and voting, but it appears that all states that voted ultimately supported the recommendation; see also Edmund Cody Burnett, *The Continental Congress* (New York: MacMillan Co., 1941), 768–769 (describing approval of recommendation).

58. See Max Farrand, *The Framing of the Constitution of the United States* (New Haven, CT: Yale University Press, 1913), 11–12 (discussing Rhode Island's unique failure to attend).

59. See Clinton Rossiter, *1787: The Grand Convention* (New York: Macmillan, 1966), 54–55.
60. See S. Doc. No. 83–170, at 13 note m (1953) (indicating that thirty-nine of the fifty-five delegates who attended signed the document).
61. To proceed to the ratification stage, the Continental Congress probably had to agree to send it to the states for ratification. Bruce Ackerman and Neal Katyal, "Our Unconventional Founding," *University of Chicago Law Review* 62 (1995): 515–517. The strong support of the Philadelphia Convention was probably an important part of why the Congress agreed to do so.
62. See Catherine Drinker Bowen, *Miracle at Philadelphia: The Story of the Constitutional Convention, May to September, 1787* (Boston, MA: Little, Brown, 1986), 13.
63. Another way of looking at the Framers' choice is that they chose nine states because that was the number of states the approval of which was required for important decisions under the Articles of Confederation. See Amar, *America's Constitution*, 311. In that case the three-fourths requirement in Article V was chosen as the closest round fraction to reflect the proportion of states required for ratification in Article VII rather than the other way around.
64. There is another possible asymmetry between the constitutional origination and the amendment processes. In the former, only those states who agreed to the Constitution were bound, but in the amendment process those states who decline ratification are nevertheless bound if the amendment obtains ratification by three-quarters of the states. One might argue that this asymmetry tends to make the original Constitution less good than amendments because, in the origination process, states were under pressure to agree to the Constitution; the alternative was being cast out of the Union with possible dire consequences. But state decisions in the negative were understood not to be final, and North Carolina and Rhode Island in fact assented after they originally rejected the Constitution. See Beeman, *Plain Honest Men*, 391–392, 405. Thus, states did not in reality face such a harsh choice. Moreover, the sponsors of the Constitution wanted all the states to ratify it because the Union would then be stronger. As a result, the incentives to propose a good original constitution in this respect may have been even greater than those to propose a good amendment because, in the latter case, it does not matter if the ultimate support is not unanimous. Thus, our judgment is that the difference in the binding nature of the origination and the amendment processes does not detract significantly from the rough symmetry between the two.
65. Both of these problems arguably affected the constitutional enactment process. When Congress and the states supported a convention, they may have expected that the results would be a true amendment of the Articles and would go

through the Articles' amendment process. When the Philadelphia Convention chose a nine-thirteenths ratification requirement, delegates could have done so with an eye toward the degree of support they expected for the constitution that they were writing.

66. We should also note one clear departure from symmetry that we have already discussed in the section on reasonable stringency—the provision that prohibits amending the states' equal representation in the Senate. Whether or not this provision can be eliminated with two amendments, the process for eliminating it is certainly stricter than was the process for enacting it.

67. Georgia produced a temporary constitution in 1776. This document is reproduced in *The Revolutionary Records of the State of Georgia*, vol. 1, ed. Allen D. Candler (Atlanta, GA: The Franklin-Turner Co., 1908), 274–277.

5. The Continuing Desirability of an Old Supermajoritarian Constitution

1. See, for example, William E. Scheuerman, "Constitutionalism in an Age of Speed," *Constitutional Comment* 19 (2002): 354–355.

2. John Harrison, "The Lawfulness of the Reconstruction Amendments," *University of Chicago Law Review* 68 (2001): 375 (seeing the Constitution as capturing popular sovereignty like "lightning in a bottle").

3. We know of no constitution made under the kind of supermajoritarian rules we endorse that expressly contemplates living constitutionalism or judicial updating. It is true that the judiciaries of many nations have engaged in judicial updating of their constitutions, just as the Supreme Court has on occasion. Ran Hirschl has detailed the worldwide movement of judicial activism and explained it as an attempt by elites to preserve a redoubt of power. See Ran Hirschl, *Toward Juristocracy: The Origins and Consequences of the New Constitutionalism* (Cambridge, MA: Harvard University Press: 2004). But the existence of such practices does not show that the enactors of these constitutions would have endorsed them.

4. In Chapter 8, we respond to arguments that, despite risk aversion, supermajority rules for constitution making encourage delegations to the future because they make it hard to obtain agreement on constitutional provisions with definite meaning.

5. See *McCulloch v. Maryland*, 17 U.S. (4 Wheat.) 316, 406–08 (1819).

6. See Philip A. Hamburger, "The Constitution's Accommodation of Social Change," *Michigan Law Review* 88 (1989): 287.

7. See Robert A. Goldwin, Comment, "Original Intent and the Constitution," *Maryland Law Review* 47 (1987): 194–195.

8. See, for example, Robert G. Natelson, "The Legal Meaning of 'Commerce' in the Commerce Clause," *St. John's Law Review* 80 (2006): 789; Randy E.

Barnett, "The Original Meaning of the Commerce Clause," *University of Chicago Law Review* 68 (2001): 101.

9. The passage of time may strengthen rather than weaken the rationale for some provisions of the Constitution. For the most part, the Framers did not understand competition among the states to be a benefit produced by federalism, but in the modern world, that competition has become a strong argument for federalism.

10. See Hamburger, "The Constitution's Accommodation," 300.

11. See John O. McGinnis, "Reviving Tocqueville's America: The Rehnquist Court's Jurisprudence of Social Discovery," *California Law Review* 90 (2002): 566. On Condorcet grounds, small numbers are less likely to reach accurate results. See Adrian Vermeule, "Common Law Constitutionalism and the Limits of Reason," *Columbia Law Review* 107 (2007): 1493.

12. See Vermeule, "Common Law Constitutionalism," 1499–1500 (making a similar point about common law constitutionalism).

13. As we discussed in Chapter 3, even a majoritarian process that tapped into the community sentiment better than the judicial process does not provide a good mechanism for aggregating preferences and judgments in the entrenchment context.

14. It might be argued that even if following the Constitution's original meaning improves the quality of decisions, it also creates additional decision costs because the original meaning is difficult to discover. But as we discuss in Chapter 11, if the courts tried to follow the original meaning, a modern culture of originalism would develop, with legal scholars and historians providing substantial assistance in discovering that meaning.

15. See William M. Landes and Richard A. Posner, "Rational Judicial Behavior: A Statistical Study" (John M. Olin Law & Econ. Working Paper, Paper No. 404, 2008), 15–16, available at http://ssrn.com/abstract=1126403 (noting that justices have recently become more polarized and susceptible to block ideological voting).

16. It is a fundamental premise of the constitutional separation of powers that each branch seeks to aggrandize its own powers. See, for example, James Madison, "Federalist No. 51," *The Federalist Papers*, ed. Clinton Rossiter (New York: New American Library, 1961), 322; see also Jonathan R. Macey, "Judicial Preferences, Public Choice, and the Rules of Procedure," *Journal of Legal Studies* 23 (1994): 631.

17. See, for example, Tracey E. George, "Court Fixing," *Arizona Law Review* 43 (2001): 38.

18. It is important to note that this tendency is not necessarily malevolent. Judges naturally want to reach a result that is fair, and their preferences are one window into the often obscure landscape of fairness.

19. Compare *Griswold v. Connecticut*, 381 U.S. 479, 530 (1965) (Stewart, J., dissenting), with *Seminole Tribe of Fla. v. Florida*, 517 U.S. 44, 72 (1996) (Rehnquist, C.J.).

20. Compare *Lochner v. New York*, 198 U.S. 45, 75–76 (1905) (Holmes, J., dissenting), with *Roe v. Wade*, 410 U.S. 113, 152–53 (1973).

21. Some scholars have suggested that a virtue of an informal amendment process, or what we call judicial updating, is the fluidity it permits. See, for example, Reva B. Siegel, "Constitutional Culture, Social Movement Conflict and Constitutional Change: The Case of the De Facto ERA," *California Law Review* 94 (2006): 1327–1328. We have shown why just the opposite is the case. It is the formal constitution-making process that brings the consensus that establishes affection for the Constitution. Even apart from this point, claims like that of Professor Siegel fail to show how such an informal process is likely to lead to high-quality constitutional provisions.

22. See Heather K. Gerken, "The Hydraulics of Constitutional Reform: A Skeptical Response to Our Undemocratic Constitution," *Drake Law Review* 55 (2007): 939.

23. Recently, scholars have argued that judicial updating constitutes part of a larger social process in which political actors other than the judiciary help advance the ideas that are ultimately used to update the Constitution (ibid., 935). Although this is undoubtedly true as a factual matter, it does not change our normative critique. The existence of this social process does not erase the judiciary's necessary discretion to choose which ideas to incorporate into the Constitution from the many advanced to the Supreme Court justices.

24. For instance, the justices have acted to protect rights of minorities only when these minority rights have significant support. When minorities do not have the requisite level of political support, the Court has been unwilling to incur the attacks that protecting the minorities would occasion. See Michael J. Klarman, "Rethinking the Civil Rights and Civil Liberties Revolutions," *Virginia Law Review* 82 (1996): 16–18.

25. Some law professors and political scientists have recently argued that the Court follows public opinion. See Barry Friedman, *The Will of the People: How Public Opinion Has Influenced the Supreme Court and Shaped the Meaning of the Constitution* (New York: Farrar, Straus and Giroux, 2009) (arguing that the Supreme Court is a political actor that responds to constituencies). We are skeptical of this claim. That the Court is an institution constrained by other institutions should not be confused with the claim that it follows popular will in the manner of a legislature. First, the legislature is structured to reflect popular opinion, while the judiciary is insulated from it. See Jesse H. Choper, *Judicial Review and the National Political Process: A Functional Reconsideration of the Role of the Supreme Court* (Chicago: University of Chicago Press, 1980),

3–70. Second, consistent with this analysis, some political scientists have suggested that there is no convincing proof of the majoritarianism of the Supreme Court. See Jeffrey A. Segal and Harold J. Spaeth, *The Supreme Court and the Attitudinal Model* (Cambridge: Cambridge University Press, 1993), 331–332. There are whole areas of the law in which the judiciary is patently out of step with the public. For instance, even a Supreme Court made up of Republican appointees offers little or no support for prayer in public schools, although huge majorities support the policy. See Michael Comiskey, "The Rehnquist Court and American Values," *Judicature* 77 (1992): 265–266. The current Court appears to act regularly against the weight of popular sentiment. See, for example, *Boumediene v. Bush*, 128 S. Ct. 2229, 2240 (2008) (habeas rights for terrorist suspects held at Guantanamo); *Kennedy v. Louisiana*, 128 S. Ct. 2641, 2646 (2008) (prohibiting the death penalty for child rapists); *Kelo v. City of New London*, 545 U.S. 469, 489–90 (2005) (permitting taking of homes for commercial development); *Grutter v. Bollinger*, 539 U.S. 306, 343 (2003) (upholding racial and ethnic preferences for admission to universities). See also Lawrence Baum and Neal Devins, "Why the Supreme Court Cares About Elites, Not the American People," *Georgetown Law Journal* 98 (2010): 1515 (arguing that justices are more influenced by elite opinion than by public opinion); Richard Pildes, "Is the Supreme Court a 'Majoritarian' Institution?" *Supreme Court Review* 2010 (2010): 103 (critiquing the thesis that the Court follows the will of the majority of either the people or the legislature).

26. For an argument in favor of such a jurisprudence, see Jeffrey Rosen, "Originalism and Pragmatism: False Friends," *Harvard Journal of Law and Public Policy* 31 (2008): 937.

27. Unless the Court was to defer absolutely to the legislature and thus abnegate judicial review, a doctrine of deference cannot furnish a complete jurisprudence. The judiciary must first determine the meaning of a constitutional provision before it can decide whether the legislature's interpretation is close enough to the original meaning to warrant deference. The legislature, in fulfilling its own duty to pass only constitutional legislation, must also determine the Constitution's meaning. It cannot simply defer to its own authority.

A theory of very substantial deference embraced for policy or philosophical reasons should be distinguished from a theory of deference that may be rooted in the original methods the enactors expected to be applied to the Constitution. In Chapter 8, we suggest that it is possible that the enactors expected the judiciary to defer to the legislature as a kind of tiebreaker when the constitutional theory supporting legislation was as plausible as any other.

28. For example, while we argue below that the nation would have passed an amendment expanding the Commerce Clause during the New Deal, once the Supreme Court broadened the clause on its own, it was unlikely that

there would be enough support for an amendment to cut it back, even though the nation would not have expanded the clause as broadly as the Supreme Court did.

29. See, for example, *Wickard v. Filburn*, 317 U.S. 111, 128–29 (1942) (holding that Congress may regulate local activities not regarded as commerce if those activities have a substantial economic effect on interstate commerce).

30. See David E. Kyvig, *Explicit and Authentic Acts: Amending the U.S. Constitution, 1776–1995* (Lawrence: University Press of Kansas, 1996), 305, 314 (arguing that Roosevelt could have passed constitutional amendments expanding federal power).

31. For discussion about why the pre–New Deal Court was correct in its construction of the clause, see Randy Barnett, *Restoring the Lost Constitution: The Presumption of Liberty* (Princeton, NJ: Princeton University Press, 2004), 274–318; Richard A. Epstein, "The Proper Scope of the Commerce Power," *Virginia Law Review* 73 (1987): 1387.

32. US Senate, "Party Division in the Senate, 1789–Present," available at http://www.senate.gov/pagelayout/history/one_item_and_teasers/partydiv.htm (accessed 1/15/10) (referring to the 75th Congress).

33. Office of the Clerk of the US House of Representatives, "Party Divisions of the House of Representatives, 1789 to Present," available at http://clerk.house.gov /art_history/house_history/partyDiv.html (accessed 1/15/10) (referring to the 75th Congress).

34. See Michael J. Dubin, *Party Affiliations in State Legislatures: A Year by Year Summary, 1976–2006* (Jefferson, NC: McFarland & Company, Inc., 2007), 28, 36, 40, 68, 82, 94, 122, 129, 137, 144, 154, 167, 174, 189 (Kansas, Maine, Massachusetts, New Hampshire, North Dakota, South Dakota, and Vermont were entirely controlled by Republicans, but the party only partially controlled California, Connecticut, Delaware, New Jersey, New York, Oregon, and Rhode Island). Iowa had one house controlled by Democrats and the other evenly divided (ibid., 65). In Wisconsin, the Progressives were the largest party in each house (ibid., 202).

35. Wallace S. Sayre, "Major Party Platforms of 1936," *Current History* (August 1936): 52.

36. See Rafael Gely and Pablo T. Spiller, "The Political Economy of Supreme Court Constitutional Decisions: The Case of Roosevelt's Court-Packing Plan," *International Review of Law and Economics* 12 (1992): 63.

37. For a discussion of the extent to which the Court-packing plan and related external pressures were responsible for the Court's switch, see Mark Tushnet, "The New Deal Constitutional Revolution: Law, Politics, or What?" *University of Chicago Law Review* 66 (1999): 1075–1076 (reviewing Barry Cushman, *Rethinking the New Deal Court* [New York: Oxford University Press, 1998]). For

an argument that internal, doctrinal factors were responsible, see Cushman, "Rethinking the New Deal Court," 3–7. Whether the Supreme Court decisions of 1937 can be reconciled with prior doctrine, later decisions like *Wickard v. Filburn,* cannot be so reconciled. Thus, we believe that judicial failure to enforce the Constitution resulted from political changes, including judicial appointments, even if there can be legitimate arguments about when that judicial failure occurred.

38. Our argument that the original meaning of the Commerce Clause accommodates changing economic and technological circumstances should not be confused with the spurious argument that cases like *United States v. Darby,* 312 U.S. 100 (1942) and *Wickard v. Filburn* accommodated change within the Constitution's original meaning. Although the meaning of the Commerce Clause is static, it accommodates change by permitting the regulation of more activities as commerce increases with the growth of the economy. The main problem with the New Deal cases is that they changed the original meaning of the term *commerce.* The difference between the originalist vision and that of New Deal justices is that between a constant principle that changes the scope of its application as the facts of the world change and a variable principle that itself mutates in meaning.

39. Gerard N. Magliocca, "Court-Packing and the Child Labor Amendment," *Constitutional Commentary* 27 (2011): 457.

40. Ibid., 458.

41. Ibid., 482–484.

42. All states had child labor laws at the time. See *Hammer v. Dagenhart,* 247 U.S. 251, 275 (1918). Many were equally stringent or more stringent than federal law. See S. Comm. on the Judiciary, 68th Cong., Child Labor Amendment 23 (Comm. Print 1924) (noting that the labor standards of thirteen states are equal to or higher than the standards of federal law).

43. See Kurt T. Lash, "The Constitutional Convention of 1937: The Original Meaning of the New Jurisprudential Deal," *Fordham Law Review* 70 (2001): 477, n. 88.

44. Ibid., 476, n. 87. It is significant that Roosevelt also did not actively promote these other amendments, further suggesting that he was not seriously interested in constitutional amendments. See Magliocca, "Court-Packing," 479.

45. See Bruce Ackerman, *We the People: Transformations* (Cambridge, MA: Belknap Press, 1998), 338 (suspecting the president would have wanted an amendment "empowering Congress to legislate for the general welfare" in the absence of effective regulation by the states).

46. See Joseph P. Lash, *From the Diaries of Felix Frankfurter* (New York: W.W. Norton and Co., Inc., 1975), 58 ("[H]e feared that an amendment to the Constitution would diminish the intrinsic character of a document that was

intended to endure and that he profoundly believed had ample resources within its original terms to meet the changing needs of successive generations.").

47. See Jane McCarthy with Alice Shorett, *Negotiating Settlements: A Guide to Environmental Mediation* (New York: American Arbitration Association, 1984), xi.

48. Consistent with this hypothesis, there has been stronger interest-group participation in the Supreme Court nomination process since the 1950s. See Michael Gerhardt, *The Federal Appointment Process* (Durham, NC: Duke University Press, 2000), 219.

49. See also Jeremy Paul, "Campaign Reform in the 21st Century: Putting Mouth Where the Money Is," *Connecticut Law Review* 30 (1998): 799 (suggesting that some of our legal culture is simply opposed to constitutional amendments).

50. See Ronald Dworkin, "Comment," in Antonin Scalia and Amy Gutmann, *A Matter of Interpretation, Federal Courts and the Law* (Princeton NJ: Princeton University Press, 1997), 119–123.

51. See John R. Vile, *Encyclopedia of Constitutional Amendments, Proposed Amendments, and Amending Issues, 1789–2002* (Santa Barbara, CA: ABC-CLIO, Inc., 2003), 177.

52. See *Frontiero v. Richardson*, 411 U.S. 677, 688 (1973) (Brennan, J., plurality opinion) (applying strict scrutiny to strike down a law that discriminated against women while the amendment was pending); *Reed v. Reed*, 404 U.S. 71, 75–76 (1971) (striking down discriminatory laws and effectively applying intermediate scrutiny while the Equal Rights Amendment was being considered). In *Frontiero*, Justice Powell concurred on other grounds but argued against strict scrutiny to allow the amendment a chance to settle the issue. See also *Frontiero v. Richardson*, 691–692. (Powell, J., concurring in judgment).

53. *Reed v. Reed*, 72–73.

54. Ibid.

55. *Frontiero v. Richardson*, 682.

56. See Suzanne Sangree, "Title IX and the Contact Sports Exemption: Gender Stereotypes in a Civil Rights Statute," *Connecticut Law Review* 32 (2000): 412.

57. See Richard A. Posner, "Professionalisms," *Arizona Law Review* 40 (1998): 7 (describing the Warren Court era as a period of judicial activism).

58. See Stephen M. Griffin, "The Nominee is . . . Article V," *Constitutional Commentary* 12 (1995): 172.

59. See, for example, Howard Gillman, "The Collapse of Constitutional Originalism and the Rise of the Notion of the 'Living Constitution' in the Course of American State-Building," *Studies in American Political Development* 11 (1997): 192–194.

60. For a discussion of the strength of the originalist interpretative methods at the time of the nation's founding, see Gilllman, "The Collapse of Constitutional

Originalism," 197–203. Originalism has been undergoing a revival since the 1970s. Jonathan O'Neill, *Originalism in American Law and Politics* (Baltimore, MD: The John Hopkins Press, 2005), 111–160.

61. See Richard A. Posner, "What Do Judges and Justices Maximize? (The Same Thing Everybody Else Does)," *Supreme Court Economic Review* 3 (1993): 28–29 (arguing that judges maximize their utility in part by following the rules). Therefore, if originalism becomes the prevailing rule, judges will want to follow it.

62. See Adrian Vermeule, "Foreword: System Effects and the Constitution," *Harvard Law Review* 123 (2009): 56.

63. Ibid.

64. Ibid., 55–56.

65. For the original statement of the theory of the second best, see R. G. Lipsey and Kelvin Lancaster, "The General Theory of Second Best," *The Review of Economic Studies* 24 (1956–1957): 11–12.

66. For the original statement of the second best in the constitutional context, see Peter B. McCutchen, "Mistakes, Precedent, and the Rise of the Administrative State: Toward a Constitutional Theory of the Second Best," *Cornell Law Review* 80 (1994): 17.

67. See McCutchen, "Mistakes, Precedent, and the Rise of the Administrative State" ("[T]wo wrongs may not quite make a right. . . ."); Lipsey and Lancaster, "The General Theory," 12, 28–31 ("[N]othing can be said about the direction or the magnitude of the secondary departures from optimum conditions made necessary by the original non-fulfillment of one condition," and making such judgments is extremely difficult).

68. As our discussion of judicial correction in Chapter 6 shows, we are open to consequentialist considerations that would overcome our general consequentialist arguments for originalism. We thus agree with Professor Vermeule that general consequentialist arguments must be tested by such calculations. See Vermeule, "Foreword," 55, 62. We disagree that second-best arguments offer a reason to do so.

69. In Chapter 10, we offer a theory of the precedent that would encourage an originalist Court to overrule many nonoriginalist precedents but would still authorize the Court to keep precedents that are necessary for the stability and desirable operation of our system. Professor Vermeule, however, appears to think that a theory for precedent in a consequentialist originalism is impossible because it will either allow too many nonoriginalist precedents, thus vitiating originalism, or too few nonoriginalist precedents, thereby requiring the overturning of fixed features of the legal landscape. See Vermeule, "Foreword," 56–57. But we answer this type of criticism in Chapter 10, where we outline an intermediate approach to precedent that avoids overturning a class of essential precedents but allows the overturning of other precedents.

70. See Vermeule, "Foreword," 60–63.
71. Vermeule overlooks such possible differences between originalism and other jurisprudences in this strategic calculus. See Vermeule, ibid.
72. See, for example, Jeffrey Rosen, "Conservatives v. Originalism," *Harvard Journal of Law and Public Policy* 19 (1996): 465.
73. See also John O. McGinnis, "Impeachable Defenses," *Policy Review* 95 (1999): 27–29 (showing that, under the intense public scrutiny of congressional hearings, even nonoriginalist scholars resort to originalism).
74. See Vermeule, "Foreword," 61.
75. See Richard H. Fallon, Jr., " 'The Rule of Law' as a Concept in Constitutional Discourse," *Columbia Law Review* 97 (1997): 48.
76. See Gerken, "The Hydraulics of Constitutional Reform."
77. See Michael W. McConnell, "Textualism and the Dead Hand of the Past," *George Washington Law Review* 66 (1998): 1127.
78. Ibid.
79. Thus, our argument provides a functional answer to the argument that the passage of time undermines the case for applying originalism. See Michael C. Dorf, "Integrating Normative and Descriptive Constitutional Theory: The Case of Original Meaning," *Georgetown Law Review* 85 (1997): 1819–1820. A supermajoritarian process designed for entrenchment compensates for the passage of time. It is better to enforce the results of the past supermajoritarian process than to enforce the decisions of current majorities in the legislature or Supreme Court.

6. Supermajoritarian Failure, Including the Exclusion of African Americans and Women

1. We focus on departures by the judiciary (rather than by other government entities) because it is the most commonly proposed alternative. Another reason to focus on the judiciary is that a legislative correction will often depend on the judiciary's cooperation. If the legislature attempted to correct the constitution, it would only take effect in most cases if the judiciary did not strike down the legislation as unconstitutional.
2. Akhil Amar, for instance, believes that the Constitution could be amended outside Article V by a national referendum. See Akhil Reed Amar, "Philadelphia Revisited: Amending the Constitution Outside Article V," *University of Chicago Law Review* 55 (1988): 1043. Others have critiqued the historical support for that view. See, for example, Henry Paul Monaghan, "We the People[s], Original Understanding, and Constitutional Amendment," *Columbia Law Review* 96 (1998): 121. In addition, such a national referendum lacks the supermajoritarian features that make for beneficial constitutionalism.

3. For a defense of the process by one who has, see Sanford Levinson, *Our Undemocratic Constitution* (New York: Oxford University Press, 2006).

4. If the legislature attempted the constitutional correction, it would face some of the same problems that beset establishing constitutional provisions by majority rule such as partisanship. Legislative correction would also not eliminate the problems of judicial correction because judicial review would require the judiciary to evaluate legislative corrections.

5. For a discussion of the legality of the Reconstruction Amendments, see Chapter 4.

6. African American freedmen, however, were eligible to vote under the same rules as whites in five states (New Hampshire, New York, New Jersey, North Carolina, and Massachusetts) at the time of the ratification. See *Dred Scott v. Sandford*, 60 U.S. (19 How.) 393, 572–573 (1856) (Curtis, J., dissenting). We know that African Americans generally voted for the Federalist Party in the antebellum period and often had a high opinion of both George Washington and Alexander Hamilton. See Leon F. Litwack, *North of Slavery, The Negro in the Free States, 1790–1860* (Chicago: University of Chicago Press, 1961), 80–81. Therefore, it seems likely that most of the few African Americans who did participate in voting for delegates to the convention supported ratification.

7. Justice Marshall famously called attention to this central problem for US constitutional law. See Thurgood Marshall, Commentary, "Reflections on the Bicentennial of the United States Constitution," *Harvard Law Review* 101 (1987): 1, 2.

8. Nevertheless, even here it is not clear what alternative was better than adhering to the Constitution. Junking the Constitution over the slavery issue likely would have led to a retreat to sectional governments. The southern governments may well have treated African Americans even worse. Perhaps more importantly, the failure of the Constitution would have retarded the progress of a liberal social order based on markets that made slavery ideologically anomalous. Trying to change the Constitution on these essential matters through nonoriginalist interpretations in the early Republic would likely have had a similar result. The different regions would have promptly spiraled into disunion.

9. U.S. Const. amend. XIII.

10. U.S. Const. amend. XIV.

11. U.S. Const. amend. XV.

12. See Akhil Reed Amar, *America's Constitution: A Biography* (New York: Random House, 2005), 349–403.

13. See, for example, Voting Rights Act of 1965, Pub. L. No. 89–110, 79 Stat. 437 (codified as amended at 42 U.S.C. sec. 1971, 1973 to 1973aa-6 (2006)).

14. The strongest argument for concluding that the Reconstruction Amendments did not fully correct the supermajoritarian failure is that they failed to prohibit

a variety of forms of discrimination against African Americans, such as discrimination in matters that would not have been treated as civil rights in 1868. The original meaning of the Reconstruction Amendments is hotly contested, but even under the most optimistic interpretations, it is quite possible that the Amendments were insufficient. For the reasons we discussed earlier in this Chapter, however, it does not follow that the enterprise of judicial correction would be on the whole beneficial.

15. We recognize that some historians believe that the subordination of African Americans in the post-Reconstruction South was largely created by social custom and private violence and that Jim Crow laws were thus largely unnecessary to achieve subordination. See Michael J. Klarman, *From Jim Crow to Civil Rights: The Supreme Court and the Struggle for Racial Equality* (New York: Oxford University Press, 2004), 59–60. But we agree with critics who see legal restrictions on African Americans as greatly facilitating their subordination by preventing defections of Southerners for whom customs would not have been in their economic and personal interest. See David E. Bernstein and Ilya Somin, "Judicial Power and Civil Rights Reconsidered," *Yale Law Journal* 114 (2004): 591, 603–604 (reviewing Klarman, *From Jim Crow to Civil Rights*). Without discrimination as to voting, African Americans would also have gained much more control over the government, which would have allowed them to act against private violence and social custom. Finally, the original meaning of the Equal Protection Clause obligates the states to act against such private violence. See U.S. Const. amend XIV, sec. 1.

16. See Klarman, *From Jim Crow to Civil Rights*, 30.

17. Ibid.

18. Ibid., 31.

19. See *Giles v. Harris*, 189 U.S. 475, 487 (1903) (refusing to compel registration when African Americans were being discriminated against in a good character test because the courts could not oversee the voting system).

20. See Amar, *America's Constitution*, 395.

21. 163 U.S. 537 (1896).

22. Ibid., 550–551.

23. See John Harrison, "Reconstructing the Privileges or Immunities Clause," *Yale Law Journal* 101 (1992): 1385, 1458–1459.

24. Ibid., 1459.

25. See, for example, Amar, *America's Constitution*, 162 (understanding the Fourteenth Amendment as an attempt to prevent restoration of racial caste).

26. See Klarman, *From Jim Crow to Civil Rights*, 93.

27. For a comparison of the views of the supporters of the Fourteenth Amendment, like Bingham and Stevens, see Jacobus TenBroek, *Equal Under Law* (New York: Collier Books, 1965).

28. For Charles Crisp's views on civil rights, see Raphael O'Hara Boyd, "Service in the Midst of a Storm: James Edward O'Hara and Reconstruction in North Carolina," *Journal of Negro History* 2001 (2001): 319, 329.

29. Act of February 8, 1894, ch. 25, 28 Stat. 36, 36 (1894).

30. For a discussion that emphasizes the importance of *Brown* in civil rights jurisprudence as an imposition of cultural values rather than an enforcement of the original meaning of the Constitution, see Robert Post, "Law and Cultural Conflict," *Chicago-Kent Law Review* 78 (2003): 485, 500. Our point here is scholars like Post miss a larger truth. Whatever the correctness of *Brown* as a matter of the original meaning, the original meaning of the Reconstruction Amendments granted such a large measure of legal equality to African Americans that if they had been enforced, *Brown* either would not have been necessary or would not have been a cultural watershed.

31. See Michael W. McConnell, "Originalism and the Desegregation Decisions," *Virginia Law Review* 81 (1995): 947, 1131–1139. McConnell's is admittedly a controversial thesis. Compare Michael J. Klarman, "*Brown*, Originalism, and Constitutional Theory: A Response to Professor McConnell," *Virginia Law Review* 81 (1995): 1881, with Michael W. McConnell, "The Originalist Justification for *Brown*: A Reply to Professor Klarman," *Virginia Law Review* 81 (1995): 1937. See also Harrison, "Reconstructing the Privileges or Immunities Clause," 1462–1463 (arguing that the original application of the Privileges or Immunities Clause would have resulted in invalidating the segregation laws at issue in *Plessy* and *Brown*).

32. The close connection between women and male relatives may mean that women's suffrage at the time of ratification would not have made as large a difference as many people believe. Indeed, we have some evidence to this effect. Women who owned the requisite amount of property were able to vote in New Jersey at this time, and politicians acted as if they would vote in the manner that men did in their area of the state. See Judith Apter Klinghoffer and Lois Elkis, "'The Petticoat Electors': Women's Suffrage in New Jersey, 1776–1807," *Journal of the Early Republic* 12 (1992): 159, 172.

33. U.S. Const. amend. XIX.

34. See Joseph W. Dellapenna, *Dispelling the Myths of Abortion History* (Durham, NC: Carolina Academic Press, 2006), 958.

35. One other potential defect is that property restrictions on the franchise in the original constitution-making process excluded some poor individuals. But Akhil Amar has recently shown that states substantially widened their franchises during the original ratification process to include most free males; see Amar, *America's Constitution*, 48. Thus, we think this is a less significant defect than those we discuss. We would respond to it, as we have responded to the other failures, by suggesting that judicial action to correct it would have more

costs than benefits. For instance, it is very difficult even to determine how poorer citizens would have wanted to change the Constitution. The federal government was not regarded at the time as a mechanism for aiding the poor, and it is unclear whether poorer citizens would have wanted more power for the federal government or the states. It is also unclear how much leverage they would have had to change the Constitution. Income redistribution through progressive taxation was not a political issue on the agenda of the eighteenth century. Perhaps the poor would have had success in putting more restrictions on government distribution of economic privileges, like monopolies, to the well connected, but the fate of such proposals remains hard to assess.

36. See Richard Beeman, *Plain Honest Men: The Making of the American Constitution* (New York: Random House, 2009), 82, 386–411 (describing state ratification conventions).

37. U.S. Const. art. V.

38. Ibid.

39. We model the influence of the Senate on judicial appointments in John O. McGinnis and Michael B. Rappaport, "The Judicial Filibuster, the Median Senator, and the Countermajoritarian Difficulty," *Supreme Court Review* 2005 (2005): 257.

40. See Richard A. Posner, *Breaking the Deadlock: The 2000 Election, the Constitution, and the Courts* (Princeton, NJ: Princeton University Press, 2001), 228–231.

41. Given the loyalty of citizens at the time of the Framing to their states rather than to a larger national entity that had not yet fully come into being, it seems fanciful that some element of representation by state could have been avoided. Even in light of that reality, it was still better to have a supermajoritarian than majoritarian process for proposing and ratifying the Constitution.

42. Small states may have disproportionate power to pass legislation in the ordinary legislative process. Even though legislation also has to be passed by the House, small states can get some items passed by trading their disproportionate power in the Senate to block legislation that large states might desire. As a result, small states tend to get more pork barrel spending per capita. See Frances L. Lee and Bruce I. Oppenheimer, *Sizing up the Senate: The Unequal Consequences of Equal Representation* (Chicago: University of Chicago Press, 1999), 156–186. Given that constitutional amendments for the last two centuries have generally concerned a single subject, however, such trades do not seem to have much affected the constitutional amendment process.

43. We already explained in Chapter 4 why state applications for a convention are largely a dead letter in the convention process.

44. See John A. Ragosta, "Trade and Agriculture, and Lumber: Why Agriculture and Lumber Matter," *Kansas Journal of Law and Public Policy* 14 (2005): 413, 439.

45. See Keith Poole, 105th Congress, available at http://voteview.com/c105/c105.htm (accessed 1/21/10).

46. Even if the Constitution did not include such a provision, a constitutional amendment to eliminate equal representation would not likely pass given that more than one-quarter of the states—the smaller ones—benefit from that equal representation.

7. Original Methods Originalism

1. Professor Larry Solum expresses the difference between positive and normative considerations well: "Semantics is about meaning. 'Normativity' . . . is about the moral or ethical status of reasons for action." See Lawrence B. Solum, "Semantic Originalism," Illinois Public Law Research Paper No. 07-24 (2008), 28–30, available at http://papers.ssrn.com/sol3/papers.cfm?abstract_id=1120244.

2. Ibid., 2–5.

3. See Randy E. Barnett, "The Misconceived Assumption about Original Assumptions," *Northwestern University Law Review* 103 (2009): 615, 642–650.

4. See Keith E. Whittington, *Constitutional Interpretation: Textual Meaning, Original Intent, and Judicial Review* (Lawrence: University Press of Kansas, 1999), 3.

5. See, for example, Arthur Selwyn Miller, *Social Change and Fundamental Law: America's Evolving Constitution* (Westport, CT: Greenwood Press, 1979), 349.

6. Ibid., 390.

7. See, for example, Steven G. Calabresi and Saikrishna B. Prakash, "The President's Power to Execute the Laws," *Yale Law Journal* 104 (1994): 541, 556.

8. For the antisurplusage rule, see *Kamper v. Hawkins*, 3 Va. 20, 88–89 (1793) ("The repetition of the term, judges, shows that it was in contemplation that both the tribunals, and the judges should be distinct and separate."), and *Marbury v. Madison*, 5. U.S. (1 Cranch) 137, 175 (1803) ("If any other construction would render the clause inoperative, that is an additional reason for rejecting such other construction, and for adhering to their obvious meaning.")

9. For example, if the term *diamond* is used in a baseball discussion, there is a presumption that it refers to the baseball field rather than to a gem.

10. *Ejusdem generis* is a canon of construction that requires that "when a general word or phrase follows a list of specific persons or things, the general word or phrase will be interpreted to include only persons or things of the same type as those listed." Bryan Garner, ed., *Black's Law Dictionary*, 7th ed. (St. Paul, MN: West Group, 1999), 535.

11. For the rule of lenity, see *McNally v. United States*, 483 U.S. 350, 359–360 (1987).

12. See, for example, *Schlottman v. Hoffman*, 18 So. 893, 895 (Miss. 1895) ("It is a

well-settled canon for the construction of wills that the court will take into consideration the attending circumstances of the testator, the quantity and character of his estate, the state of his family, and all facts known to him which
may reasonably be supposed to have influenced him in the disposition of his
property.")

13. The term *ex post facto law* appears to have had these different meanings in 1787
as well. James Madison had assumed that it covered retroactive civil laws, but
John Dickinson examined Blackstone and concluded that it covered only retroactive criminal laws. See Max Farrand, ed., *The Records of the Federal
Convention of 1787*, vol. 2 (New Haven, CT: Yale University Press, 1911),
448–449.

14. See Frederick Schauer, "Statutory Construction and the Coordinating
Function of Plain Meaning," *The Supreme Court Review* 1990 (1990): 231, 234,
n. 6 (depending on its context, a word can be given a legal rather than ordinary
meaning).

15. See, for example, *Garcia v. United States*, 469 U.S. 70, 76, n.3 (1984) (resort to
legislative history only if statute is ambiguous).

16. Richard S. Kay, "Adherence to the Original Intentions in Constitutional
Adjudication: Three Objections and Responses," *Northwestern University Law
Review* 82 (1988): 227, 230.

17. See Larry Alexander and Saikrishna Prakash "'Is that English You're Speaking?' Why Intention Free Interpretation Is an Impossibility," *San Diego Law
Review* 41 (2004): 967, 974–977; Raoul Berger, *Government by Judiciary: The
Transformation of the Fourteenth Amendment* (Indianapolis, IN: Liberty Fund,
1977), 363; Whittington, *Constitutional Interpretation*, 110–159.

18. Kay, "Adherence to the Original Intentions," 230.

19. See, for example, ibid., 245–251.

20. See Gary Lawson and Guy Seidman, "Originalism as a Legal Enterprise,"
Constitutional Commentary 23 (2006): 47, 65 (arguing that the majority's views
may determine the authority of the law without determining its meaning). One
possibility is that the enactors delegated to a subgroup of people the authority to
decide the meaning of the Constitution. See ibid., 64–65 (discussing this issue).
If one is to view the determination of meaning as a delegation, we believe it is
best viewed as a delegation to the results of a process in which the applicable
interpretive rules are applied.

21. There are various formulations of this view. Most original public meaning
theorists rely on a reasonable reader or author. See Lawson and Seidman,
"Originalism as a Legal Enterprise", 74–76 (requiring that the constitution
be interpreted based on the intentions of a reasonable, intelligent, and knowledgeable person); Randy E. Barnett, *Restoring the Lost Constitution: The
Presumption of Liberty* (Princeton, NJ: Princeton University Press, 2004), 92

("Originalism seeks the public or objective meaning that a reasonable listener would place on the words used in a constitutional provision at the time of its enactment"); Antonin Scalia, *A Matter of Intepretation: Federal Courts and the Law* (Princeton, NJ: Princeton University Press, 1997), 16–17, 37 (suggesting that originalism looks to the intent that a reasonable person would gather from the constitutional text, understood as a brief charter of government). Other theorists seem to imply a reasonable reader or author; see, for example, Vasan Kesavan and Michael Stokes Paulsen, "Is West Virginia Unconstitutional?" *California Law Review* 90 (2002): 291, 398 ("[T]he meaning the language would have had (both its words and its grammar) to an average, informed speaker and reader of that language at the time of its enactment into law."). While Larry Solum focuses on how the Constitution would have been understood by a competent speaker of American English at the time it was adopted (Solum, "Semantic Originalism," 51–54), we believe that he supplies that speaker with additional knowledge of the constitutional context and the division of linguistic labor that makes him behave as both reasonable and knowledgeable in the respects with which we are concerned. See ibid., 55, n. 169.

22. See Barnett, *Restoring the Lost Constitution,* 92 (discussing the ascendency of original public meaning); Vasan Kesavan and Michael Stokes Paulsen, "The Interpretive Force of the Constitution's Secret Drafting History," *Georgetown Law Journal* 91 (2003): 1113, 1144–1145 (arguing that public meaning originalism corrects for original intent's shortcomings); Lawson and Seidman, "Originalism as a Legal Enterprise," 47–48 (arguing that the concept of a reasonable person at the time of the framing is the measure of constitutional meaning); Solum, "Semantic Originalism," 2 (suggesting a "theoretical foundation for original public meaning originalism").

23. *Compare* Lawson and Seidman, "Originalism as a Legal Enterprise," 80 (supporting inclusion of interpretive tools), *with* Barnett, "The Misconceived Assumption," 659 (opposing their use).

24. Barnett, "The Misconceived Assumption," 659.

25. Barnett, *Restoring the Lost Constitution,* 89–117; Barnett, "The Misconceived Assumption," 629.

26. Barnett, *Restoring the Lost Constitution,* 100.

27. Ibid.

28. Indeed, as Mikko Wennberg observes in a comment on Professor Barnett's own contract theory: "[T]he meaning of the terms of contract is determined by law. Of course, most words have meaning independent of their legally defined meaning, but *as the terms of the contract* their meaning depends ultimately on the law. The conventional meaning of some term is its legal meaning only if there is an—explicit or implicit—legal rule according to which contract terms are interpreted according to their conventional meaning. The rules of a

contract law determine how the terms are to be interpreted. If the meaning of terms of contract are determined by law, then the conventional meaning of the *contract terms* are determined by *how people expect the terms to be interpreted in courts.* The reasonable meaning is thus not independent of existing law and legal practices." Mikko Wennberg, "On Barnett's Theory of Default Rules," *Canadian Journal of Law and Jurisprudence* 16 (2003): 147, 153.

29. Barnett, "The Misconceived Assumption," 659.

30. In his book, Barnett also argues in favor of original public meaning on normative grounds because it is a means of locking in the meaning of the Constitution (Barnett, *Restoring the Lost Constitution*, 103–104). If locking in meaning is the goal, however, then interpretive rules are a far superior means of promoting that goal than the constitutional construction advocated by Barnett that seems to undermine lock-in.

31. See Barnett, "The Misconceived Assumption," 630.

32. To be clear, we are not necessarily asserting that *ejusdem generis* or the rule of lenity was widely deemed applicable to the Constitution, although we are inclined to believe that both were. Their applicability requires additional research. The point is that these rules are exactly the type that might have been widely treated as applicable and, if so, they would have been accepted as binding.

33. Solum, "Semantic Originalism," 110–111.

34. Ibid.

35. Ibid.

36. Solum also discusses legal meanings as terms of art, analyzing them through the device of a linguistic division of labor. Solum doubts that all terms in the Constitution are legal terms of art. We agree with him that there is little reason to believe that all or most constitutional terms are legal terms of art.

37. As discussed earlier, these legal interpretive rules differ from legal meanings. In fact, the legal interpretive rules sometimes choose ordinary meanings over legal meanings. The key point is that it is the legal interpretive rules that decide which meaning is selected.

38. U.S. Const. art. VI.

39. U.S. Const. amend. IX ("The enumeration in the Constitution, of certain rights, shall not be construed to deny or disparage others retained by the people.").

40. *Compare* Laurence H. Tribe and Michael C. Dorf, "Levels of Generality in the Definition of Rights," *University of Chicago Law Review* 57 (1990): 1057, 1100 (Ninth Amendment has substantive content but is also a rule of construction), *with* Kurt T. Lash, "A Textual-Historical Theory of the Ninth Amendment," *Stanford Law Review* 60 (2008): 895, 903 (Ninth Amendment is a rule of interpretation, not a substantive grant of rights).

41. Charles J. Cooper, "Limited Government and Individual Liberty: The Ninth Amendment's Forgotten Lessons," *Journal of Law & Policy* 4 (1987): 63, 64.
42. Alexander Hamilton, "Federalist No. 84," *The Federalist Papers*, ed. Henry Cabot Lodge (New York: G.P. Putnam's Sons, 1888), 537.
43. Barnett, *Restoring the Lost Constitution*, 54–55.
44. *Expressio unius est exclusio alterius* means "the expression of one thing is the exclusion of another." Bryan Garner, ed., *Black's Law Dictionary*, 7th ed. (St. Paul, MN: West Group, 1999), 1635.
45. 128 S. Ct. 2783, 2789 (2008).
46. See, for example, *Copeman v. Gallant*, 1 P. Wms. 314, 24 Eng. Rep. 404 (1716), cited in *District of Columbia v. Heller*, 129 S.Ct. 2783, 2789 (2008). One reason for the venerable canon is that "the remedy often extends beyond the particular act or mischief which first suggested the necessity of the law." Joel Prentiss Bishop, *Commentaries on the Written Laws and Their Interpretation* (Boston: Little, Brown, and Co., 1882), sec. 51.
47. A difficulty for Justice Stevens's dissent is that he does not rebut this rule. See *District of Columbia v. Heller*, 2822, 2825 (Stevens, J. dissenting). Thus, he can only deploy the prefatory language if he can show that it clarifies an ambiguity in the phrase "the right of the people to keep and bear arms."
48. See St. George Tucker, "View of the Constitution of the United States," *Blackstone's Commentaries: With Notes of Reference, to the Constitution and Laws, of the Federal Government of the United States; and of the Commonwealth of Virginia*, vol. 1, ed. app. (Philadelphia, PA: William Young Birch and Abraham Small, 1803), 151; Thomas Jefferson, "Opinion on the Constitutionality of a National Bank (Feb. 15, 1791)," *Thomas Jefferson: Writings*, ed. Merrill D. Peterson (New York: Library of America, 1984), 416, 421. For a discussion of the relation of compact theory to strict construction, see Kurt T. Lash, "'Tucker's Rule': St. George Tucker and the Limited Construction of Federal Power," *William & Mary Law Review* 47 (2006) 1343. For an excellent discussion of Jefferson's position, see H. Jefferson Powell, "The Political Grammar of Early Constitutional Law," *North Carolina Law Review* 71 (1993): 949, 956.
49. See *Gibbons v. Ogden*, 22 U.S. (1 Wheat) 187–188 (1824).
50. Joseph Story, *Commentaries on the Constitution of the United States*, vol. 1 (Boston: Hilliard, Gray, and Company, 1833), 411–418 (discussing the Marshall-Tucker dispute and siding with Marshall).
51. One passage in the *Federalist* might be thought to militate against reliance on legal interpretive rules. Alexander Hamilton states: "Even if these maxims [of legal interpretation] had a precise technical sense, corresponding with those who employ them on the present occasion which, however, is not the case, they would still be inapplicable to a Constitution of government. In relation to such a subject, the natural and obvious sense of its provisions, apart from any technical

rules, is the true criterion of construction." Alexander Hamilton, "Federalist No. 83," *The Federalist Papers*, ed. Clinton Rossiter (New York: Signet Classic, 2003), 496. We do not read this passage as barring the use of legal rules in constitutional interpretation. First, in the same essay, Hamilton argues that the two maxims can be properly applied to the Constitution (ibid., 496–497, showing how both "a specification of particulars is an exclusion of generals" and "the expression of one thing is the exclusion of another" are properly applied to the Constitution). Second, elsewhere in the *Federalist*, Hamilton himself relies on legal rules in expounding the Constitution. See, for example, ibid., "Federalist No. 32," 196 (applying "what lawyers call a negative pregnant," involving an interpretive rule that says the negation of one thing is the affirmance of another"); ibid., "Federalist No. 84," 513 (applying the antisurplusage rule). Moreover, in his famous opinion on the bank of the United States, Hamilton is even more explicit about the utility of legal rules of construction: "the intention [of the Constitution] is to be sought according to the usual and established rules of construction." Alexander Hamilton, "Opinion on the Constitutionality of an Act to Establish a Bank (1791)," *Papers of Alexander Hamilton*, vol. 8, ed. Harold Syrett (New York: Columbia University Press, 1965), 111 (emphasis added).

Given Hamilton's regular embrace of legal interpretive rules to construe the Constitution, how are we to understand the passage in "Federalist No. 83"? While it is possible to view Hamilton's claim as being a careless argument made in a rush of enthusiasm against his opponents, we believe that the passage can be construed to be consistent with Hamilton's overall views. When the Constitution was enacted, there was a general view that the Constitution's plain meaning was controlling. By contrast, ambiguous or vague provisions could be resolved with the help of interpretive rules. Thus, Hamilton is reasonably read as suggesting that even if hypertechnical rules could alter the plain meaning for some other category of law, they cannot change the plain meaning of the Constitution.

Our reading also accords with the context of the passage. Hamilton here is arguing against the claim that, by requiring a jury trial in criminal cases, the Constitution abolishes the right to trial by jury in civil cases (Hamilton, "Federalist No. 83," ed. Rossiter, 496–498). As Hamilton shows, this is a poor argument because requiring trials for criminal cases hardly prohibits them for civil cases. Hamilton is clearly concerned to show that these interpretive rules have been misapplied. Thus, Hamilton observes that "rules of legal interpretation are rules of common sense" to show that these legal rules cannot have the absurd application that is being suggested. But nothing he says denies that properly applied legal rules that have been developed by the common wisdom of courts can clarify ambiguous or vague constitutional provisions.

52. Under an original intent foundation, the interpretive rules are those that the enactors actually thought applied to the Constitution. Under an original public meaning foundation, the interpretive rules are those that an informed observer would have reasonably believed applied to the Constitution.

53. See, for example, Charles C. Thach, Jr., *The Creation of the Presidency 1775–1789: A Study in Constitutional History* (Baltimore, MD: Johns Hopkins Press, 1969), 34–35 (observing that the New York Constitution served as a model for executive power provisions in the federal constitution); Hans A. Linde, "First Things First: Rediscovering the States' Bills of Rights," *University of Baltimore Law Review* 9 (1980): 379, 381–382 (showing that state constitutions served as models for the federal Bill of Rights).

54. See Joseph Biancalana, "Originalism and the Commerce Clause," *University of Cincinnati Law Review* 71 (2002): 383, 396 (showing that the Philadelpha Convention ultimately changed the vague federal powers under the Virginia Plan to the specific enumeration of federal power). Another example compares the federal Bill of Rights, which employed the legally enforceable "shall," and the Virginia Bill of Rights, which used the more maxim-oriented "ought." *Compare* U.S. Const. amends. I–VIII *with* Virginia Const. art. I sec. 3, 4, 10, and 11.

55. See H. Jefferson Powell, "The Original Understanding of Original Intent," *Harvard Law Review* 98 (1985): 885, 898–900 (arguing that statutes were an important interpretive model for the Constitution).

56. Article VI is consistent with this analogy because it provides parallel treatment to the Constitution and statutes: Both are Supreme law of the Land. See Henry P. Monaghan, "Our Perfect Constitution," *New York University Law Review* 56 (1981): 353, 392–393. In the *Federalist Papers*, Alexander Hamilton also makes an express analogy between the interpretation of the Constitution and the legal interpretative rules that have been applied to statutes. Hamilton, "Federalist No. 78," ed. Lodge, 486; cf. *Marbury v. Madison*, 176 (resolving constitutional question by "recognize[ing] certain principles, supposed to have been long and well established").

57. See *McCulloch v. Maryland*, 17 U.S. (1 Wheat.) 316, 415 (1819).

58. See Lawson and Seidman, "Originalism as a Legal Enterprise," 59, 71–72.

59. See John C. Yoo, "The Judicial Safeguards of Federalism," *Southern California Law Review* 70 (1997): 1311, 1375.

60. See Hamilton, "Federalist No. 78," ed. Lodge, 487; *Marbury v. Madison*, 176.

61. The objection discussed in the text does not merely overstate the degree to which legal meaning is hard for nonlawyers to understand. It also exaggerates the transparency of ordinary meaning. For example, advocates of original public meaning argue that the text's meaning should be understood as a well-informed speaker of the language would understand it. See, for example,

Lawson and Seidman, "Originalism as a Legal Enterprise," 73; see also Kay, "Adherence to the Original Intentions," 27–29 (collecting citations for this position). Such a speaker might have far more knowledge than an average reader of the document.

62. In arguing for judicial review, Alexander Hamilton also called attention to lawyers' specialized knowledge (Hamilton, "Federalist No. 78," ed. Lodge, 490).

63. For an attack on the use of "expected applications," see Jack Balkin, *Living Originalism* (Cambridge, MA: Harvard University Press, 2011), 293.

64. See Saikrishna Prakash, "The Constitution as Suicide Pact," *Notre Dame Law Review* 79 (2004): 1299, 1312.

65. Michael B. Rappaport, "A Textual and Historical Derivation of the Constitutional Interpretive Rules" (unpublished manuscript on file with the authors).

66. In this book, we do not determine the amount of evidence needed to establish the interpretive rules that are binding today. If the interpretive rules derive from a constitutional provision, the evidence required is not likely to differ from that needed to establish any constitutional norm as a matter of original meaning. But in this chapter, we assume that the interpretive rules apply because the enactors would have used them to determine the Constitution's meaning. Determining the amount of evidence needed to establish these rules may be more complicated. One issue that would bear on this issue is whether there is an alternative to the interpretive rule available. For example, one might wonder whether the rule of lenity applies to the Constitution's criminal provisions. Because the ordinary interpretive rules would apply in the absence of the rule of lenity, one might require strong evidence to apply the rule of lenity instead of (or in addition to) those rules. In contrast, there may be questions that are more basic, such as whether one looks primarily to text or intent. In this situation, there is no default rule and therefore one might simply select the interpretive rule that has the stronger support.

67. There is not necessarily a sharp distinction between these two forms of originalism, given that a text is naturally understood in light of the purposes of its drafters. See Monaghan, "Our Perfect Constitution," 375.

68. Tucker, "View of the Constitution," *60 (emphasis omitted).

69. Ibid., *61.

70. Ibid.

71. William N. Eskridge, Jr., "All About Words: Early Understandings of the 'Judicial Power' in Statutory Interpretation, 1776–1806," *Columbia Law Review* 101 (2001): 990. While Eskridge argues against an originalist/textualist conception in favor of an equity of the statute approach, he does not present evidence in favor of a dynamic conception of statutory interpretation, at least not one where the statute is updated through the application of evolving principles in the manner of the living Constitution. Ibid., 999, 1003–1004. For example, the

only instance of a statutory interpretation that Eskridge explicitly describes as "dynamic" simply involves the judiciary's refusal to interpret a recent statute to reach a result so inequitable that it cannot believe the legislature would have intended it (ibid., 1018, n. 126, 1023. We understand this court's action as having chosen a static intentionalist approach in preference to a textualist one, not as having adopted an approach that interprets based on changing values or circumstances over time, which is how Eskridge presents the dynamic approach in other scholarship. See William N. Eskridge, Jr, "Dynamic Statutory Interpretation," *University of Pennsylvania Law Review* 135 (1987): 1479.

72. See, for example, Raoul Berger, "Activist Indifference to Facts," *Tennessee Law Review* 61 (1993): 9; Raoul Berger, "Some Reflections on Interpretivism," *George Washington Law Review* 55 (1986): 1.

73. Matthew Bacon, *A New Abridgement of the Laws of England*, vol. 4 (London: Majesty's Law-Printers, 1768), 647–648 ("Statute" I(5)), *quoted in* Raoul Berger, "Some Reflections," 3 n. 18.

74. See James Wilson, "Of the Study of the Law in the United States," *The Works of James Wilson*, vol. 1, ed. Robert G. McCloskey (Cambridge, MA: Belknap Press of Harvard University Press, 1967), 69, 75, *cited in* Berger, "Activist Indifference," 10–11.

75. Thomas Rutherforth, *Institutes of Natural Law* (Baltimore, MD: William & Joseph Neal, 1832), 405, cited in Berger, "Activist Indifference," 10.

76. While we view this intentionalist approach to statutory interpretation as genuine, some commentators have claimed that the method is not really intentionalist, but rather an attempt to impose equitable principles on statutes. See Eskridge, "All About Words," 1001–1002; John F. Manning, "Textualism and the Equity of the Statute," *Columbia Law Review* 101 (2001): 1, 34–36. We disagree with this view because we see reference to equity as essentially an effort to discern intent rather than seeing reference to intent as essentially a way of imposing equitable principles. First, the traditional approach generally described its task as determining the intent of the legislature and justified departures from the text on that basis, not on the basis of equity. See Tucker, "View of the Constitution," *59–62; James Wilson, "Of the Study of the Law in the United States," *The Works of James Wilson*, vol. 2, ed. Robert G. McCloskey (Cambridge, MA: Belknap Press of Harvard University Press, 1967), 478. Second, the operation of intentionalism at the time naturally depended on references to principles. In a world where there was no recorded legislative history and where statutes were not carefully drafted, departing from statutory text that seemed questionable in favor of widely held principles was a reasonable method for discerning the legislature's intent. See Robert N. Clinton, "Original Understanding, Legal Realism, and the Interpretation of 'This Constitution,'" *Iowa Law Review* 72 (1987): 1177, 1197–1120. When legislative history did arise concerning

the US Constitution, this history was in fact consulted by some interpreters as a means of discerning the enactors' intent. Third, other aspects of the traditional statutory interpretive approach are also consistent with a jurisprudence of intentionalism, but not with one of equitable principles. For example, when the legislature had indicated in the text that it had considered an issue, the court was supposed to apply the textual resolution, even if it deemed it unreasonable, thereby giving effect to the legislature's expressed intent. See Tucker, "View of the Constitution," *91 ("[T]here is no court that has the power to defeat the intent of the legislature, when couched in such evident and express words, as leave no doubt whether it was the intent of the legislature or no.").

In determining the applicable interpretive rules for the Constitution, one would naturally consider the traditional statutory interpretation approach along with the other interpretive rules discussed here. But if one somehow believed that the traditional statutory interpretation approach was the sole approach applicable to the Constitution, that method would still constitute a type of originalism. Applying that approach to the Constitution, an interpreter would give effect to the original meaning of the text unless he concluded, based on values at the time of the enactment, that it did not reflect the enactors' intent. It might be argued, however, that the traditional statutory interpretation approach should be applied differently to a document that had legislative history. If such history provided evidence of intent, then the traditional approach might consider that as well as the values of the enactors' generation.

77. Powell, "The Original Understanding," 895. Powell also shows that some writers believe that the meaning of *statute*, referred to as King's "intent," was ascertained only by the text of the law (ibid.).

78. Manning, "Textualism," 52–54, 85–102.

79. Another reason that reliance on text grew is that legislatures appeared to engage in more careful drafting, and therefore the text of the statute was seen as better reflecting the legislature's intent. See ibid., 54; Sir Peter Benson Maxwell, *On the Interpretation of Statutes* (London: William Maxwell & Son, 1875), 230.

80. See Manning, "Textualism," 52–54; William D. Popkin, *Statutes in Court: The History and Theory of Statutory Interpretation* (Durham, NC: Duke University Press, 1999), 19.

81. See Manning, "Textualism," 85–102.

82. Philip Hamburger, *Law and Judicial Duty* (Cambridge, MA: Harvard University Press, 2008), 54.

83. Ibid.

84. Ibid.

85. Dean Michael Treanor has offered an interesting challenge to the view that the Framers' generation deployed textualism in constitutional interpretation. See

William Michael Treanor, "Against Textualism," *Northwestern University Law Review* 103 (2009): 983. We have responded to that view at length and show that cases on which Dean Treanor relies are not as opposed to textualism as he makes out and that, in any event, their analysis is generally within the broad family of originalism. See John O. McGinnis and Michael B. Rappaport, "Original Methods Originalism: A New Theory of Interpretation and the Case Against Construction," *Northwestern University Law Review* 103 (2009): 751, 794–802.

86. See Hamilton, "Opinion as to the Constitutionality of an Act to Establish a Bank" 111. James Madison also endorsed looking principally to the original textualist meaning of the Constitution: "I entirely concur in the propriety of resorting to the sense in which the Constitution was accepted and ratified by the nation. In that sense alone it is the legitimate Constitution. And if that be not the guide in expounding it, there can be no security for a consistent and stable . . . exercise of its powers." James Madison, "Letter from James Madison to Henry Lee (June 25, 1824)," *The Writings of James Madison*, vol. 9, ed. Gaillard Hunt (New York: G.P. Putnam's Sons, 1910), 192. For another example of textualist interpretation, see Gouverneur Morris, "Letter from Gouverneur Morris to Timothy Pickering (Dec. 22, 1814)," *Records of the Federal Convention of 1787*, vol. 3, ed. Max Farrand (New Haven, CT: Yale University Press, 1966), 420.

87. *Sturges v. Crowninshield*, 17 U.S. 122 (1819) (Marshall, C.J.).

88. See Christopher Wolfe, *The Rise of Modern Judicial Review: From Judicial Interpretation to Judge Made Law* (Lanham, MD: Rowman & Littlefield Publishers, Inc., 1994), 41–63.

89. See Clinton, "Original Understanding," 1186–1220; Charles Lofgren, "The Original Understanding of Original Intent?" *Constitutional Commentary* 5 (1988): 77; Barnett, *Restoring the Lost Constitution*, 96–100. The arguments for textualism also rely in part on the fact that the Constitution was drafted carefully to express the intent of the body. See Gouverneur Morris, *Records*, 420 ("Having rejected redundant and equivocal terms, I believed [the Constitution] to be as clear as our language would permit"); see also Clinton, "Original Understanding," 1190 ("the framers at Philadelphia . . . picked words quite carefully to convey precisely what they meant, no more and no less. Debates over the connotations of constitutional terms reflected a desire to avoid both imprecision and linguistic redundancy").

90. Annals of Cong., vol. 5, 776 (1796).

91. Clinton, "Original Understanding," 1186–1120.

92. Ibid.

93. Annals of Cong., vol. 2, 1409–1410 (1790) (statement of Elbridge Gerry); ibid., 1945 (remarks of James Madison).

94. Annals of Cong., vol. 5, 761 (1796), cited in Clinton "Original Understanding," 1203.

95. We recognize that some have contested our basic claim that the Constitution was a legal document and thus subject to legal interpretive rules. For instance, according to Larry Kramer, the Constitution was a "special form of popular law, law made by the people to bind their governors, and so subject to rules and considerations that made it qualitatively different from . . . statutory or common law." Larry D. Kramer, "Foreword: We the Court," *Harvard Law Review* 115 (2001): 4, 10. For criticism of Kramer's claims, see Saikrishna Prakash and John Yoo, "The Origins of Judicial Review," *University of Chicago Law Review* 70 (2003): 887, 904, 906–914; Gerald Leonard, "Iredell Reclaimed: Farewell to Snowiss's History of Judicial Review," *Chicago-Kent Law Review* 81 (2006): 867. While we do not have space here to fully rebut these contentions, we believe they do not undermine our argument that the enforceable meaning of the constitution was a legal one, subject to legal methods of interpretation.

    Before the Constitution, during its ratification, and in the early days of its consideration, interpreters relied on legal interpretive methods to construe constitutions throughout the United States. Before the enactment of the Constitution, Dean Treanor has shown that the rich traditions of statutory interpretation in the English-speaking world were deployed in interpreting state constitutions. See William Michael Treanor, "Judicial Review Before *Marbury*," *Stanford Law Review* 58 (2005): 455. In the debate over the Constitution, important proponents and opponents assumed it was subject to legal interpretive rules. See Powell, "The Original Understanding," 908–912. For instance, the famous Anti-Federalist Brutus complained that the judges would use legal construction to interpret the Constitution inconsistently from its plain meaning and so consolidate powers not granted in the federal government. See Brutus, "Essays of Brutus No. 12," *The Complete Anti-Federalist*, ed. Herbert Storing (Chicago: University of Chicago Press, 1981), 424–425. In the *Federalist*, Hamilton responded to these arguments, not by denying that judges would construe the Constitution according to rules of legal interpretation, but that they would do so reasonably. See Hamilton, "Federalist No. 78," ed. Lodge, 486–88. After the ratification of the Constitution, participants in debates in the First Congress regularly referred to interpretive rules in debating issues such as presidential power over cabinet departments. See Caleb Nelson, "Originalism and Interpretative Conventions," *University of Chicago Law Review* 70 (2003): 519, 573–574.

96. See Howard Gillman, "The Collapse of Constitutional Originalism and the Rise of the Notion of the 'Living Constitution' in the Course of American State-Building," *Studies in American Political Development* 11 (1997): 191, 205–209.

97. Professor Jack Balkin offers a single remark of Representative Monroe at the time of Reconstruction as evidence that those who enacted the Reconstruction Amendments embraced quite open-ended methods of interpretation. See Balkin, *Living Originalism*, 355 n. 18. We believe that this remark is at best ambiguous and is most likely read as simply recognizing that constitutional rules can apply in unexpected ways to new circumstances. As Monroe stated, "A new application of a well-known principle . . . takes us by surprise . . . ; and yet it is only what is required by the most logical consistency." See Cong. Globe, 42nd Cong., 1st Sess. 370 (statement of Rep. Monroe). A focus on logical consistency hardly seems inconsistent with originalism.

8. Original Methods versus Constitutional Construction

1. See, for example, Randy E. Barnett, *Restoring the Lost Constitution: The Presumption of Liberty* (Princeton, NJ: Princeton University Press, 2004), 118–131 (discussing construction based on theory of justice); Keith E. Whittington, *Constitutional Constructions: Divided Powers and Constitutional Meaning* (Cambridge, MA: Harvard University Press, 1999), 3–9 (viewing construction as a political process that fills in "textual indeterminacies"); Jack M. Balkin, "Original Meaning and Abortion," *Constitutional Commentary* 24 (2007): 291, 301–302 (arguing that the results of successful social movements should determine the application of constitutional provisions).
2. Barnett, *Restoring the Lost Constitution*, 123.
3. Ibid.
4. Lawrence B. Solum, "Semantic Originalism," Illinois Public Law Research Paper No. 07–24 (2008), 75–79, available at http://papers.ssrn.com/sol3/papers .cfm?abstract_id=1120244.
5. In his initial description of the distinction between interpretation and construction, Larry Solum indicated that construction occurred when the constitutional language was ambiguous or vague. See Solum, "Semantic Originalism," 69. But over time, Solum developed his theory so that he now holds that interpretation involves determining the linguistic meaning of a provision, whereas construction involves giving legal effect to the semantic context of a legal text. See Lawrence B. Solum, "The Interpretation-Construction Distinction," *Constitutional Commentary* 27 (2010): 95, 103. Consequently, construction occurs in all adjudications, even though it is largely invisible when the meaning is clear. In this chapter, we describe construction as limited to situations where ambiguity or vagueness renders the meaning unclear because that is the more common understanding. Even under Solum's later understanding, judges would have to supplement the original meaning only in cases where the language was ambiguous or vague.

6. We identify as constructionists Randy Barnett, Larry Solum, Keith Whittington, and Jack Balkin. See Barnett, *Restoring the Lost Constitution*, 118–131; Whittington, *Constitutional Constructions*, 3–9 (viewing construction as a political process that fills in "textual indeterminancies"); Solum, "Semantic Originalism," 63–86; Jack M. Balkin, *Living Originalism* (Cambridge: Harvard University Press, 2011), 3–6.

7. In this chapter, we discuss what we regard as the dominant approach to construction: the view that construction is not governed by the Constitution and allows judges to choose the approach to resolve issues of construction. Under this view, judges will have discretion as to how resolve matters of construction. We believe that this approach largely captures the approaches of Randy Barnett and Jack Balkin. Other approaches to construction are not as clearly covered by our criticism, but neither are they clearly outside it. Larry Solum has argued strongly for the distinction between interpretation and construction, but he has not, to our knowledge, proposed a method for resolving questions of construction. Keith Whittington believes that construction is primarily a matter for the political branches, although he has stated that some construction can occur in the judiciary. See Keith E. Whittington, "Constructing a New American Constitution," *Constitutional Commentary* 34 (2010): 119.

    It is possible that an approach to construction might be developed that would make its enterprise more a function of legal than political judgment. One possibility is that questions of construction might be resolved in part through the application of precedent. Another possibility is to imagine construction questions being decided based on some other source of laws, such as general constitutional law or the common law generally. Because our focus in this chapter is on existing approaches to construction, we assume judges are allowed policy or political discretion as to how to resolve questions of construction. In any event, we think that even legal approaches to construction would give substantial discretion to judges because they would have to make choices about what precedent rules to apply and how to mold the common law to create a tool for construction.

8. While we describe our point in term of ambiguities and vagueness that can be resolved by the application of rules of interpretation, it is not limited to such rules. One can well imagine that rules of punctuation or some other custom or usage favor one meaning over another, even when both are reasonable.

9. We are not certain whether judicial deference is properly understood as an interpretive rule. If so, it would be a different interpretive rule from the others we discuss because it would only apply to judicial interpretation. Alternatively, it might conceivably be seen as an aspect of the judicial power. One of us has discussed the status of the rule at greater length: See John O. McGinnis, "Is Judicial Deference Part of Originalism?" (copy on file with authors).

10. Another rule that avoids ambiguity and vagueness is one that strictly construes constitutional delegations of power to the federal government. The Jeffersonians argued that this was the correct rule for interpreting the Constitution on the ground that the Constitution was a compact among the states and that delegations to the federal government involved grants from a sovereign that traditionally were narrowly construed. See H. Jefferson Powell, "The Principal of '98: An Essay in Historical Retrieval" *Virginia Law Review* 80 (1994): 689, 692. One version of this rule would apply it only to resolve ties about whether or not the federal government possessed a power. A stronger version would apply it to deny a power to the federal government even in some cases when the weight of the evidence supports its possession of that power. This rule is similar to, but in some ways the opposite of, the rule discussed in the text that grants deference to the legislature. But in contrast to the legislative deference rule, which applies only to decision making by the judiciary, this rule would also apply to decisions made either by the judiciary or the legislature.

11. To be sure, this kind of evidentiary rule applies only to the judiciary. Because the legislature is the institution to which the rule directs deference, the rule is of no help to the legislature itself in interpreting the Constitution. Nevertheless, we do not believe that the legislature is likely to face many cases of interpretive equipoise. The substantive considerations that provide factors to interpret ambiguous or vague provisions are many—purpose, structure, and historical context, to name a few—and it seems unlikely that two interpretations of a provision are likely to be equally plausible after giving each factor its due weight. In any event, this view would leave the few instances of construction entirely to the political branches. This conclusion would comport analytically with that of constructionists like Whittington (see Whittington, "Constructing a New American Constitution") who see construction as largely the particular province of the legislature, even as it made the enterprise of legislative construction of little normative importance to constitutional law as a whole.

12. For examples of early decisions where the Court considers close cases by determining which is the stronger interpretation, see *Marbury v. Madison*, 5 U.S. 137 (1803), *Martin v. Hunter's Lessee* 14 U.S. (6 Cranch) 304 (1816), and *McCulloch v. Maryland*, 17 U.S. (4 Wheat) 316 (1819). These opinions also include in some instances weighing the evidence for the appropriate interpretive rules with which to fix the meaning of the Constitution. For instance, *McCulloch v. Maryland* pivoted on the question of whether there was better support for the rule that the Constitution was to be narrowly construed because the Constitution emanated from the states or the rule that it should be more broadly construed because it emanated from the people. See *McCulloch v. Maryland*, 17 U.S. (4 Wheat. 316 (1819).

13. While a comprehensive history of the methods of constitutional interpretation

in the early Republic remains to be done, we believe that, with few exceptions, judges made their decisions by assessing the strength of the argument for the meaning of words in their legal context. To be sure, in the very early Republic, a few judges seemed occasionally to consider extrinsic sources in rendering judgments about the Constitution. See, for example, *Chisholm v. Georgia*, 2 U.S. (2 Dall.) 419, 453 (1793) (opinion of Wilson) (considering general jurisprudence and the laws of different states, but relying "chiefly" on the Constitution of the United States). But even in that case, other justices focused only on the document. See, for example, *Chisholm v. Georgia*, 400, 466 (opinions of Blair and Chase). Thus, we believe that judges like Wilson were outliers. Dean Treanor has also suggested that the opinions in the early case of *Hylton v. United States*, 3 U.S. Dall. 171, 171 (1796) were anti-textualist. See William Treanor, "Against Textualism," *Northwestern Law Review*: 103 (2009): 985, 994–996. But we see them as broadly originalist, even though in general we do not find them very persuasive. See John O. McGinnis and Michael B. Rappaport, "Original Methods Originalism and the Case Against Construction," *Northwestern University Law Review* 103 (2009): 751, 800–802.

14. Our discussion of interpretive rules that confer deference to the legislature's interpretations naturally brings to mind Thayer's rule of clear mistake, which requires the judiciary to defer to the legislature and uphold legislation unless the statute clearly contravenes the Constitution. See James B. Thayer, "The Origin and Scope of the American Doctrine of Constitutional Law," *Harvard Law Review* 7 (1893): 129. Thayer sought to justify his rule based on both history and policy analysis (Thayer, "The Origin and Scope," 135, 140–141), whereas showing that such a rule was an original interpretive rule requires a focus on history (and inferences from the Constitution itself). As the text suggests, our reading of the history suggests that deference for the legislature's interpretation is considerably narrower than Thayer suggests.

15. To the reply that construction permits interpreters to choose only within a range not forbidden by the public meaning, we refer back to our earlier discussion in this chapter. If construction is not to be trivial theory, it must permit the choice of the less well-founded interpretations among a range of reasonable interpretations. The power to choose less well-founded interpretations and make them constitutional law binding on other actors is one that rational Framers of the Constitution are unlikely to have chosen.

16. Certain versions of construction are also in fundamental tension with the judicial function in constitutional law because they permit judges to declare binding obligation even though no law guides them. Other versions may avoid this criticism if they apply other existing bodies of law, such as precedent or the common law. But even these versions are open to the criticism that they apply nonconstitutional law to override federal statutes and state law.

17. Sir William Blackstone, *Commentaries on the Laws of England in Four Books*, vol. 1, ed. George Sharswood (Philadelphia, PA: J.B. Lippincott Co., 1893), *61.

18. See Joseph Story, *Commentaries on the Constitution of the United States* (Boston: Hilliard, Gray and Company, 1833), 411–418.

19. See, for example, Barnett, *Restoring the Lost Constitution*, 118–121.

20. There are cases where early courts might be interpreted as either relying on natural law or fundamental rights to reach decisions. The proper way to characterize these cases is not always obvious, with some commentators construing many of the cases as involving general constitutional law in diversity cases. See Jason Mazzone, "The Bill of Rights in the Early State Courts," *Minnesota Law Review* 92 (2007): 1, 59–64. Others view them as natural law deemed applicable to the Constitution through the Ninth Amendment or some other way. See Barnett, *Restoring the Lost Constitution*, 235. Still others view them as fundamental principles derived from the Anglo-American tradition. See John F. Hart, "Human Law, Higher Law, and Property Rights: Judicial Review in the Federal Courts, 1789–1835," *San Diego Law Review* 45 (2008): 823. But even if natural law or fundamental rights applied, they would not represent an example of construction where these principles applied because the original meaning ran out. Instead, these principles would apply either because they were incorporated by the positive law or because they were deemed to be higher law that applied regardless of the positive law.

21. Solum, "Semantic Originalism," 68.

22. See *Gibbons v. Ogden*, 22 U.S. 1, 187–188 (1824).

23. Barnett, *Restoring the Lost Constitution*, 158–159.

24. *The Writings of James Madison*, vol. 6, ed. Gaillard Hunt (New York: G.P. Putnam's Sons, 1910), 27.

25. Ibid.

26. Barnett, *Restoring the Lost Constitution*, 125.

27. Letter from Thomas Jefferson to Wilson Cary Nicholas (September 7, 1803) (emphasis added), in *The Writings of Thomas Jefferson: 1801–1806*, ed. Paul Leicester Ford (New York: G.P. Putnam's Sons, 1897), 247–248.

28. Ibid.

29. Thomas Jefferson, "Opinion on the Constitutionality of the Bill for Establishing a National Bank" (February 15, 1791), in *The Papers of Thomas Jefferson*, vol. 19, ed. Julian P. Boyd (Princeton, NJ: Princeton University Press, 1974) 275–276.

30. Ibid., 277.

31. See Whittington, *Constitutional Constructions*, 20–72.

32. See ibid., 27–28 (stating that Chase argued that impeachment applied only to illegal behavior).

33. See ibid., 31–32 (stating some Federalists saw impeachment "in effect as a *mode*

of removal, and not as a charge and conviction of high crimes and misdemeanors.").

34. Ibid., 38 (showing that voting record supports this view).

35. Ibid., 68 ("[B]oth sides turned to external political principles to supplement what was discoverable in the text [of the Constitution] itself").

36. We recognize that amendments subsequent to the original constitution are best interpreted according to the interpretive rules extant at the time of the amendment. Thus, it would be possible to argue that construction developed at a time later than the Framing. But we have not yet seen substantial evidence of construction in the nineteenth and early twentieth centuries, where originalism was still the dominant philosophy of interpretation.

37. Jack M. Balkin, "Original Meaning and Constitutional Redemption," *Constitutional Commentary* 24 (2007): 427, 455.

38. There are studies of risk aversion in finance, showing that the overwhelming majority of people are risk-averse in regard to financial investments. William A. Klein and John Collins Coffee, *Business Organization and Finance*, 5th ed. (Westbury, NY: Foundation Press, 1993), 233–234. Balkin has provided no reason to believe they would feel otherwise in political investments, like a constitution.

39. Again there is an analogy to finance: the more equity is at risk, the more risk-averse management will be. See Lawrence J. White, "The S&L Debacle," *Fordham Law Review* 59 (1991) S57, S60.

40. In Chapter 3, we argue that supermajority rules help reduce the extent of those costs by minimizing the risk of bad outcomes. But whether supermajority rules succeed in doing that, citizens remain risk-averse about the prospect of bad outcomes.

41. Mark Tushnet, "The Warren Court as History," in *The Warren Court in Historical and Political Perspective*, ed. Mark Tushnet (Charlottesville: The University Press of Virginia, 1993), 17 ("The justices who formed the core of the late Warren Court . . . found that they had been placed in a position where they had a fair amount of discretion to do what they believed right, and they believed that they were authorized, by virtue of their selection for that position, simply to do what they believed right").

42. See Suzanne Sangree, "Title IX and the Contact Sports Exemption: Gender Stereotypes in a Civil Rights Statute," *Connecticut Law Review* 32 (2000): 381, 412.

43. Of course, provisions that are supported by a consensus might not be proposed if individual groups or even members of a majority believe that they can secure their preferred policies through alternative means. But if constitutional enactments are genuinely checked by a supermajoritarian requirement, then these groups will be forced to propose provisions supported by a consensus.

44. See, for example, *Creating the Bill of Rights: The Documentary Record from the First Federal Congress*, eds. Helen E. Veit et al. (Baltimore, MD: The Johns Hopkins University Press, 1991) 66, 77 (remarks of Madison, J.).

45. See A. E. Dick Howard, "Rights in Passage: English Liberties in Early America," in *The Bill of Rights and the States*, eds. Patrick T. Conley and John P. Kaminski (Madison, WI: Madison House Publishers, 1992), 3, 11.

46. See, for example, Thomas B. McAffee, "Restoring the Lost World of Classical Legal Thought: The Presumption in Favor of Liberty over Law and the Court over the Constitution," *Cincinnati Law Review* 75 (2007): 1499, 1537 (noting Federalist fear that a bill of rights could endanger the Constitution's structural protections for liberties).

47. Supreme Court decision making also does not have the other desirable characteristics of the supermajoritarian amendment process. For example, while constitutional amendments are enacted behind a limited veil of ignorance, because it is hard to know the effects of these amendments in future circumstances, Supreme Court decisions can simply be distinguished so that they do not apply in ways the justices do not desire.

48. Keith Whittington's theory of constitutional construction focuses more on construction by the political branches than by the judiciary, and thus its is not subject to this objection. But even construction through ordinary politics does not provide the kind of deliberation that makes for entrenchments of sufficient beneficence that they should be enforced against subsequent majorities.

49. It might be objected that lawyers on whom people relied in the constitution-making process were also elites. This is true, to some extent, but it is a matter of degree. The hundreds of representatives to state ratifying conventions are, to be sure, more elite than ordinary citizens, but as a group, they are more diverse and less elite than the nine justices on the Court.

50. Barnett, *Restoring the Lost Constitution*, 118–121.

51. Ibid., 169 (arguing that one should choose the presumption of liberty as the principle of construction).

52. Ibid., 261.

53. Balkin, "Original Meaning and Abortion," 301–302.

54. 198 U.S. 45 (2005).

55. 410 U.S. 113 (1973).

9. Precedent, Originalism, and the Constitution

1. Michael Stokes Paulsen, "The Intrinsically Corrupting Influence of Precedent," *Constitutional Commentary* 22 (2005): 289.

2. Gary Lawson, "Mostly Unconstitutional: The Case Against Precedent Revisited," *Ave Maria Law Review* 5 (2007): 1.

3. Thomas W. Merrill, "Originalism, Stare Decisis and the Promotion of Judicial Restraint," *Constitutional Commentary* 22 (2005): 271.

4. Henry Paul Monaghan, "Stare Decisis and Constitutional Adjudication," *Columbia Law Review* 88 (1988): 723.

5. See Lawson, "Mostly Unconstitutional," 1; Gary Lawson, "The Constitutional Case Against Precedent," *Harvard Journal Law & Public Policy* 17 (1994): 23.

6. See Lawson, "Mostly Unconstitutional," 6; Lawson, "The Constitutional Case," 32.

7. It might be thought that this argument would forbid not only horizontal but vertical precedent. Lawson, however, argues that lower federal courts would still be obliged to follow Supreme Court precedent because they are "inferior" to the Supreme Court. See Steven G. Calabresi and Gary Lawson, "Equity and Hierarchy: Reflections on the Harris Execution," *Yale Law Journal* 102 (1992): 255, 276, n. 106. While it raises fascinating questions, we leave aside the question whether, and if so, to what extent, this conclusion is compatible with Lawson's overall approach.

8. This interpretation also has implications outside the judiciary. Presumably, the executive would be forbidden from following judicial precedents under this view. While Lawson argues that the executive would be required to follow judicial judgments on the ground that the term *judicial power* implies binding decisions, the executive would be forbidden from following judicial precedents that it believes are mistaken. See Gary Lawson and Christopher D. Moore, "The Executive Power of Constitutional Interpretation," *Iowa Law Review* 81 (1996): 1267, 1290–1292, 1302. More radically, Michal Paulsen also appears to argue that presidents are required to not follow judicial precedents (and even judgments), but he takes much of it back, arguing that three principles require the president to moderate his decisions. See Michael Stokes Paulsen, "The Most Dangerous Branch: Executive Power to Say What the Law Is," *Georgetown Law Journal* 83 (1994): 217, 332; see also Michael B. Rappaport, "The Unconstitutionality of 'Signing and Not-Enforcing,'" *William & Mary Bill of Rights Journal* 16 (2007): 113, 118, n. 18 (raising questions about the constitutionality and legitimacy of Paulsen's principle of accommodation).

9. While it would be unconstitutional for courts to follow precedent in statutory cases under ordinary circumstances, it is possible that Congress could pass a law allowing for Supreme Court precedent in statutory cases. Congress might enact a statute providing that a Supreme Court statutory interpretation decision should be understood as having the effect of amending the statute. It is by no means clear that such a statute would conform to the original meaning of the Constitution.

10. Lawson, "Mostly Unconstitutional," 12.

11. Ibid., 12.

12. Ibid., 12–13.

13. In contrast to Lawson's textual arguments against precedent, other originalists rely on conceptual or normative arguments. For example, Randy Barnett argues that originalism is logically inconsistent with precedent because "[o]riginalism amounts to the claim that the meaning of the Constitution should remain the same until it is properly changed," and only a constitutional amendment is capable of changing its meaning. See Randy E. Barnett, "Trumping Precedent with Original Meaning: Not as Radical as It Sounds," *Constitutional Commentary* 22 (2005): 257, 258–259. Whatever the merits of Barnett's normative argument, we believe that it is missing a key ingredient; namely, it does not purport to show that the Constitution itself precludes precedent. If the Constitution expressly told judges to follow precedent in certain circumstances, an originalist would not argue that judges should decline to follow the constitutional text because originalism precludes it. Instead, the originalist would concede that the original meaning requires the following of precedent. Our argument is of the same form because we believe the Constitution implicitly allows for precedent.

14. For a view of the history of precedent that is similar in many respects with ours, see Richard W. Murphy, "Separation of Powers and the Horizontal Force of Precedent," *Notre Dame Law Review* 78 (2003): 1075, 1085–1101.

15. See Henrici De Bracton, *On the Laws and Customs of England*, ed. Sir Travers Twiss (London: Longman, 1878; repr. Buffalo, NY: W.S. Hein, 1990), 9 (page references are to 1990 edition) ("If, however, any new and unaccustomed cases shall emerge, and such as have not been usual in the realm, if, indeed any like cases should have occurred, let them be judged after a similar case, for it is a good occasion to proceed from like to like.").

16. See Sir Carleton Kemp Allen, *Law in the Making* (Oxford: Clarendon Press, 1964), 205–207 (discussing sixteenth- and seventeenth-century emphasis on precedents in both procedural and substantive matters).

17. Sir Edward Coke, *Coke upon Littleton*, bk. 3, eds. Francis Hargrave and Charles Butler (Philadelphia, PA: Robert H. Small, 1853), ch. 7 sec. 420.

18. See Thomas Healy, "Stare Decisis as a Constitutional Requirement," *West Virginia Law Review* 104 (2001): 43, 64.

19. Michael McConnell highlights Coke's reliance on custom and precedent. McConnell writes that, even in cases of first impression, Coke would not fill the gap with abstract reason, but instead would "cast the net of his antiquarian research farther afield," and in the famous *Calvin's Case*, came "up with a 200-year-old precedent." See Michael W. McConnell, "Tradition and Constitutionalism Before the Constitution," *University of Illinois Law Review* (1998): 173, 179–180.

20. Sir Mathew Hale, *The History and Analysis of the Common Law of England*

(London: Printed by J. Nutt, assignee of Edw. Sayer, Esq., for J. Walthoe, 1713; repr. Birmingham, AL: Legal Classics Library, 1987), 68 (page references are to the 1987 edition).

21. William Blackstone, *Commentaries on the Laws of England*, vol. 1 (Chicago: University of Chicago Press, 1979), 69–70. Facsimile of first edition of 1765–1769 (last emphasis added).

22. See Caleb Nelson, "Stare Decisis and Demonstrably Erroneous Precedents," *Virginia Law Review* 87 (2001): 1, 32.

23. See Blackstone, *Commentaries*, vol. 1, 70. In the passage quoted above in the text, Blackstone adopted a declaratory view of law, writing that when a decision is overruled or not followed, "the subsequent judges do not pretend to make a new law, but to vindicate the old one from misrepresentation. For if it be found that the former decision is manifestly absurd or unjust, it is declared, not that such a sentence was *bad law*, but that it was *not law*" (ibid). Some commentators have viewed Blackstone's view as being largely inconsistent with the notion of precedent because it adopts the declaratory view of the law. For example, Thomas Lee argues that the declaratory theory "presupposes a relatively weak (if not nonexistent) doctrine of stare decisis." Thomas R. Lee, "Stare Decisis in Historical Perspective: From the Founding Era to the Rehnquist Court," *Vanderbilt Law Review* 52 (1999): 647, 660. According to Lee, "the classic declaratory theory left ample room for departing from precedent under the fiction that prior decisions were not law in and of themselves but were merely evidence of it" (ibid).

    While it is possible that most practitioners of the declaratory theory held a "relatively weak" view of precedent, Lee's argument that there is a strong connection between the declaratory theory and weak precedent does not necessarily hold. There is a basic distinction between the effect of a mistaken decision and the discretion of a court to refuse to follow earlier decisions. While the declaratory theory holds that the effect of a mistaken decision is that it is treated as if it were never the law, this does not mean that it also has a weak standard for recognizing that a precedent was mistaken. As Blackstone's own position seems to suggest, one could believe that prior judicial decisions should usually be followed while also believing that, when an old decision is not followed, it had never been law and the new decision applies retroactively. In fact, some contemporary judges, such as Justice Scalia, argue for applying judicial decisions retroactively precisely because it will discourage judges from overruling precedents. See *James B. Beam Distilling Co. v. Georgia*, 501 U.S. 529, 549 (1991) (Scalia, J., concurring).

24. Mansfield certainly was aggressive in overturning various decisions, but he "never entirely ignored precedents." Healy, "Stare Decisis," 71 (quoting David Lieberman, *The Province of Legislation Determined: Legal Theory in Eighteenth Century Britain* (Cambridge, England: Cambridge University Press, 1989), 126).

In the same vein, he sometimes followed rules he did not agree with because "the authorities are too strong" or "the cases cannot be got over." Allen, *Law in the Making*, 212.

25. Allen, *Law in the Making*, 211–212 (emphasis omitted).

26. Theodore Plucknett writes that during the Year Book period of the Middle Ages, a single case would have only limited authority, but a series of cases was "a well established custom" and was entitled to significant weight. See Theodore F. T. Plucknett, *A Concise History of the Common Law* (London: Butterworth, 1956), 347. The authority of a series of decisions continued to be recognized as the strength of precedent grew over time. Still, Plucknett writes, "[U]nder a developed system of precedents one case is as good as a dozen if it clearly covers the point, and at the present day citations are consequently few and to the point. The eighteenth century, however, still seems tempted to find safety in numbers, and to regard the function of citations to be merely that of proving a settled policy or practice" (ibid., 349); see also Healy, "Stare Decisis," 68 (greater weight given to a series of decisions).

In 1612, John Davies wrote in his *Irish Reports* that "a custom doth never become a Law to bind the people, until it hath been tried and approved time out of mind, during all which time there did thereby arise no inconvenience." See J. G. A. Pocock, *The Ancient Constitution and the Feudal Law* (Cambridge: Cambridge University Press, 1990), 32 (quoting John Davies). Coke also noted that "wherein the laws have been by the wisdom of the most excellent men, in many successions of ages, by long and continual experience, (the trial of light and truth) fined and refined, which no one man, (being of so short a time) albeit he had in his head the wisdom of all the men in the world, in any one age could ever have effected or attained unto. . . . [N]o man ought to take it on himself to be wiser than the laws" (ibid., 35, quoting Sir Edward Coke in *Calvin's Case*).

27. See, for example, *Morecock v. Dickins*, 27 Eng. Rep. 440, 441 (Ch. 1768); see also Healy, "Stare Decisis," 69 ("[M]ost judges agreed [in 1760] that precedent should be followed in cases involving property or contracts, where certainty was essential."); Lee, "Stare Decisis in Historical Perspective," 688 (noting that, by the time the *Morecock* decision was handed down, a "distinction had already taken hold in the English courts" between "commercial cases and other decisions"); Lee J. Strang, "An Originalist Theory of Precedent: Originalism, Nonoriginalist Precedent, and the Common Good," *New Mexico Law Review* 36 (2006): 419, 451–452 ("Stare decisis was applied more vigorously in cases involving property or contract.").

28. For a similar view of the use of precedent in England, see Philip Hamburger, *Law and Judicial Duty* (Cambridge, MA: Harvard University Press, 2008), 228–229.

29. See Allen, *Law in the Making,* 219, n. 1 (arguing that the modern theory developed in the nineteenth century); Plucknett, *A Concise History,* 349–350 (same); William S. Holdsworth, "Case Law," *Law Quarterly Review* 50 (1934): 180 (arguing that the modern theory "was reached substantially by the end of the eighteenth century").

30. See Healy, "Stare Decisis," 55–56, 66–73; Lawson, "Mostly Unconstitutional," 12–13; Lee, "Stare Decisis in Historical Perspective," 659–662; Michael Stokes Paulsen, "Abrogating Stare Decisis by Statute: May Congress Remove the Precedential Effect of Roe and Casey?" *Yale Law Journal* 109 (2000): 1535, 1576–1577 (endorsing Lee's argument).

31. See Healy, "Stare Decisis," 55–56, 66–73; Lawson, "Mostly Unconstitutional," 12–13; Lee, "Stare Decisis in Historical Perspective," 659–662; Paulsen, "Abrogating Stare Decisis by Statute," 1576–1577.

32. Leonard W. Labaree, *Royal Government in America: A Study of the British Colonial System Before 1783* (New Haven, CT: Yale University Press, 1930), 4–5.

33. Evarts Boutell Greene, *The Provincial Governor in the English Colonies of North America* (New York: Longmans, Green, and Co., 1898), 113, 140–144.

34. Labaree, *Royal Government in America,* 5.

35. Healy states that, during the seventeenth century, the colonists were "struggling to survive on a strange continent" and therefore employed a legal system that relied on adaptability rather than restraint. Healy, "Stare Decisis," 73–74. He suggests—without actually asserting—that precedent was not followed (ibid). See also Strang, "An Originalist Theory of Precedent," 457 ("During the seventeenth century such a doctrine was weak, but in the eighteenth century, as the colonial legal system became increasingly complex, the doctrine of precedent came to resemble its English counterpart"). But even if precedents were not followed at this early date, this fact would have little relevance for the meaning of the Constitution. In the undeveloped colonies of the seventeenth century, the colonists displayed a "strong dislike of lawyers," and therefore may not have followed accepted legal forms such as precedent. See Healy, "Stare Decisis," 74. But as time progressed, the colonies developed and came to embrace the Anglo-American legal system (ibid., 74–75; Strang, "An Originalist Theory of Precedent," 456). The Americans, who were writing the Constitution in developed political communities, would no doubt have relied on the ordinary legal forms that had developed in England and in the colonies for the last several generations. They would not have assumed that the forms employed by new undeveloped colonial outposts would govern or be relevant.

36. See, for example, Strang, "An Originalist Theory of Precedent," 457.

37. Morton J. Horwitz, *The Transformation of American Law, 1780–1860* (Cambridge, MA: Harvard University Press, 1977), 8.

38. Ibid.

39. See William E. Nelson, *Americanization of the Common Law: The Impact of Legal Change on Massachusetts Society, 1760–1830* (Cambridge, MA: Harvard University Press, 1975), 18–20.

40. John Adams, *Diary and Autobiography of John Adams*, vol. 1, ed. L. H. Butterfield (Cambridge, MA: Belknap Press of Harvard University Press, 1961). As Chief Justice of the Massachusetts Supreme Court, Thomas Hutchinson had expressed similar views, emphasizing the need for known and certain law and arguing that the common law provided the rule of decision and prevented judicial legislation. See Horwitz, *The Transformation*, 5.

41. See Horwitz, *The Transformation*, 8.

42. *Somerville v. Johnson*, 1 H. & McH. 348, 353–54 (Md. 1770), cited in Strang, "An Originalist Theory of Precedent," 457.

43. Healy questions the claim that colonial courts generally followed the English precedent doctrine (Healy, "Stare Decisis," 75–76). But Healy's arguments focus on the modern notion of strong precedent. Thus, many examples that he proposes, while inconsistent with strong precedent, are entirely consistent with the weaker view of precedent. For example, Healy cites as evidence against precedent that James Otis had "argued in a 1761 case that it is '[b]etter to observe the known Principles of Law than any one Precedent'" (Healy, "Stare Decisis," 76). This statement is not inconsistent, however, with the English conception of precedent that conferred limited weight to single decisions. Where a single case is inconsistent with known principles of law, which were derived from previous cases, courts would often not follow the single decision. But that did not imply that precedent was not given weight and that a series of decisions was not given significant weight. A similar analysis applies to Healy's discussion of *Belt v. Belt*, a Maryland decision from 1771, in which the Court "disregarded the decision in a previous case and instead followed the teachings of Mansfield." See Healy, "Stare Decisis," 76 (discussing *Belt v. Belt*, 1 H. & McH. 409, 418 (Md. 1771), 1771 WL 13, at *6). But, again, it was entirely consistent with the accepted system for the court to not follow a single decision that was inconsistent with "the authorities in the books" that had been derived from other cases. See *Belt v. Belt*, 418, *6.

44. Horwitz, *The Transformation*, 8 [quoting *Watts v. Hasey*, Quincy's Mass. Rep. 194 (1765)].

45. See *Somerville v. Johnson*, 353–354, *quoted in* Strang, "An Originalist Theory of Precedent," 457.

46. See Nelson, *Americanization of the Common Law*, 18, n. 62.

47. James Wilson, *The Works of James Wilson*, vol. 2, ed. James DeWitt Andrews (Chicago: Callaghan and Co., 1896), 144.

48. Thomas Jefferson, *The Writings of Thomas Jefferson*, vol. 12, eds. Andrew A. Lipscomb and Albert Ellery Bergh (Washington, DC: Issued under the

auspices of the Thomas Jefferson Memorial Association of the United States, 1907), 299.

49. Ibid.

50. James Kent, *Commentaries on American Law*, vol. 1, (New York: O. Halsted, 1826).

51. Because Kent's treatise was written in 1826—nearly forty years after the Framing—its ability to shed light on the Constitution's original meaning is limited. Nonetheless, the treatise's adoption of the Blackstone–Wilson approach suggests the continuity of that view.

52. While Kent did not have a strong or modern conception of precedent, he certainly believed that precedent could change the results that judges would otherwise reach. And Kent's writings certainly recognize that precedents can be overruled: "But I wish not to be understood to press too strongly the doctrine of *stare decisis*. . . . It is probable that the records of many of the courts in this country are replete with hasty and crude decisions; and such cases ought to be examined without fear, and revised without reluctance. . . . Even a series of decisions are not always conclusive evidence of what is law; and the revision of a decision very often resolves itself into a mere question of expediency, depending upon the consideration of the importance of certainty in the rule, and the extent of property to be affected by a change of it." See Kent, *Commentaries*, vol. 1, 444. But as the quotation in the text makes clear, Kent also strongly affirmed precedent. Clearly, Kent had a nuanced view that noted that overrulings are a matter of trade-offs—in particular, trade-offs between reliance and accuracy. Kent also recognized that a series of decisions is of greater weight than a single decision, and while not impregnable, a series of decisions is entitled to substantial weight.

53. See, for example, *Goodell v. Jackson*, 20 Johns. 693, 720 (N.Y. 1823) (Kent, C.); *Packard v. Richardson*, 17 Mass. (17 Tyng) 122, 143 (1821); *Kerlin's Lessee v. Bull*, 1 Dall. 175, 178 (Pa. 1786); *Bush v. Bradley*, 4 Day 298, 309–10 (Conn. 1810) (opinion of Smith, J.); *Minnis v. Echols*, 12 Va. (2 Hen. & M.) 31 (Va. 1808) (opinion of Roane, J.); *Respublica v. Roberts*, 1 Yeates 6, 7 (Pa. 1791). For an extended discussion of several of these cases, see Nelson, "Stare Decisis and Demonstrably Erroneous Precedents," 14–17 and accompanying footnotes. See also James Madison, *The Mind of the Founder: Sources of the Political Thought of James Madison*, ed. Marvin Meyers (Hanover, NH: University Press of New England, 1981), 391 ("Because it is a reasonable and established axiom, that the good of society requires that the rules of conduct of its members should be certain and known, which would not be the case if any judge, disregarding the decision of his predecessors, should vary the rule of law according to his individual interpretation of it"). But see *Commonwealth v. Posey*, 8 Va. (4 Call) 109, 116 (1787) (opinion of Tazewall, J.) (writing that "the uniformity of decisions"

about the correct interpretation of a statute "does not weigh much with me," because "although I venerate precedents, I venerate the written law more").

Thomas Jefferson and the Virginia committee on law revision also expected precedent to apply to written laws. See Jefferson, *The Writings of Thomas Jefferson*, 299. Zephaniah Swift expected the same. See Zephaniah Swift, *A System of the Laws of the State of Connecticut* (Windham, CT: John Byrne, 1795), 46 ("[The Connecticut courts] have by a series of decisions ascertained the construction of the statutes, by which many very important points, and principles have been settled").

54. Some of the judges during this period followed what appeared to be a weak (but nonetheless genuine) view of precedent. For example, in a treatise written in 1795, Connecticut lawyer and later Chief Justice Zephaniah Swift discussed the role of English and Connecticut precedents under Connecticut law. Swift seemed both to endorse precedent (precedent "is founded in the highest wisdom, and produces the best effects") and to dismiss or limit it ("the institution [of precedent], is a principle established which corrects all errors and rectifies all mistakes"). See Swift, *A System of the Laws*, 40–41. One way to reconcile Swift's apparently conflicting views is to interpret him as following Blackstone's notion that only clear errors can be reversed and that precedent should otherwise be followed.

However one interprets Swift's meaning, it seems clear that he believed that Connecticut decisions were entitled to at least a moderate amount of precedential weight because Swift drew a distinction between English and Connecticut decisions. Swift wrote "[t]hat part of the English common law, *which has been thus approved by the [Connecticut] courts*, may be considered as our common law by adoption" (ibid., 44 [emphasis added]). By contrast, "that part which has not been thus adopted, may . . . be considered obligatory, so far as it is consistent with reason, adapted to our local circumstances, and conformable to the policy of our jurisprudence" (ibid.). Because Connecticut decisions are entitled to greater precedential weight than English decisions, Swift views Connecticut decisions as having real, significant precedential weight.

A similar view is expressed by Vermont Chief Justice Nathaniel Chipman. Chipman wrote that "[i]f no reason can be assigned, in support of [English] rules or precedents, not already adopted in practice [in Vermont]," then they should not be adopted. See Nathaniel Chipman, *Reports and Dissertations in Two Parts* (Rutland, VT: Anthony Haswell, 1793), 65. Clearly, when Vermont courts had actually adopted such English rules, which might be relied on, even precedents that seemed unreasonable might have been followed. Similar views of relatively weak precedent were held by other judges. See Nelson, "Stare Decisis and Demonstrably Erroneous Precedents," 31 (discussing Jacob Radcliff of the Supreme Court of New York, who agreed that "common-law decisions could be erroneous" and should not be followed unless overruling them would have retrospective influence or affect preexisting rights); see also ibid. (discussing the similar view of Edmund Pendleton).

55. Herbert J. Storing and Murray Dry, eds., *The Complete Anti-Federalist*, vol. 2 (Chicago: University of Chicago Press, 1981), 234–244 (emphasis added).

56. Ibid, 441.

57. Alexander Hamilton, James Madison, and Jon Jay, "Federalist No. 78," ed. Clinton Rossiter (New York: Mentor, 2003), 470.

58. Hamilton, Madison, and Jay, "Federalist No. 37," 225.

59. Stephen B. Weeks, *State Records of North Carolina*, vol. 12, eds. William L. Saunders and Walter Clark (Goldsboro, NC: Nash Bros., 1907).

60. Madison adhered to these ideas concerning precedent throughout his life. Later examples involve his decision to sign the bill reauthorizing the bank of the United States because precedent supported its constitutionality, although he had a contrary view. See Ira C. Lupu, "Time, the Supreme Court, and The Federalist," *George Washington Law Review* 66 (1998): 1324, 1334. Many years later, Madison returned to this subject, articulating a view that was consistent with his earlier ideas but more elaborate. He wrote: "Yet, has it ever been supposed that [the judge] was required or at liberty to disregard all precedents, however solemnly repeated and regularly observed, and, by giving effect to his own abstract and individual opinions, to disturb the established course of practice in the business of the community? . . . There is, in fact and in common understanding, a necessity of regarding a course of practice, as above characterized, in the light of a legal rule of interpreting a law, and there is a like necessity of considering it a constitutional rule of interpreting a Constitution." Madison, *The Mind of the Founder*, 390, 392.

61. We are indebted for the cases we discuss here to Thomas Lee, "Stare Decisis in Historical Perspective," and Lee Strang, "An Originalist Theory of Precedent," who have provided very useful pictures of precedent in the Marshall Court.

62. In addition to the Supreme Court, the lower federal courts also appear to have followed precedent. See Strang, "An Originalist Theory of Precedent," 468 ("There are countless similar examples showing that stare decisis was a ubiquitous feature of early federal court legal practice as employed by litigants, the courts, and even the reporters"). A notable example involves Judge Chase's decision for the federal circuit court concerning the constitutional definition of treason, where the judge relied on two previous federal court interpretations. According to Chase, "[t]hese decisions, according to the best established principles of our jurisprudence, became a precedent for all courts of equal or inferior jurisdiction; a precedent which, though not altogether obligatory, ought to be viewed with great respect, especially by the court in which it was made, and ought never to be departed from, but on the fullest and clearest conviction of

its incorrectness." Case of Fries, 9 F. Cas. 924 (C.C.D. Pa. 1800) (No. 5127) (discussed in Strang, "An Originalist Theory of Precedent," 470). Chase also "considered the law as settled by those decisions" (ibid., 936).

63. The two decisions where the Court actually overruled prior cases involved situations in which a contrary practice had evolved after the overruled decision; see *Gordon v. Ogden*, 28 U.S. 33, 34 (1830) (overruling *Wilson v. Daniel*, 3 U.S. 401 (1798), on the basis of the fact that "a contrary practice" to the decision had "since prevailed"), and where the full record had not been before the Court in the previous decision. See *United States v. Percheman*, 32 U.S. 51, 88–89 (1833) (overruling *Foster v. Neilson*, 27 U.S. 253 (1829)). Thus, there were special circumstances that justified these overrulings. See also Lee, "Stare Decisis in Historical Perspective," 679–681.

Two decisions are normally mentioned as overrulings, but they were not true overrulings. In *Hudson v. Guestier*, 10 U.S. 281 (1810), Marshall himself recognized that he had counted votes incorrectly in the previous case of *Rose v. Himely*, 8 U.S. 241 (1808) 10 U.S. at 285 (Marshall, J., dissenting). The majority thus did not overrule *Rose* on the issue before it. See Lee, "Stare Decisis in Historical Perspective," 677–678. *Green v. Neal's Lessee*, 31 U.S. 291 (1832), also does not provide an example of overruling precedent that had any claim to binding effect, despite its failure to follow the previous cases of *Patton's Lessee v. Easton*, 14 U.S. 476 (1816), and *Powell's Lessee v. Harman*, 27 U.S. 241 (1829). *Neal's Lessee* merely held that, when Tennessee law had changed on the decisive question at issue, the new Tennessee law should have been followed. See 31 U.S. at 295, 299–301; see also Lee, "Stare Decisis in Historical Perspective," 678.

64. 8 U.S. 75, 100–01 (1807).

65. In *Ogden v. Saunders*, 25 U.S. 213, 266 (1827), Bushrod Washington notably said that he would follow the conclusion of *Sturges v. Crowninshield*, 17 U.S. 122 (1819), which permitted states to pass bankruptcy laws to discharge debts, despite his continued disagreement with its holding.

66. *Ex parte Bollman*, 101 (Johnson, J., dissenting).

67. See Lee, "Stare Decisis in Historical Perspective," 669.

68. *Ex parte Bollman*, 103–104 (Johnson, J., dissenting).

69. In another part of the opinion, Justice Johnson indicated that it is only a single decision that must be addressed because the second decision merely cited the first (ibid., 104).

70. 17 U.2S. 316 (1819).

71. 6 U.S. 358, 396 (1805).

72. We also do not believe Marshall's occasional decision not to prominently cite a precedent in an opinion reflected his rejection of precedent. In *Cohens v. Virginia*, 19 U.S. 264, 290–310 (1821), Marshall engaged in a lengthy analytical discussion to conclude that the Supreme Court had appellate authority to

review state court judgments. Only after justifying the conclusion did Marshall cite *Martin v. Hunter's Lessee*, 14 U.S. 304 (1816), which had decided the question previously. See *Cohens v. Virginia*, 310. While this practice seems inconsistent with modern practice, it is not necessarily inconsistent with the weaker theory of precedent. By answering the question again with a slightly different theory and without significantly relying on the previous decision, the Court lent independent authority to its conclusion regarding one of the most significant issues in constitutional law at the time. Under the weaker version of precedent, a single decision may not be entitled to great weight, but a series of decisions was entitled to more weight, and therefore the manner in which *Cohens* was decided helped to solidify the law in this area.

73. See Lee, "Stare Decisis in Historical Perspective," 668.

74. *McCulloch v. Maryland*, 401. Similarly, in *Stuart v. Laird*, 5 U.S. 299 (1803), Justice Patterson upheld circuit riding in large part because the practice had been used in case after case (ibid., 309, "[T]he practice and acquiescence under it for a period of several years, commencing with the organization of the judicial system, affords an irresistible answer, and has indeed fixed the construction").

75. One possible objection to our reliance on the history of precedent is that it is consistent with what Lawson describes as the epistemological case for precedent. See Lawson, "Mostly Unconstitutional," 18–22. Under the epistemological view of precedent, one can rely on precedent if it is the "best evidence of the right answer" (ibid., 19). Thus, one might argue that the weak version of precedent we discuss might be justified on epistemological grounds because prior decisions could be evidence of the correctness of these decisions, and a series of decisions would be strong evidence of their correctness. In this way, one might attempt to make Lawson's view consistent with at least some of the history.

This argument does not work. Lawson argues that the circumstances in which an epistemological version of precedent should hold sway are very narrow indeed and are much narrower than the tradition of precedent we discuss. First, these precedent rules regularly held that precedents about property rights were entitled to greater weight because the reliance interest was larger. Because it is reliance, not accuracy, that is the main value, it is clear that epistemology cannot account for this rule. Second, even if one puts to the side the property-right precedent rule, the leading authorities on precedent, such as Blackstone and Kent, argued that precedent was also based on values other than accuracy, like predictability and judicial constraint. The weak precedent rules are hard to understand as simply being about accuracy. Finally, it should not be surprising that there is some connection between precedent and accuracy. Desirable precedent rules promote a variety of benefits, including accuracy. Real-world precedent rules—both today and historically—cannot be understood as being solely about accuracy, as Lawson himself recognizes (ibid., 21).

76. See Murphy, "Separation of Powers," 1084 ("[I]t seems quite clear that the Framers expected the new federal courts to treat their past decisions as evidence of law and to adhere to them absent a strong justification to the contrary").

77. U.S. Const. art. III, sec. 1.

78. See Saikrishna B. Prakash and Michael D. Ramsey, "The Executive Power over Foreign Affairs," *Yale Law Journal* 111 (2001): 231, 252. For another example, see our argument that the members of Congress possess as constitutional powers some of the authority traditionally enjoyed by members of Parliament. See John O. McGinnis and Michael B. Rappaport, "The Rights of Legislators and the Wrongs of Interpretation: A Further Defense of the Constitutionality of Legislative Supermajority Rules," *Duke Law Journal* 47 (1997): 327, 332–336.

79. See John Harrison, "The Power of Congress over the Rules of Precedent," *Duke Law Journal* 50 (2000): 503, 524.

80. Ibid.

81. John Harrison views precedent rules as evidentiary rules about the nature of the law. He then argues that just as regularly applied evidentiary rules for facts, such as the hearsay rule, were not incorporated into the judicial power, precedent rules were also not so incorporated. See Harrison, "The Power of Congress," 524. We agree that the hearsay rule was not made part of the judicial power, but disagree that this implies that no aspects of precedent are part of the judicial power. Precedent rules were applied by more judges and to a more distinctively judicial task than hearsay rules. Precedent rules were applied by all judges compared to hearsay rules, which were mainly applied by trial judges. Precedent rules involve judicial decisions by judges on the law rather than decisions made largely in aid of jury decision making. In addition, at the time of the Framing, the hearsay rule was a relatively recent development. See John H. Wigmore, *Evidence*, v. 5, ed. John H. Chadbourn (Boston: Little, Brown, 1974), sec. 1364, at 18 (dating origin of hearsay rule to between 1675 and 1690). By contrast, while we have shown that some form of precedent was followed consistently from at least the time of Coke, precedent was thought to be part of the English legal system from the earliest periods; see James Kent, *Commentaries on American Law*, ed. O. W. Holmes, Jr. (Boston: Little, Brown, 1873), 473–478, or even to predate it, see James Wilson, *Works of James Wilson*, vol. 2, ed. Robert G. McCloskey (Cambridge, MA: Belknap Press of Harvard University Press, 1967), 342 (suggesting that the doctrine of precedent was brought to England by the Romans). Thus, while the hearsay rule was certainly one of the broader common law rules, it did not have the generality, history, and connection with judicial decision making that precedent had.

82. John Harrison argues against incorporating precedent into the judicial power

on the ground that the constitutional enactors would have viewed civil law judges, who did not formally follow precedent, as exercising the judicial power. See Harrison, "The Power of Congress," 522, n. 61. This argument, however, fails to recognize that the term *judicial power* would have had different meanings depending on the context. Because the enactors were enacting a legal document within the Anglo-American legal system, they would be presumed to have in mind the judges of that legal system, who employed precedent. For the same reason, terms within the Constitution are often given their common law meaning rather than looking to their meaning under the civil law. It is true, no doubt, that the enactors would have deemed civil law judges as exercising judicial power in some sense of the term, but that does not mean that they used that foreign or secondary sense of the term in the Constitution.

83. See Bradford R. Clark, "Federal Common Law: A Structural Reinterpretation," *University of Pennsylvania Law Review* 144 (1996): 1245; William A. Fletcher, "The General Common Law and Section 34 of the Judiciary Act of 1789: The Example of Marine Insurance," *Harvard Law Review* 97 (1984): 1513.

84. See Harrison, "The Power of Congress," 525–526. It seems clear that the Constitution was written with an understanding that general law would apply because constitutional provisions make that assumption. For example, consider cases involving interstate border disputes, which are within the original jurisdiction of the Supreme Court. The law governing such disputes needs to include some common law because it cannot be entirely federal statutory law—because Congress has no enumerated power to legislate on border disputes—or state law because one state cannot have authority to resolve a border dispute with another. Given the text and overall structure of the Constitution, it seems that the constitutional enactors expected the Supreme Court to resolve such disputes in accordance with the general law.

85. Thus, in our view, except for the minimal concept of precedent commanded by the "judicial power," the Court's precedent rules are similar to default rules that the people acting through their representatives can vary.

86. The Supremacy Clause provides that "this Constitution, and the laws of the United States which shall be made in Pursuance thereof; and all Treaties made, or which shall be made under the Authority of the United States, shall be the supreme Law of the Land." See U.S. Const. art. VI, sec. 1, cl. 2.

87. Because it is not the supreme law of the land, the general law would not be binding on state courts when these courts construe federal law. We do not address how precedent would operate in state courts.

88. See Harrison, "The Power of Congress," 525–529. While we follow Harrison's view of precedent as a matter of general law, we do disagree with his view that the Constitution does not incorporate any notion of precedent under the judicial power. See ibid., 518–521.

89. Ibid., 525.

90. Ibid, 521–523.

91. Harrison does argue persuasively, however, that precedent in federal courts is at best understood as reflecting a mixture of statutory structure and general law. See Harrison, "The Power of Congress," 525–531.

92. We leave aside the question of whether the application of such state laws to federal courts would be unconstitutional, as Harrison believes. See ibid., 525 (citing *McCulloch v. Maryland*), or whether they would simply be preempted under the statutes establishing federal courts.

93. Ibid., 529.

94. See Zephaniah Swift, *A Digest of the Laws of the State of Connecticut*, vol. 1 (New Haven, CT: S. Converse, 1822) ("Stare decisis is a fundamental maxim of the common law"); see also *Carroll v. Lessee of Carroll*, 57 U.S. (16 How.) 275, 286 (1850) (Curtis, J.) (referring to "the maxim of the common law, *stare decisis*").

95. See Harrison, "The Power of Congress," 532–534; William Van Alstyne, "The Role of Congress in Determining Incidental Powers of the President and of the Federal Courts: A Comment on the Horizontal Effect of 'The Sweeping Clause,'" *Ohio State Law Journal* 36 (1975): 788, 793–794.

96. See Harrison, "The Power of Congress," 532–534.

97. Thus, the distinction between rules that constitute the original meaning of the Constitution and precedent rules that govern the internal operation of the Court is crucial to the argument here. Congress lacks the power to change the meaning of the Constitution. For instance, it could not enact interpretive rules that would tell the Court to look for modern meanings rather than original meanings or to emphasize text more than intent. As we discussed in Chapter 7, the interpretive methods deemed applicable to the Constitution at the time of its enactment provide the rules for constituting the Constitution's meaning, and Congress cannot change these rules any more than it can change the words of the Constitution. While Congress's authority to pass genuine precedent rules is a significant power, the power to enact interpretive rules that would change the meaning of the Constitution would be awesome and would be inconsistent with the constraint that is an essential aspect of a constitution.

98. See U.S. Const. art. VI, sec. 2 ("any Judges in every State shall be bound thereby, any Thing in the Constitution or Laws of any State to the Contrary notwithstanding").

99. Our understanding of the relationship between the Supremacy Clause and precedent also derives support from an unlikely source—from Lawson's own scholarship. While Lawson believes that the Supremacy Clause prohibits horizontal precedent—the Supreme Court following its own prior decisions—he also believes that it allows vertical precedent—lower courts following Supreme

Court decisions. Lawson's attempt to distinguish horizontal from vertical precedent is problematic, and a reading of the Supremacy Clause that would allow vertical precedents would be close to the one that we adopt here.

Lawson grounds the permissibility of vertical precedent in the "hierarchical structure of Article III"—presumably Article III's reference to "one Supreme court" and "such inferior Courts." See Calabresi and Lawson, "Equity and Hierarchy," 276, n. 106. But this reference to a Supreme Court does not specifically require that vertical precedents be followed. One can easily read the Constitution's use of the term *Supreme Court* more narrowly to refer to a court that might possess supreme authority as to its orders, but not as to its precedents. Such a Supreme Court might have the power to require a lower court to follow the order it issues in the particular case under review, but not have the power to compel lower courts to follow its opinion as a precedent in future cases. This distinction between orders and precedents is a familiar one among departmentalists, and is adopted by Lawson himself concerning the obligation of the executive to follow judicial orders. Given that the Supreme Court can be understood as having authority to issue orders rather than precedents, we believe Lawson's interpretation of the Supremacy Clause should not merely prohibit horizontal precedents but also vertical precedents. After all, allowing vertical precedents would permit lower courts to follow the Supreme Court's nonoriginalist decisions in future cases rather than following the Constitution itself. By contrast, countenancing vertical precedents requires that one both understand precedent as an essential characteristic of the Supreme Court (and the judicial power) and then see that characteristic as mandating a narrower interpretation of the Supremacy Clause. It is such an interpretation of the Supremacy Clause that we adopt.

10. The Normative Theory of Precedent

1. Antonin Scalia, A *Matter of Interpretation*, ed. Amy Guttman (Princeton, NJ: Princeton University Press, 1997) 45–46; Antonin Scalia, "The Rule of Laws as the Law of Rules," *University of Chicago Law Review* 56 (1989): 1175, 1178–1179, 1184–1185.
2. See Thomas W. Merrill, "Originalism, Stare Decisis, and the Promotion of Judicial Restraint," *Constitutional Commentary* 22 (2005): 271, 278 (precedent provides a thicker body of norms to constrain judges).
3. Ibid., 276–277.
4. See Emily Sherwin, "A Defense of Analogical Reasoning in Law," *University of Chicago Law Review* 66 (1999): 1179, 1190–1193.
5. Some commentators have argued strong precedent rules are justified because they protect the institutional legitimacy of the Court. See, for example,

Suzanna Sherry, "The Eleventh Amendment and Stare Decisis: Overruling *Hans v Louisiana*," *University of Chicago Law Review* 57 (1990): 1260, 1262–1263. This argument is troubling because it suggests that hiding and perpetuating errors is superior to acknowledging and correcting them. Such an argument would never be applied to other parts of the government. If the president violated the Constitution, few commentators would suggest the appropriate response is to cover up the violation, rather than criticize it, because to do so would "undermine the President's legitimacy." We believe the same analysis applies to the Court, and we wonder what else could justify this difference in treatment.

6. 381 U.S. 479 (1965).

7. 410 U.S. 113 (1973).

8. See Jack Balkin, *Living Originalism* (Cambridge, MA: Belknap Press of Harvard University Press, 2011), 471–481.

9. Ibid., 475.

10. Ibid.

11. *Helvering v. Davis*, 301 U.S. 619 (1937); *Steward Mach. Co. v. Davis*, 301 U.S. 548 (1937).

12. *Juilliard v. Greenman*, 110 U.S. 421 (1884); *Knox v. Lee*, 79 U.S. 457 (1870); *Hepburn v. Griswold*, 75 U.S. 603 (1869).

13. See, for example, Richard A. Epstein, "The Proper Scope of the Commerce Power," *Virginia Law Review* 73 (1987): 1387.

14. *INS v. Chadha*, 462 U.S. 919, 967 (1983) (Powell, J., concurring in the judgment). For a partial list of the affected statutes, see ibid., 1003–1013.

15. While the enormous costs of the cases in this category of precedent seem to justify keeping them regardless of the factors that might argue for the return to original meaning, one can identify precedents that would impose lesser costs if they were overturned. These costs should be deemed one factor in the analysis of determining whether a precedent should be followed or overturned. Certainly, *Chadha* would fall into this category, as would a large number of other cases.

16. 295 U.S. 602 (1935).

17. 497 U.S. 654 (1988).

18. 130 S.Ct. 3138 (2010).

19. It might be argued that permitting the president to remove all executive officials at will would generate enormous costs because of the importance of the independence of the Federal Reserve to the stability of the economy. Currently, the chairman and other governors of the Federal Reserve are, by statute (12 USCS, sec. 242), insulated from presidential removal without cause. Such independence can be justified as a policy matter by the concern that a

federal reserve under too much influence from the president could manipulate the money supply for political ends—for instance, to create an economic boom to aid the reelection of the president or a successor of his party. On other hand, in an advanced democracy like the United States, it is not clear how much undue influence the president could exercise on the chairman because the president would be constrained by both popular and elite opinion from rash firings of a well-known figure whose independence was widely understood as important to the economy. But if one believed that eliminating the legal protections of independence from the Federal Reserve would have enormous costs, that would justify making exception for those positions on the grounds that the Federal Reserve plays, as it surely does, a unique role in the economic life of the nation. A rule giving the president removal powers with this single exception is a clear and workable one that still moves the interpretation of the Constitution much closer to its original meaning (assuming, of course, that that meaning precluded independent agencies).

20. 347 U.S. 483 (1954).

21. For instance, the sex discrimination cases of the 1970s (discussed in Chapter 5) represent such a consensus even if they do not reflect an accurate understanding of the Fourteenth Amendment.

22. On rational ignorance, see Arthur Lupia and Mathew D. McCubbins, *The Democratic Dilemma: Can Citizens Learn What They Need to Know?* (Cambridge: Cambridge University Press, 1998), 20.

23. The justices here are constrained by having to find a precedent whose principle is to be tested for consensus.

24. 381 U.S. 479 (1965).

25. For the same reasons, the Supreme Court should not attempt to predict whether political conflicts—partisan or otherwise—would interfere with the constitutional amendment. For example, it might be thought that liberals and conservatives could not agree on the proper way to define intermediate scrutiny because they might attempt to grandstand in order to promote other positions, such as their differing views on abortion. But these problems should be ignored because they are difficult to predict, may change over time, and do not really go to the basic point of whether there is support for the underlying principle.

26. Another question involves the time at which a precedent must have consensus support. One view is that the precedent should have consensus support at the time when it is to be applied. Another view is that the precedent could satisfy the consensus requirement at any time after it was decided, even if it no longer had consensus support at the time it was to be applied. We believe the first rule is superior for four reasons.

First, if the precedent does not command a consensus at the time the Court is to apply it, the original meaning it displaces still has a claim to presumptive beneficence. Thus, the argument for precedent displacing originalism is much weaker. Second, in those circumstances, a decision by the Court to discard a precedent in favor of the original meaning is not so costly in terms of the justices' reputations because there is no current consensus. Third, it is much more difficult for the Court to determine whether there ever existed the requisite consensus than to assess whether the requisite consensus exists currently. Therefore, the disciplinary framework for such decision making would be less reticulated and the error costs accordingly higher. Finally, requiring consensus at the time the Court is to apply the precedent differentiates a precedent from a constitutional amendment that remains binding even if the consensus in its favor dissipates. Such a differentiation helps preserve incentives to make constitutional changes through amendment rather than through judicial decision.

27. See *United States v. Lopez*, 514 U.S. 549, 554–561 (1995).
28. See Michael J. Gerhardt, "Super Precedent," *Minnesota Law Review* 90 (2006): 1204, 1206, 1216 (discussing Chief Justice Roberts's and Justice Alito's testimony at the Senate Committee on the Judiciary hearings in which superprecedents were mentioned).
29. 410 U.S. 113 (1973).
30. 505 U.S. 833 (1992).
31. See *Confirmation Hearing on the Nomination of Samuel A. Alito, Jr. to Be an Associate Justice of the Supreme Court of the United States: Hearing Before the S. Comm. on the Judiciary*, 109th Congress (2006), 321 (statement of Sen. Arlen Specter, Chairman, S. Comm. on the Judiciary); *Confirmation Hearing on the Nomination of John G. Roberts, Jr. to Be Chief Justice of the United States: Hearing Before the S. Comm. on the Judiciary*, 109th Congress (2005), 144–145 (statement of Sen. Arlen Specter, Chairman, S. Comm. on the Judiciary).
32. At one time, we offered a third rule of precedent—one we described as involving corrective precedent—to reflect the fact the some precedents may represent reasonable attempts to correct supermajoritarian failure. For example, assume (which we are not inclined to do) that *Brown v. Board of Education* was wrongly decided as a matter of original meaning. It might be possible to think that the Court would be justified in following it under our doctrine of corrective precedent. Had African Americans been fully included in the constitution-making process in 1866 (or even 1787), it is likely that they would have placed a high priority on obtaining a general prohibition on racial discrimination in regard to important government benefits, such as public schooling. Thus, even had the Court been wrong about the Constitution's original meaning in *Brown*, we argued there would have been no reason to disturb the ruling because it rectified a likely supermajoritarian failure.

    Nevertheless, on balance, we believe corrective precedent is unjustified as a category. The courts would have to decide whether precedents were plausibly corrective and, given the difficulty of determining judicial corrections, this decision would be difficult and potentially ideologically divisive. The basic difficulty is the one we noted in Chapter 6 on supermajoritarian failure. Judicial correction requires judges to answer many difficult questions (made all the more difficult because some are counterfactual.) For instance, one would have to decide whether or not African Americans would have been politically situated to insist on a prohibition on discrimination in public schooling. As a result of the sheer number of considerations, these determinations would likely be more difficult than deciding whether a precedent created enormous costs or represented the kind of supermajoritarian consensus that would prompt a constitutional amendment in its favor. The questions attending judicial correction are more ideologically charged and depend on inquiries into more distant history than the question of whether overruling a decision would force Congress to act immediately or whether a decision now enjoys a popular consensus.

33. Caleb Nelson, "Stare Decisis and Demonstrably Erroneous Precedents," *Virginia Law Review* 87 (2001): 1, 13–14.
34. One of the virtues of clarity is that it helps treat similarly situated litigants equally, and such equal treatment is thus a virtue that rides on clarity. Originalism, of course, has the same virtue when original meaning is clear, and thus the benefits of equal treatment do not always favor precedent over originalism.
35. The limitation here that the precedent must be within the range of uncertainty of the original meaning is essential. If a court were to interpret an uncertain provision in a clearly mistaken way, then the costs of following the precedent would be much greater because it would be clearly departing from the original meaning. Our discussion here of uncertainty in the original Constitution overlaps with the common claim that precedent should be followed if it represents a plausible construction of the original meaning. If one interprets a plausible construction as one that is within the range of uncertainty of the original meaning, then the two factors are identical.
36. For a discussion of how judges' prior beliefs or "priors" can be changed, see Richard Posner, *How Judges Think* (Cambridge, MA: Harvard University Press, 2008), 68.
37. See Randy E. Barnett, *Restoring the Lost Constitution: The Presumption of Liberty* (Princeton, NJ: Princeton University Press, 2005), 267.
38. One way that the precedent rule might allow reliance to be shown is to establish that a significant number of private actions have been taken based on the precedent. Another method, which would avoid this difficult showing, might be to presume that a long-standing precedent of a couple of generations has been relied upon.

39. There are other possible precedent rules that should be evaluated. One rule with a strong historical pedigree suggests that courts should follow precedents that have been repeatedly affirmed unless these precedents are obviously erroneous. The requirement of repeated affirmation serves to show that interpretation has remained stable through changing factual and political circumstances. This consensus though the years provides some epistemic evidence that the interpretation has a claim to correctness (although this evidence of epistemic correctness will be strong only if the courts are relatively free to depart from this precedent until it has been repeatedly reaffirmed). Repeated affirmations also suggest that rule is likely to be relatively clear and that there has been time for diffuse reliance on the precedent.

40. 505 U.S. 833, 854–869 (1992) (plurality opinion).

41. The precedent analysis of *Casey* has been relied upon subsequently by the Court. See *S. Cent. Bell Tel. Co. v. Alabama*, 526 U.S. 160, 166 (1999); *Adarand Constructors, Inc. v. Pena*, 515 U.S. 200, 233 (1995).

42. To be sure, some of the rules may require a court to consider multiple issues but nevertheless such rules should be cast in terms of criteria that must be satisfied rather than flexible balancing tests. Rules provide more constraint on judges than do balancing tests and offer more transparency in their application.

43. *Planned Parenthood v. Casey*, 855 ("Although *Roe* has engendered opposition, it has in no sense proven 'unworkable'. . . .").

44. Ibid.

45. We are not suggesting that originalists would often confront such a situation. To be a remnant, the nonoriginalist precedent must be inconsistent not with simply one other precedent but with several.

46. *Planned Parenthood v. Casey*, 855.

47. See, for example, *United States v. Darby*, 312 U.S. 100 (1941).

48. 381 U.S. 479 (1965).

49. See Barnett, *Restoring the Lost Constitution*.

50. Ibid., 258–259.

51. Ibid., 263–266.

52. Ibid.

53. See Merrill, "Originalism," 272–273. Another important article that is more tentative, but points to much the same position, is Henry Paul Monaghan, "Stare Decisis and Constitutional Adjudication," *Columbia Law Review* 88 (1988): 723, 771–772 (suggesting that originalism plays an "increasingly subordinate [role]" compared to precedents in constitutional adjudication).

54. Merrill, "Originalism," 273. Part of his argument for the judicial restraint that adherence to precedent provides is that it helps treat similarly situated litigants alike (ibid., 276).

55. Ibid., 278.
56. See Frank H. Easterbrook, "Ways of Criticizing the Court," *Harvard Law Review* 95 (1982) 802, 805–807.
57. See John O. McGinnis and Michael Rappaport, "A Pragmatic Defense of Originalism," *Northwestern University Law Review* 101 (2007): 383, 389–390.
58. 163 U.S. 537, 537–538 (1896).
59. While the constitutionality of *Brown* under the original meaning raises two significant issues—whether separate but equal is constitutional and whether the right to attend a public school is a civil right—the precedential effect of *Plessy* is limited to the question of the correctness of separate but equal because the right to make a contract with a railroad company seems plainly to constitute a civil right. In our view, *Plessy* is plainly wrong on the question of separate but equal. In that case, African Americans and railroad companies were denied the opportunity to contract to sit in certain coaches (those restricted to whites) in which they wished to sit (ibid., 538–39). The fact that whites were also denied the right to contract to sit in other coaches (those restricted to African Americans) is irrelevant because it was the equality in contracting for a particular set of coaches (those in which whites also sat) that was at issue. See John Harrison, "Reconstructing the Privileges or Immunities Clause," *Yale Law Journal* 101 (1992): 1385, 1459, 1462. See also Chapter 4 (providing additional arguments for why separate but equal is wrong). The question of whether the equality guarantee of the Fourteenth Amendment applies to public schools is a harder one, but we are inclined to believe it does. See Michael W. McConnell, "Originalism and the Desegregation Decisions," *Virginia Law Review* 81 (1995): 947.; Steven G. Calabresi and Sarah E. Agudo, "Individual Rights Under State Constitutions When the Fourteenth Amendment Was Ratified in 1868: What Rights Are Deeply Rooted in American History & Tradition?" *Texas Law Review* 87 (2008): 7.
60. 428 U.S. 153 (1976).
61. 408 U.S. 238 (1972).
62. John Hart Ely, *Democracy and Distrust* (Cambridge, MA: Harvard University Press, 1980), 65.
63. One might also see the decision as justified because *Furman* itself did not follow the rules of precedent in striking down the death penalty.
64. 514 U.S. 549 (1995).
65. See Andrew Koppelman, "How 'Decentralization' Rationalizes Oligarchy: John McGinnis and the Rehnquist Court," *Constitutional Commentary* 20 (2003): 11, 20–21.
66. See Richard H. Fallon, Jr., "Constitutional Precedent Viewed Through the Lens of Hartian Positivist Jurisprudence," *North Carolina Law Review* 86 (2008): 1107, 1157 (discussing how *Lopez* invalidated a federal statute as beyond

Congress's authority but did not overrule any previous cases, including any New Deal decisions).

67. Robert Bork, for instance, has stated that, to overrule that reading of the New Deal would "overturn much of modern government and plunge us into chaos." See Robert Bork, *The Tempting of America* (New York: Touchstone, 1991), 158.

68. 426 U.S. 833 (1976).

69. 392 U.S. 183 (1968).

70. Unlike the other overrulings discussed in this section, we do not mean to suggest that *National League of Cities* captures the original meaning. But for an argument that it does based on the meaning of states and their structural position in the Constitution, see Michael B. Rappaport, "Reconciling Textualism and Federalism: The Proper Textual Basis of the Supreme Court's Tenth and Eleventh Amendment Decisions," *Northwestern University Law Review* 93 (1999): 819, 819–820.

71. 505 U.S. 833 (1992).

72. 410 U.S. 113 (1973).

73. 381 U.S. 479 (1965).

74. See Mark Tushnet, "Response: Liberal Political Theory and the Prerequisites of Liberal Law," *Yale Journal of Law and the Humanities* 11 (1998): 469, 473, n. 13.

75. See, for example, Nelson Lund and John O. McGinnis, "*Lawrence v. Texas* and Judicial Hubris," *Michigan Law Review* 102 (2004): 1555. In that article, one of the authors of this book argued in favor of overruling *Griswold* (ibid., 1611–1612). The concept of entrenched precedent offered here had not been developed at the time. He now believes that the entrenched precedent analysis should control and that *Griswold* should not be overruled.

11. *Imagining an Originalist Future*

1. See, for example, Jack Balkin, *Living Originalism* (Cambridge, MA: Belknap Press of Harvard University Press, 2011).

2. See, for example, William J. Cuddihy, *The Fourth Amendment: Origins and Original Meaning* (New York: Oxford University Press, 2009); Kurt T. Lash, "The Lost Original Meaning of the Ninth Amendment," *Texas Law Review* 83 (2004): 331.

3. See, for example, Michael D. Ramsey, *The Constitution's Text in Foreign Affairs* (Cambridge, MA: Harvard University Press, 2007).

4. See, for example, Robert Bork, *The Tempting of America* (New York; Free Press, 1997); Raoul Berger, *Government by Judiciary: The Transformation of the Fourteenth Amendment* (Cambridge, MA: Harvard University Press, 1977).

5. See, for example, Randy E. Barnett, *Restoring the Lost Constitution: The Presumption of Liberty* (Princeton, NJ: Princeton University Press, 2005).

6. See, for example, Balkin, *Living Originalism*.

7. U.S. Const. amend. II.
8. Nelson Lund, "Outsider Voices on Guns and the Constitution," *Constitutional Commentary* 17 (2000) 701: 704–708.
9. Warren E. Burger, "The Right to Keep and Bear Arms," *Parade Magazine*, January 14, 1990, 4.
10. Balkin, *Living Originalism*, 62.
11. Ibid.
12. Ibid., 60.
13. Ibid.
14. Bruce Ackerman, *We the People: Foundations* (Cambridge, MA: Belknap Press of Harvard University Press, 1993), 267–294.
15. Ibid., 105.
16. See Michael W. McConnell, "The Forgotten Constitutional Moment," *Constitutional Commentary* 11 (1994): 115, 142–143 (arguing that, under certain criteria, eleven eras in US history could be considered constitutional moments).
17. Edmund Burke, "Reflections on the Revolution in France" in *The Writings and Speeches of Edmund Burke,* vol. 8 (Oxford: Oxford University Press, 1990): 147.

ACKNOWLEDGMENTS

This volume began as a book on a different subject. For over ten years, we had worked on the role of supermajority rules as an instrument of governance and as a central feature of the US Constitution. We saw such voting rules as a key to understanding the Constitution and as the Founding's most distinctive contribution to political structure.

But two things happened to change our course. First, in the process of writing an article, "Our Supermajoritarian Constitution," we realized that supermajority rules offered a way to put originalism on a firmer normative foundation. Second, we watched a revival of interest in originalism in the academy and in the wider world. The time was ripe for a comprehensive defense of the most pervasive interpretive theory in the history of US constitutional law.

Another advantage of the pivot to originalism was the opportunity it afforded to take advantage of the conferences and scholarly debate generated by the renewed focus on the subject. In particular, we are grateful for comments on portions of this work from a number of friends and colleagues: Larry Alexander, Akhil Amar, Robert Bennett, Rebecca Brown, Steve Calabresi, Laurie Claus, Tom Colby, Neal Devins, Lee Epstein, Richard Fallon, Barry Friedman, Mark Graber, Chris Green, Jamal Greene, Philip Hamburger, Tonja Jacobi, Eugene Kontorovich, Andrew Koppelman, Nelson Lund, John Manning, Mike McConnell, Tom Merrill, Frank Michelman, Mark Movsesian, Caleb Nelson, Richard Parker, Jim Pfander, Richard Posner, Sai Prakash, Mike Ramsey, Nick Rosenkranz, Adam Samaha, Mike Seidman, Scott Shapiro, Steven Smith, Ilya Somin, Kevin Stack, Peter Strauss, and Mark Tushnet. In addition we have benefited from substantial exchanges with Jack Balkin, Randy Barnett, Larry Solum, and Keith Whittington, who are themselves responsible for much of originalism's renewal. Our continuing disagreement with these scholars may suggest to them we still have not benefited enough, but our work has been strengthened by trying to be more precise about the locus of our disputes.

We have also profited from the discussions at various law schools where one or the other of us has presented portions of this work to faculty members. These institutions include Capital Law School, Columbia Law School, Florida State College of Law, Georgetown Law School, University of Illinois Law School, University of Southern California Law School, University of Texas Law School, and Vanderbilt Law School.

Portions of Chapter 1 are reprinted from "A Pragmatic Defense of Originalism," 101 *Northwestern Law Review* 395 (2007). Portions of Chapter 3 are reprinted from "Majority and Supermajority Rules: Three Views of the Capitol," 85 *Texas Law Review* 1115 (2007); and "The Condorcet Case for Supermajority Rules," 16 *Supreme Court Economic Review* 67 (2007). Portions of Chapters 4 and 5 are reprinted from "Our Supermajoritarian Constitution," 80 *Texas Law Review* 703 (2002); and "Originalism and the Good Constitution," 98 *Georgetown Law Review* 1693 (2009). Portions of Chapter 6 are reprinted from "Originalism and the Good Constitution" 1693 (2009). Portions of Chapters 7 and 8 are reprinted from "Original Methods Originalism: A New Theory of Interpretation and the Case against Construction," 103 *Northwestern Law Review* 751 (2009). Portions of Chapters 9 and 10 are reprinted from "Reconciling Originalism and Precedent," 103 *Northwestern Law Review* 803 (2009). We are grateful to the editors of each of those articles.

We are also grateful for the support of our own institutions. In particular, John recognizes that his deans have been instrumental in the genesis of this book: David Van Zandt, in encouraging him to write it, and Daniel Rodriquez, in supporting it. Mike also recognizes the significant support of Deans Kevin Cole and Stephen Ferruolo.

At home, each of us has acquired debts. John is grateful to his wife, Ardith, for enduring a first year of marriage in which not one, but two books were being pushed over the finish line. John's father has often wondered when this book, so long in gestation, would become a living thing. His jokes on the subject have been a spur to completion. Mike is grateful for the support of his family, who has also indulged in jokes about the book's completion. He will always remember the probing questions asked by his two children about originalism.

INDEX

Accuracy perspective: nature and function of, 47–48; under supermajority rules, 47–58, 60–61; representatives reflecting, 48; framework of, 48–51; independence and decision maker numbers within, 51–52; supermajority favorable due to bad entrenchment proposals under, 54–56; insurance rationale for supermajority rule from, 56–57; summary of, 57–58; supermajority producing good entrenchments under, 60–61

Accuracy rate, 50–51, 52–54, 61

Ackerman, Bruce, 205–206

Adams, John, 162

Affirmative action, 108–109

African Americans: originalism problem stemming from treatment of, 9–10, 11; supermajoritarian originalism defense on exclusion of, 16–17; enactment process excluding, 106–111; good constitution and supermajority rules undone by exclusion of, 107; Reconstruction Amendments correcting enactment exclusion of, 107–108; amendment enforcement failure impact on, 109–110; civil rights enforcement failure involving, 110. *See also* Affirmative action

Allen, C. K., 160

Amar, Akhil, 6–7, 63, 70

Ambiguity and vagueness: as constructionist justification, 8, 139, 140, 141, 152–153; original methods approach to, 141, 152–153; defined, 141–142; interpretive rules addressing, 141–144; interpretive rules evidence for interpreting, 142–143; enactor resolution of, 143–144; legislature resolving, 143–144; Constitution not addressing, 144, 147, 148; of judicial power in Article III, 168; of Supremacy Clause, 173

Amendments and amendment process: Constitutional correction through, 17, 28, 85; stringency reasonable for, 64–65, 66, 69; living constitutionalism undermining, 65; technological and social change leniency in, 66, 69; proposals defeated in, 66–69; Child Labor, 67–68, 90–92; Nineteenth, 69, 111–112; Seventeenth, 69; Civil War, 69–71; Fourteenth, 69–71, 110; enactments, 69–72; slavery, 70, 107–108; state de facto authority in, 71; Twenty-sixth, 71–72; Eighteenth and Twenty-first, 72; difficulty level, 73–74; comparative analysis of, 73–75; defects of, 75–77, 100, 112–113, 114; origination rough symmetry with rules of, 77–80; origination differences with, 78–79; judicial updating inferior to, 81–82, 85–90; consensus required for, 85–86, 88, 89, 151; high-quality likelihood from, 86; judicial updating undermining, preempting, or displacing, 88–90, 92–94, 96, 201–202; Roosevelt's treatment of, 90–92; Supreme Court Commerce Clause circumvention of, 90–92; New Deal undermining, 92; judicial correction undermining, 105–106; Reconstruction, 107–111; enforcement failures, 109–111; women enactment exclusion corrected by, 111–112; by state, 112–113, 114; interpretive rules supported by, 126–127; Ninth, 126–127; Second, 127, 200; original meaning preserving, 176; entrenched precedent compared to, 184; originalism future reinvigoration of, 201–203; people given constitutional power through, 202, 206–207. *See also* Article V; Article VII; Enactment process, supermajoritarian; Proposal, defeated

objectivity of, 204–206; formal compared to higher, 205. *See also* Constitutional law or provisions; Judicial updating or review; Precedent; Statutes; Supreme Court

Lawson, Gary, 155, 156–157, 172–174

Legal change and decision making: good constitution addressing, 83–84; within supermajoritarian constitution, 84; constructionist originalism approach to, 151–152; original meaning promoting good, 202–203

Legislation: supermajoritarian theory on, 2; constitutional law trumping ordinary, 11, 205; majority rule for ordinary, 12, 36; supermajoritarian constitution superior to, 20, 28; marginal, 36–37; Christmas tree, 43. *See also* Condorcet Jury Theorem

Legislators. *See* Representatives

Legislature: vote trading causing unstable, 46–47; factions within, 50; aberrational elections danger to judgment of, 53; supermajority rule restraining agenda of, 54; judicial updating deference to, 88; ambiguity and vagueness resolved by, 143–144; precedent power of, 171–172

Legitimacy and legality, 69–71, 151

Leniency, 66, 69

Living constitutionalism, 118; defined, 1–2; from constructionist originalism, 8; Supreme Court constitutional power through, 13–14, 81, 94; amendment process undermined by, 65; enactor intent in opposition to, 83; constitutional law consequences from, 87–88; law's objectivity undermined by, 204–206

Madison, James, 1, 145–146, 166

Majority rule: for ordinary legislation, 12, 36; supermajority rules compared to, 12, 33–61; in Supreme Court, 14, 87, 89–90; voting rights under, 35; preference perspective under, 35–47; marginal legislation under, 36–37; consensus, 39; partisan entrenchment from, 39–40, 41, 52–53; narrow preference in, 43–44, 46, 60; vote trading in, 46–47; entrenchment accuracy rate low under, 52–53; future consideration undermined by, 52–53; repeal, 58; Constitution ratified by state, 63; collective enactor intent

understood through, 122. *See also* Condorcet Jury Theorem

Mansfield, Lord, 160

Marshall, Thurgood, 9

Marshall Court, 137, 145, 166–167

Merrill, Tom, 192–193

Minorities: supermajority rules protecting, 12, 13, 16, 33, 42–43, 60; good constitution providing protection for, 22, 42; supermajoritarian constitution protecting, 60

Nation, 38

Nelson, William, 161

New Deal, 92, 184, 199, 205

Nineteenth Amendment, 69, 111–112

Ninth Amendment, 126–127

Nonoriginalism, 10, 18, 96–97, 199–200. *See also* Judicial updating or review; Supreme Court

Nonpartisanship, 12, 33, 39–41, 46, 86

Normative interpretive theory, 117–118, 150–153

Original intent: original public meaning compared to, 116–117, 121; as positive interpretive theory, 117, 121–123; nature of, 121; text-oriented theories contrasted with, 121–122

Originalism: challenges for, 1; constitutional interpretation incorporating, 1; defined, 1; Supreme Court support for, 1, 94, 96–97, 127–128; welfare treatment in, 1–2; "dead hand" governance in, 8–9; African American and women treatment impacting, 9–10, 11; exclusion problematic for, 9–10; nonoriginalist, or Supreme Court, precedent troubling, 10, 18; beneficial judicial review requiring form of, 13; constructionist justification lacking for, 15; precedent reconciled and consistent with, 17–18, 154–155, 156–157, 168–174, 195–196; obligation and adherence to, 19–21, 96–97; supermajoritarian constitution followed through, 82–83; compromise unpredictable, 97; presumptive, 97–98; supermajoritarian failure response in applying defective, 100–101; *Brown v. Board of Education* compatibility with, 111; precedent supposed conflict with, 156–157; clarity, predictability, and judicial constraint stemming

Supermajoritarianism and supermajoritarian
theory, as originalism defense, 5, 6; normative defense and consequentialist perspective
of, 11, 15–16, 17–18; rules-based judicial constraint in, 11–12, 17–18, 24, 165–166, 174; structure of, 11–12; good constitution created and
preserved through, 12–14, 19, 26; "dead
hand" governance response, 15–16; on gen-
erational equality and constitutional inheritance, 15–16; on African American and
women exclusion, 16–17; precedent reconciled with originalism in, 17–18; precedent
justifications in, 18
Supermajority rules: legitimate and desirable
entrenchments from, 11, 12–13, 34–35; good
constitution created and preserved through,
12, 14, 26, 62–63, 64, 84, 149–150; majority
rules compared to, 12, 33–61; minorities
protected by, 12, 13, 16, 33, 42–43, 60; partisanship dampened and nonpartisanship promoted by, 12, 33, 39–41, 46, 86; long-term
decision making encouraged by, 12–13; Constitution created and amended using, 13,
62–64; consensus promoted and protected
by, 31, 33, 38–39, 60, 149; preference perspective under, 35–47, 59–60; marginal legislation under, 36–37; marginal entrenchments
under, 37; enactment stringency of, 37–38,
64–77; veil of ignorance established by
entrenchment, 42–43, 46, 50, 54; unequal
intensity and vote trading with, 45–46; vote
trading under, 46–47; accuracy perspective
under, 47–58, 60–61; accuracy rate increase
under, 50, 53–54; insurance rationale for,
50–51, 56–57; legislative agenda restrained
by, 54; public interest supported by, 54; bad
entrenchment proposal proportion favoring,
54–56; good entrenchments supported by,
58–61; Article V for amendment using, 63,
77, 78, 201–202; African American exclusion
undermining, 107; amendments rectifying
failure of, 107–108; constitutional construction from, 148–150. *See also* Condorcet Jury
Theorem
Supremacy Clause, 126, 156, 172–174
Supreme Court, 152; originalism support from,
1, 94, 96–97, 127–128; originalism troubled

by nonoriginalist precedent of, 10, 18; living
constitutionalism and constitutional power
given to, 13–14, 81, 94; majority rule in, 14,
87, 89–90; ERA undermined by nonoriginalist, 68, 72, 93–94, 201–202; on voting
rights in *Oregon v. Mitchell*, 71; Constitution's general terms constraining, 84–85;
consensus not reflected by, 86, 88–89, 151;
ideological bias on, 86; law preferences in
interpretation and self-aggrandizement by,
86; veil of ignorance lacking for, 86–87, 89;
amendment process undermined in
Commerce Clause alteration by, 90–92;
Roosevelt "packing," 91–92; general constitutional provision interpretation by, 92–93;
compensating adjustment difficulty for,
95–96; civil rights enforcement failure by,
110; interpretive rules supported by, 127–128;
construction not recognized by early, 145;
precedent for, 166–167, 189–191; precedent
rules contrasted with *Casey* from, 189–191;
precedent rules applied to previous decisions
of, 193–196; originalist future reconciled
with nonoriginalist past, 199–200. *See also*
Entrenched precedent; Living constitutionalism; Marshall Court

Technology, 66, 69, 199
Text, 136–138
Text, of Constitution, 126–128, 133, 156
Text-oriented theories, 121–122
"Theory of the second best," 95
Thick theory, 5
Transparency, 105
Twenty-first Amendment, 72
Twenty-sixth Amendment, 71–72

Unequal intensity, 44–47
United States v. Lopez, 194–195
US Constitution. *See* Constitution

Veil of ignorance: high discount rate as
limiting, 42; nature and benefits of, 42;
entrenchment mutability weakening, 42–43;
supermajority entrenchment rule establishing, 42–43, 46, 50, 54; constitutional provisions for, 43–44; appropriate stringency